INDEPENDENT SCOTCH

The History of Independent Bottlers

DAVID STIRK

For Dawn.
For everything and all that you mean to me.

And in loving memory of Piet Molenkamp.
"Remember when you were young?
You shone like the sun."

First Published in the United Kingdom in 2023
Copyright © 2023 by David Stirk

Cover Design by Katy Coltart
Cover image courtesy of Whisky Auctioneer

Interior Design by Adam Hay Studio

ISBN: 978-1-399-94553-0

Contents

Foreword

By Serge Valentin
Creator of whiskyfun.com,
Keeper of the Quaich

I visited my first distillery in Scotland, The Glenlivet, in the late 1970s. At that time, I had not had an opportunity to cross the path of any independent bottlers, even if Cadenhead's and Gordon & MacPhail were active (as I later discovered they were). In France, only the large brands of blends, as well as Glenfiddich and Cardhu (official bottlings) were really available. Eventually came the Classic Malts, also Macallan, Laphroaig, Bowmore and Springbank but it's only when visiting liquor shops in Scotland, in the '90s, that I first came across 'unknown distilleries, all packaged the same'. I remember that was my first impression of the 'independent bottlings', which I had only seen mentioned in Michael Jackson's first 'Companion', as well as in Wallace Milroy's little handbook.

I believe my first real encounter with a larger selection of independent bottlings happened at Robertson's in Pitlochry; there were also these wee miniatures by Gordon & MacPhail, which you could find in tourist shops. All of a sudden, from a dozen names, the scope went to almost one hundred of them! Including Brora, which I had never heard of before, and Millburn, Glen Spey or Convalmore, to name but a few. What's more, most independent bottlings were very lousily packaged, which did actually send the right message: 'it's the liquid and variety that count!' There is absolutely no doubt that without the indies, I'd have remained a casual drinker. I also remember getting excited(!) when spotting an ex-bourbon matured Macallan whilst the distillery was only bottling ex-Sherry matured expressions. Or, naturally, all those names that

Picture opposite courtesy of Whisky Auctioneer.

the distillers were keeping for blending, with the notable exception of the Italian market where some brands had already exported one or two 'official' expressions in the 1970s and 1980s. Such as, say Glenesk.

Unlike the '70s, when I trekked across Scotland in search of 'The Glenlivet', the internet has changed the amount of information available. It is perhaps unheard of for a whisky drinker to not know or own an independent bottling. What would the whisky landscape be today without the internet? Certainly, for me, my journey would have remained a personal one – not shared with thousands on a near daily basis.

What is sure is that there are more and more independent bottlers, many only armchair bottlers or sub-sub-sub-bottlers but it's passion that counts in the end. What is interesting is that I am continually hearing 'you can't find great casks at a fair price anymore' or 'independent bottling is finished'. I've heard that in the 1990s, in the 2000s, in the 2010s, and now in the 2020s, while there's always more IBs, some only selling to their home markets.

In David's excellent book we find out why so many independent bottlers now exist. He takes us through the 'unique' market conditions that have led the industry into supporting hundreds of smaller brands and bottlers. David also divulges his own path giving an insight into how a bottling company starts, nearly collapses, then flourishes, and then like so many hundreds of independent companies before, gets bought out and disappears. Pour yourself a nice glass of whatever whisky you like to drink whilst reading and explore the fascinating history and times of the independent bottler. And if you're feeling really brave, check out many of their bottlings on whiskyfun.com.

Notes from the author

Whisky or whiskey, whichever you prefer, is a made up word. It is a bastardised connotation of the Gaelic *Uisge Beatha* which in English is roughly translated as Water of Life. Likely the term 'whisky' was coined by English soldiers posted in Ireland who found asking for a glass of Uisge Beatha too long winded (and likely too colloquial for their liking). It is even possible that the term whisky was a slight mickey-take of the slurring drinkers at the bar asking for another 'Uisge'. Who knows? Likewise when one part of the world started spelling whiskey with an 'e' and other parts without, no-one really knows why, and I for one have never cared. If it has an 'e' it does not mean it is Irish, nor unpeated, nor triple distilled, nor smoother, nor correct, nor incorrect, ad nauseum. Perhaps the 'e' was dropped when advertisements were paid by the letter (those canny Scots).

Whisky possibly came to Scotland from Ireland. Possibly through the Kintyre peninsula (it is the closest part of Scotland to Ireland so makes sense). But however it got to Scotland it is the Scots that certainly had the greatest success with exporting it to the world. Once certain legalities were sorted and lines drawn, the mixing of rich, powerful Highland malts with mass produced, softer Lowland grains (I am surmising now, don't write in) resulting in mainstream acceptance meant the market for blended Scotch whisky breached London and through the tentacles of the British Empire, the world (give or take a few countries).

A product made exclusively from cereals malted, milled, mashed, fermented and distilled at least twice, with no additives (other than occasionally some *light* colouring) and only the water, peat fires (when used) and oak maturation to influence flavour (yes I know, yeast strains, mashing temperatures, fermentation times, still shape, middle cut size etc all have a part to play – are you sure you should be reading this section?). Blends became brands and brands became sought after. Johnnie Walker, Ballantine's, Buchanan's, Black & White, Dewar's, Dimple, Haig, White Horse... these became household names. Men throwing Molotov cocktails in the Second World War would stop, check the label on the bottle and only after ensuring it wasn't their favourite brand would then add the rag before lighting (I'm joking, again don't write in).

A lot of prior knowledge has been taken for granted in writing this book. So much so, that whilst I have promised in the Introduction not to go into too much detail I think some information and explanation is required. If you're long in the tooth (or liver) drinking whisky then you can skip this part. If you have happened upon this book by chance or been given it (or are now wondering how it ended up in this used book store) then this section may help with some background knowledge. For any further information regarding facts and figures of production, consumption and revenue please visit the Scotch Whisky Association's website where information is freely provided www.scotch-whisky.org.uk.

Today we have several classifications of Scotch whisky (this book is really only dealing with the Scottish side of things – apologies if you were looking on information regarding bottlers of whisky from other countries) that may need explaining in order to understand parts of the book.

Single Malt Scotch Whisky
Whisky distilled from 100% malted barley and taken from one
distillery using pot stills. This can be a vatting of different whiskies
(for example different years, cask types, peating levels etc).

Blended Malt Scotch Whisky
This is single malts from different distilleries blended together.

Single Grain Scotch Whisky
This is grain whisky (any grain) that is distilled either in pot
stills or continuous stills (even if this is single malt through a
continuous still) taken from one distillery.

Blended Grain Scotch Whisky
Grain whisky from different distilleries blended together.

Blended Scotch Whisky
Grain and malt whisky blended together (doesn't matter
if they are from different distilleries or not).

Single Cask Scotch Whisky
Whisky taken from a single cask. This generally implies the whisky has remained in the same cask, or at least not been blended if moved from one cask to another. This can be a difficult definition when we come to vatted or blended whiskies taken from a single cask.

Finished Whisky
This is not a legal term but refers to whisky that has spent time maturing in one type of cask before being transferred to another. This can be done as many times as desired and does not have to be disclosed to the consumer. Again, this can be misconstrued especially when used together with the above term 'single cask'.

The age on a bottle of whisky signifies the youngest whisky in the bottle. It is against the labelling regulations to mention on the label, bottle or packaging any information that would suggest any other age than the youngest constituent part of the whisky.

I'm not going to go into the extra terms listed above. To find out what pot and continuous stills are, or the production process there are numerous excellent websites and books that go into a detail to satisfy the biggest geeks. However, a few myths to dispel before reading on:-

Scotch whisky is not whisky until aged in oak for three years in Scotland. Before that it is known as 'New Make' or Scottish spirit if in the cask[1]. New make is clear like water, all of the colour comes from the maturation process (and/or the colouring agent E150). There is no such thing as a Double or even Triple malt. That would be a Blended Malt Scotch Whisky (see terms above). Double and triple malt are terms for beer. There is also really no such thing as Double or Triple Matured – see term above for 'Finished Whisky'. Either a whisky is matured or it isn't – it cannot be done twice.

Scotch malt whisky is distilled twice, occasionally three times (there are a couple exceptions where a part distillation occurs of some of the spirit – look up Mortlach or Springbank, actually, don't look them up, just go buy a bottle). For grain whisky you'll need to look up 'Continuous' or 'Coffey' still. Scotch whisky almost entirely utilises 'used' oak casks[2] – that is casks that have previously held a different alcoholic beverage. This goes back to the beginning of the industry when oak casks freshly emptied of wines would be filled to transport and store spirit. By happy accident[3] it was found that this

1. The moment it turns three years old it is then Scotch whisky.
2. When it is fresh oak the industry uses the term 'virgin' – as in 'not kissed by alcohol' (the virgin part is true, I made up the last bit).
3. The storage of liquids moving from amphoras to wooden casks was that 'happy accident'.

housing process would yield quite different results depending upon previous contents and time spent in casks. Casks that previously held Bourbon are the most common type of cask currently being used although they are not the most traditional (unless you can provide evidence to me that the Country Squire in the 17th Century was quaffing down Jim Beam with his grilled pheasant and turnip). Other cask types include Spanish & Portuguese fortified wines (such as Madeira, Port and Sherry), wine casks from France and Italy (mainly), and casks that have held spirit such as Cognac & Brandy. (For a truly funky experience a few Scotch whiskies have been matured in ex-Tequila casks and even an ex-Tabasco cask – although not sure the latter was allowed to be described as 'Scotch' whisky. The industry needs some boundaries...).

Old whisky does not always equal good whisky but almost always means it costs more. Good whisky is a completely subjective thing (but the consensus suggests some are better than others). Expensive whisky likewise does not signify quality. It can often be as a result of an overspend in packaging or marketing or PR. Or in some extreme cases, all three.

Introduction

"You'll never be an expert on whisky."

Hopefully, I've never referred to myself as being an expert. Those sorts of terms are for professors, court room testimonies and eulogies. Let's get something straight from the start; there is no such thing as an 'expert' on whisky. Sure there are those, some who work in white coats, that have doctorates in studies such as Yeast Strains, or Scatter Analysis, or Brewing & Distilling and whilst these people are very much experts in their fields, they are not, and generally do not consider themselves, experts on whisky.

There are respected palates, professional blenders and writers who have a way with description – but again, I don't recall any of these wonderful people describing themselves as an 'expert' on whisky. Well, apart from one – but we'll get to him later. Even those that become intimately familiar with, say a single distillery's output, would struggle to identify their own malt if taken from a single cask and put up against similar makes and ages.

Instead the journey of whisky, no, wait, let's call it an odyssey (it sounds better and I like the idea of it being 'longer' than a journey), the odyssey of the whisky drinker (that already sounds better) is a personal one – and very much unprofessional. It cannot be steered by anything other than your own personal preference. No other person is an expert on your palate in the same way that 'matchmakers' are usually a pain in the arse, busy-bodies. I have often heard people say 'I'm not an expert on whisky' to which the obvious reply is 'do you like this?'. Assuming they have an opinion, they are an expert on what whiskies they like. This isn't the world of wine after all (nudge, nudge, wink, wink).

As this is not a history of whisky in its entirety I feel no need to start at the beginning of the story[4]. I'm guessing that readers will already be acquainted with the term 'Whisky' (Uisge Beatha, Aqua Vitae, Water of Life) and it's rather foggy, but oft repeated, history. The constant reminders of its earliest references in around 1494; it's possible migration to Scotland from Ireland; it's origins most likely in Persia or somewhere nearby. Similarly much more will be assumed such as knowledge of the production methods and rules of whisk(e)y making and marketing[5].

As I intertwine my own tale, I will try to recall those incidents that were funny, embarrassing, revealing and interesting. For those that know me well, the title of this book will be amusing to you. I first moved to Scotland in January 2002 – Campbeltown to be precise. Twelve years later Scotland would have its first Independence Referendum and I was 'noted' for being a vocal supporter of retaining the Union. You'll be glad to read, dear reader, that I will not go anywhere near this live grenade of a topic. It is quite possible that soon after these words are in print Scotland may have indeed voted for full independence. In which case *'Nemo me impune lacessit'*.

To understand why there are independent bottlers and in particular their recent explosion, we need to head back and look at the industry from the 1940s onwards. Much of what happened, the decisions taken and at times fractious nature of the industry, caused the expansion of the '50s and '60s, the overproduction, recession and mergers of the next 20 years and the workings of a new, modern industry. I will explore what caused these decisions and what implications they had on the industry. Along the way I will tell my own story; simply as a glimpse into what it is like to start and run an independent bottling company.

I am concentrating upon the part of the industry that has fascinated and involved me the most; independent bottlers. That is, bottlers of Scotch whisky with no attachment to the distillers of the liquid inside the bottles. At the end of the book is a list of the main bottlers of the last 30-40 years and I will touch on many of these companies throughout. With one notable exception however. Whilst I will from time to time mention Gordon & MacPhail, much of their impact is excluded due to the size and difference in how they operate but mainly because their story deserves its own tome[6]. For any company, person or outfit that has been overlooked, I apologise – with the ever-changing nature of this industry, an exhaustive book was never going to be possible.

[Please note that where applicable these are my memoirs, notes and

---

4. There are several excellent books on the early history of the whisky industry. "The History of the Distillers Company 1877-1939" by R.B. Weir and "Scotch: The Formative Years" by Ross Wilson are two I recommend.
5. And isn't everyone an expert in this field?
6. Long overdue...

observations. Those that have contributed and/or are included in this book do not necessarily share my views and were not consulted prior to printing – other than on texts or an interview they provided.]

David Stirk, Thornhill, 2023

CHAPTER 1

WHY WHISKY?

"My first whisky was a Balvenie 10 year old Founder's Reserve - not so surprising, most bottles I consumed at the early stage were proprietary bottlings. However, I was lucky enough to get a few Cadenhead's Authentic Collection green bottles in the US in the 1990s, and also lucky enough later around the year 2000 to get some Signatory dumpy bottles and Douglas Laing Old Malt Cask ones when I came back to Taiwan. These ones really opened my eyes, since no one cared about single malts at the time. For me, independent bottlers allow you to explore a distillery in a new way. The IB acted as a window for whisky lovers when there were often only blended whiskies available; however, now that single malt is so popular and easy to get, IBs plays a role of introducing whisky lovers to something new. This is the value of the independent bottler."

HO-CHENG YAO (AKA KINGFISHER)
Master Keeper of the Quaich

If you're reading this I'm going to guess you're a whisky drinker. And having established that, I'm going to go out on a limb and suggest that you once had your 'moment' with the drink; your epiphany if you will. What Michael Jackson (the whisky writer, RIP) referred to as his 'road to Damascus moment'. Mine came in the Autumn of 1996 before a night-out in Skipton and in the form of a bottle of Glenlivet Aged 21 Years. Poured by a friend at the time it was the ice-breaker before the beer drinking began but I can only really remember that whisky from the whole night.

And that was it really. Just one dram of a rather decent Glenlivet 21 year old and I was hooked. Up until that point whisky, for me, had been an old man's drink – and not really the discerning drink of choice either. First experiences with the drink tended to be Bell's & Coke[7] and in reality, had you asked my peers what whisky they would drink the standard answer would have been Southern Comfort; such was the ignorance and detachment from the category[8]. The Glenlivet 21 year old knocked all of my prejudices out of the park. It wasn't rough like the cheap blends I had drunk. It was softer, and fruity and there was an oaky sweetness. It glided down the throat and coated the mouth with an aftertaste that made me want another sip. My friend, who had poured the dram, noted my surprise and delight and quickly returned his bottle to the cabinet.

That was it though, one small dram of a great malt whisky and I had been caught; hook, line and sinker. That whisky got under my skin and I realised there must be others like it. In the same year I had that Glenlivet I turned twenty and headed off to University so a fairly pivotal year in my life. Prior to that epiphany, I had not a clue what I wanted to do - I was about to start a four year degree in Business & Management at Bradford University[9] with no understanding or direction of either the course or what it could progress me to. I can't pretend to have worked much at Uni, which I am sure my fellow students can attest to, but I did manage to steer everything towards the whisky industry. My student loans were spent seeking out rare whisky books and buying the occasional bottle (sadly all too occasional[10]).

By far the single most important event during my Uni years was my tour of Scotland in the name of charity. This was in the summer of '99 and was fuelled more by boredom than a real sense of charity. I was working for an

7. A rather failed attempt by Bell's at the time was to pre-mix the two in cans. It was a poor imitation of what is, possibly, the world's easiest cocktail.
8. So much so that if someone arrived to a party with a full bottle of whisky and no mixer they were generally viewed with suspicion.
9. In 1995, when I applied to attend Bradford University, it was one of the top 20 Management Schools in the UK. When I left it had slipped down that list 100 places. I take full responsibility.
10. One of the most notable bottles I bought was a 15 year old Laphroaig bottled by Cadenhead's and sold through Loch Fyne Whiskies. This cask strength expression was passed around my friends, although consuming it straight after a 'Bradford' curry resulted in a few coughing fits. I loved it...

electricity company in Northern Ireland as part of my gap year (in order to get my Honours degree). In all honesty I had chosen Northern Ireland because of a girlfriend, that lasted just a few months, and also I could live rent-free with my dad who had moved across the Irish sea in 1996. The job was, for the most part, thoroughly mind-numbing. The company and in particular the Media & Communications Department I was part of were in a period of massive upheaval and change. Whilst this did come with some interesting moments (for instance I learned how large companies restructure to avoid declaring profits – they didn't teach me that at Business School[11]) the role was basically a skivvy, glorified tea boy, for the department (mostly consisting of scanning any printed media for any mention of the company, its subsidiaries and/or related to power). To this day, still the lowest paid job I've ever had.

The job did allow me to drive all over Scotland, collecting whisky (as I mentioned, for charity[12]) and meeting some of the nicest people, in what is, unquestionably, one of the best industries. That year out, as painful and as economically challenging as it was, was the real 'light bulb' moment for me. The plan was to drive from Glasgow to the Islay ferry, and thus the first day of the five day tour was visiting all of the Islay distilleries, then the ferry to Oban before finishing late at Ben Nevis. This was also going to be a 'dry' tour[13]. Ha! As if...

The first distillery on the tour was the newly re-opened Ardbeg. It was a glorious day and the three of us (I was not alone in this endeavour), having been entertained the night before in Port Ellen by 'Islay-Mick' and his talking crow, were at the distillery as early as possible. [Islay-Mick was quite the B&B operator. He was a widower who lived with a crow that was also a recent widow. He would talk to the bird as if it was human and the crow would listen and nod as if it understood. At dinner, Mick asked the three of us if we wanted beer with the meal. He then presented us with three different beer mugs and told us the pub several doors down would fill these up for us. And the pub duly complied - Islay, what a place!] We arrived at Ardbeg and parked in the completely empty car park. Strolling up in our kilts and matching jumpers we were greeted by Jackie Thomson with one of the warmest and most welcoming smiles you could possibly wish for.

"You'll be wanting a dram then." Jackie said with a grin. It was not yet 10am. Again, Islay, what a place!

And that was the end of the 'dry' tour. We were each given a dram of the newly launched Ardbeg 17 years old and as we sat in front of a (short-lived)

---

11. I also met Pierce Brosnan's stunt double. Yeah, he was just how you would expect.
12. The charity was MenCap – Mentally Handicapped Children
13. Northern Ireland, being a fairly religious country, meant we got a fair bit of coverage from the media for this supposedly 'dry tour'

video of a certain whisky writer making out he had single-handedly saved Ardbeg, drew lots over who would be the driver for the day. A praying man would have been on his knees – luckily for me I didn't lose.

Jackie, and the team at Ardbeg were wonderful. So was Iain Henderson at Laphroaig, Donald Renwick at Lagavulin, Jim McEwan at Bowmore, David Hardy at Caol Ila and John MacLellan at Bunnahabhain. Each gave of their time, proudly showing us around their 'unique distillery' explaining what made their whisky different and going into detail about the history and tradition that they were a part of. Each and every one finished their tour with a dram. Iain Henderson proudly showed us his First Edition of Barnard's "Distilleries of the United Kingdom" (I fawned over it but did not admit I had my own facsimile copy). Donald chatted to us about moving to the Island, having not long been transferred as part of Diageo's Distillery Management shuffling policy. Jim & John filled us with stories of the Island and life there. Jim McEwan, a true Illeach[14], is still there having left Bowmore to be part of the Bruichladdich team (revived in 2000) and now retired[15]. Jim, at the time of writing, is still with us whereas John has sadly joined the great distillery in the sky. I can add little to all that has been written and said about John. He was always a joy to be around and whilst he could enjoy a good grump every now and then it was always done with a wry smile and an infectious twinkle.

A further memory of David Hardy; as I had the pleasure of bumping into him a few more times. Some point after meeting him at Caol Ila he managed Dalwhinnie Distillery and after giving me a tour invited me into his office for a dram. I was surprised to see him pull out from his safe (all distillery managers should have a safe in their office) a bottle of Cragganmore Distiller's Edition. I think I said something along the lines of 'You're the first manager of a distillery to not offer me a dram from their distillery'. To which he replied something akin to 'Maybe, but what would you pour me if you worked here?'. The Cragganmore was very much enjoyed.

Back to Islay and this 'charitable dry tour' that I was part-way through. I should explain here that my travelling colleagues and I were Islay-virgins and in reality, distillery tour virgins. Now, I don't mean those bused-around tours where facts, figures, myths and legends are regurgitated for the benefit of those who enjoy such things. No, these were the old-fashioned, non-visitor centre, and zero knowledge (or acknowledgment at least) of any warehouse regulations; the 'no social media' tours. Remember those? For those of you that do, take a long, nostalgia-filled sigh. There are few greater sights in life than

14. An Illeach is a native of Islay.
15. Maybe, or working still... hard to keep a good man down.

a distillery manager reappearing into a cold, damp, earthen-floor warehouse with a bung hammer, vallinch[16] and glasses.

It is worth noting here that there are normal sized drams and there are 'Islay' sized drams (a tradition that is not necessarily unique to the Island). By the time we got to Port Askaig for the ferry back to the mainland, myself and the other 'drinker' had consumed at least six 'Islay' drams (I seem to recall Iain Henderson offered us more than one whisky, as did David Hardy, as did Bowmore – heck they probably all did). In metric terms we're talking about 40-50ml each dram (a miniature in other words – fourteen of these in a bottle). I think the ferry was mid-afternoon and I remember nothing about the journey. I do recall getting to Ben Nevis Distillery in the dark and giggling for most of the tour. John Carmichael, now infamous I'm reliably informed, showed us around and adorned us with Ben Nevis branded jumpers on the sole condition that we wore them around Speyside (for a laugh). At the end of the first day, at least two of us were no longer Islay virgins.

I'm pretty sure I was completely smitten by the first greeting we encountered at Ardbeg Distillery – but certainly by the end of our few hours on Islay I was convinced that the whisky industry was for me. I wanted to be a part of the passion and tradition and at the time did not mind what job it would be. Every employee we encountered from the managers to someone sweeping the steps would go out of their way, and with visible pride, to tell you about their distillery. I could not recall another industry that had such universal passion. More than that, the locals were also immensely proud of their little Island's incredible contribution and place in the world. This would be replicated throughout Scotland – it has always been a small country punching above its weight and with a people willing to travel to every continent to raise a toast.

Our charitable endeavours were greatly helped by many of the distilleries we visited. We had, cheekily, asked every company to donate a bottle from each distillery that we visited so that we could raffle them to raise money. Most of the companies were incredible in their response (I believe only Glenfiddich refused although apparently this was due to our letter not getting to the distillery manager but someone else). Chivas went above and beyond. They kindly collated all of the bottles from the several distilleries (including some we could not get to) and also raised over £500 internally through raffle tickets.

It was an incredible and life-changing week. I met people who are still friends to this day and several who are no longer with us. Somehow, and I've forgotten why, it got me an invite to the second ever Spirit of Speyside whisky Festival[17]

16. A valinch is a long, often copper, tube with holes at each end. It is used for withdrawing a small amount of liquid from a cask – usually for sampling purposes. It is about 50% fit for purpose.
17. Not sure it was even called that then – may have just been the Speyside Whisky Festival

to host a tasting at the Whisky Shop, Dufftown by then owner Fiona Murdoch. Fiona also got me an invite to be part of a 'Scotch' panel that would go head to head with a similar panel of Irish whiskey connoisseurs (trying hard not to use 'that' word).

The 'head to head' filled the Royal Dublin Society; three Irish advocates and three Scotch drinkers. A famous Irish radio DJ, Gerry Ryan (I'd never heard of him) was the compere for the evening. It was all meant to be light-hearted, good natured fun and we were all geared up behind the curtain ready to come on stage when we noticed that quite a large number of the crowd got up and left before the 'debate' began. It quickly became apparent that upon sitting down and spying the six glasses in front of them, the patrons, not wishing to waste an evening hearing some meaningless pitter-patter, swiftly necked each glass and speedily retreated to no doubt a few Guinness's to take away the flavour of whichever whisky they liked the least.

Despite this, we began and I recall Fiona being particularly unimpressed with one of the more 'fruity' Irish whiskies (I think she had brought Mortlach 16 year old, the Flora & Fauna bottling). On the Irish panel was a certain John Ryan (seventh generation from the original James Power or Power's Irish Whiskey fame, sadly no longer with us) who, with his soft accent and lyrical manner, eloquently described the discussion his chosen Irish Whiskey (Midleton I think) was having with him. It was chatting him up on the nose, gave a gentle kiss on the palate and left with some soft, caressing whispers as it slowly disappeared.

I was impressed. I had chosen, as a show stopper, Laphroaig 10 year old cask strength. I had prepared a little speech but after hearing John's majestic and ever-so-slightly erotic prose I quickly changed my mind and informed the one hundred plus Irish audience that peated Scotch whisky also talks to you. I took a sip.

Yep, this whisky is saying "Feck Off![18]"

I had not judged my audience, nor my fellow panellists soundly – the laughter I had anticipated was instead a deafening silence broken only by the occasional sound of shuffling feet, tutting and cracking of knuckles. Hey ho, live and learn…

18. It's a Father Ted thing…

CHAPTER 2

WWII – *Restrictions and Export*

"For centuries the Scottish whisky industry has benefitted from the efforts of independent companies. They were the entrepreneurs who brought Scotland's 'Water of Life' to the attention of the world, perhaps most notably in North America. Today they continue to push the boundaries of what is possible – rather than what is predictable."

GRAHAM USHER
Owner of Whisky Drop, Canada

It is unknown when the term 'Independent Bottler' was first coined and certainly what we now think of as an independent bottler is only a recent phenomenon. To understand where the modern day IB has come from we need to understand how the Scotch whisky industry began and evolved. Much of the early and 19th Century I will gloss over as there are incredibly thorough and well written books on the subject (see Bibliography). The independent Scotch whisky companies that will be referred to are the buyers, blenders, bottlers and brokers that were common place from the 1880s onwards.

These independent buyers, blenders, bottlers and brokers lived side by side, in harmony, with the distillers, using their output to make blends and brands that would go on to carry the name, quality and legend of Scotch whisky to all four corners of the globe. Distillers at this time were not in the business of bottling their own whisky as a 'brand'; most had been built in order to sell their output through agents and/or direct to blenders. Some of these blenders became so successful it allowed them to buy up some of the supplying distilleries to ensure quality and supply of their brand's constituents. The household names of today, the likes of Teacher's, Johnnie Walker, Chivas Regal & Bell's (among many others) all began as merchants; general stores that sold everything from coffee to gloves and of course, wine and spirits – and in particular; whisky.

And for much of the 19th Century this is how the industry continued. Some brands came and went and the practice of distilling industrialised as ever new inventions[19], methods[20] and preferences[21] were introduced. A whisky boom in the 1880s brought a crash, caused almost single-handedly by the Pattison Brothers in 1898[22]. This subsequently caused a period of consolidation and closures; mainly by The Distillers Company Ltd (DCL), who were able to buy up failing or bankrupt distillers at knock-down prices. Created in 1877[23] The DCL originally began as an amalgamation to fight off, buy up and control the cheap grain whisk(e)y that was coming into Scotland from Ireland and England. Their success led some small and medium-sized companies, such as Jas Stewart & Co of Saucel Distillery and Menzies & Co of Caledonian Distillery

---

19. Such as the Coffey Still.
20. The use of peat for kilning the barley was slowly phased out by most distilleries from the late 19th Century onwards. Malting companies, as opposed to floor maltings at each distillery, also became more prominent from the early parts of the 20th Century.
21. There was a continual move towards a lighter style of Scotch blends. Less peaty and matured for longer.
22. The Pattison's had built up a lavish business buying, blending and brokering Scotch whisky. By obtaining large credits from distillers, they massively oversubscribed their business and eventually collapsed. Their debts were estimated at £500,000 – around £76 million inflation adjusted to 2022.
23. By the owners of Port Dundas, Carsebridge, Cameron Bridge, Glenochil, Cambus and Kirkliston grain distilleries.

to ask to join[24]. As is often the case when a part of an industry attempts to monopolise, independent firms retaliate, and in a theme we shall see continue, North British grain distillery was built in 1885 to prevent the DCL controlling grain whisky prices.

The creation of the North British Distillery forced the DCL into believing that it needed to control more of its malt whisky supply and they built Knockdhu Distillery in 1894. After the aforementioned Pattison crash, the DCL reacted by heavily regulating the grain output (thought to be a large contributor to the overproduction that partly led to the price crash of 1898) – this included the purchase of Loch Katrine distillery (otherwise known as Adelphi) and the Ardgowan distillery (both acquired in 1902 but closed in 1907). Several more, large grain outfits, were bought at a fraction of their original cost and subsequently closed.

Between 1900 and 1914 DCL were involved with at least one amalgamation or buyout per year and by the start of World War One were claimed to be the largest distillers in the world and they continued their policy of consolidation throughout the 20s and 30s.

Despite this in 1930 Aeneas MacDonald, recording from the "Directory of Whisky Brands and Blends" noted that there were 4,044 brands of whisky; 3,428 were Scotch, 487 Irish and an incredible 128 that were blends of Scotch and Irish[25]. It is interesting to note that in 1900, just two years after the Pattison crash, there were over 150 distilleries at work in Scotland and between 1932 and 1933 just 15 distilleries operated – and none of those were working full time.

Prior to the '40s the Scotch industry had seen a flurry of North American investment. Hiram Walker-Gooderham & Worts, a distilling company in Canada, having built up contacts during Prohibition in America, began to purchase Scottish distilleries[26]. Glenburgie Distillery was bought first in 1930, before Miltonduff, the whisky blending outfit of J & G Stodart, the Stirling Bond Company and George Ballantine & Son, all in 1936. This now formidable outfit was renamed Hiram Walker (Scotland) Ltd and began building Dumbarton grain distillery (which also briefly housed a new malt distillery named Inverleven) in 1938. At the time this was the largest grain distillery in Scotland.

Another large Canadian distiller who set up a subsidiary in the UK was Seagram. This 19th Century company from Ontario, were later taken on by the Bronfman brothers (at the time this was a joint venture with The Distillers

---

24. In a bid to help control their own prices and market share. Interestingly the Caledonian Distillery proposal was accepted but Saucel Distillery was rejected. Twenty-one years later the DCL did finally take over Saucel and closed it two years later in 1903.

25. Irish (and English) grain whiskey was commonly used in vatting with Scotch grain whisky before being blended with malt whisky and called Scotch.

26. Canadian distillers did very well despite Prohibition and not necessarily because the Canadians were drinking more...

"SCOTCH WHISKY" FROM JAPAN.

Disclosure in Glasgow Court.

A remarkable account of the efforts of the Japanese to imitate Scotch whisky—even to the length of naming a Japanese town "Aberdeen" and calling the Japanese-made spirit "Aberdeen"—was given at Glasgow Sheriff Court yesterday.

The allegations were made at the resumed hearing of the case in which Messrs. Henderson & Turnbull, a Glasgow firm, are charged with applying the false trade description "Scotch whisky" to each of 500 bottles of a blend containing 33 per cent. Scotch malt whisky and 67 per cent, Irish grain whisky.

Messrs. Henderson & Turnbull have pleaded not guilty to the charge

Mr. Hastie, a director of White Horse Distillers, in evidence, described visits of Japanese men to the North of Scotland when he was there engaged on research.

The case for the defence was opened . Richard Francis Nicholson (73), chairman and managing director of J. & W. Nicholson & Co., Ltd., distillers and rectifiers, Bromley and Clerkenwell, London, said he had been in the thick of the controversy as to what was Scotch whisky and what was Irish whisky from an early date in his career. He had been in the business for over 51 years and it had been going on all that time and it had happened before that.

Speaking of the blending done by his firm, Mr. Nicholson said that they had never by indication on the label or otherwise described these blends as Irish malt blended with English grain or Scotch malt blended with English grain. They considered that it was universally acknowledged and known and they took the view that they were all British-made spirits belonging to the same category. His firm had never throughout its long history made any secret of the fact that they blended English grain or Scotch grain or Irish grain with Scotch malt in order to produce blended Scotch whisky.

The Court adjourned until to-day.

Northern Whig, December 1938

Company Ltd who liked the 'arms-length' distance from the smuggling of products into the US). In 1935 the Bronfman's, using the business links of Jimmy Barclay, bought Robert Brown Ltd, a Paisley based business with extensive stocks. The following year Seagram Distillers Co was registered. This business would be highly active after World War Two.

In the 1938-39 distilling season the industry had produced 10.6 million proof gallons[27] of malt whisky and 27 million proof gallons of grain whisky. In fact, the two seasons before the outbreak of the 'phony war' the industry produced nearly 18 million proof gallons of malt spirit and over 33 million proof gallons of grain spirit. By 1939 there was a record amount of just over 144 million proof gallons of Scotch spirit sitting in warehouses in the UK. By 1947

27. An Imperial Proof Gallon is 2.59 litres of alcohol litres (proof gallons are measured at 50% alcohol by volume).

25

the maturing stocks were almost halved from the 1939 figure (and included a much higher percentage of grain whisky than pre-war).

On the 1st March 1940 the Ministry of Food, as part of the 'Potable Spirits Order'[28] assumed control over the entire production of Scotch whisky. With the writing on the wall of War between Britain and Germany, overseas importers made a desperate attempt to 'stock up' and total exports jumped to over £16 million[29] (of which the US was more than £10 million). This was nearly one third higher than 1939.

During the war years of 1940-'45 the Scotch whisky industry, due to restrictions placed upon them by the Ministry of Food, produced around 16 million proof gallons of malt and 25 million proof gallons of grain spirit. It is interesting to note that as grain was rationed distillers operated their malt distilleries in preference to their grain operations. The huge stocks of existing grain spirit and the complexities of running a large continuous still with limited grain will have also persuaded distillers to favour malt whisky[30] production.

In combination with measures to assist the war effort the world was suffering from poor harvests and continual demands for grains to feed the population and armies (in addition to issues with shipping being sunk). Supplies of bottled Scotch whisky to the 'Home[31]' market were cut by the Scotch Whisky Association (SWA)[32] in 1940 by 20% as the export of products became imperative to assist with the war economy (7 million proof gallons were exported that year, mostly to the US). In 1941 the Ministry of Food again cut supplies to the home market by a further 50% of the pre-war level. This was combined with attempted price fixing by the SWA and tax hikes by the Chancellor. By the end of the war, the UK tax on a bottle of spirits had more than doubled as had its retail price. This punitive tax increase was seeking to reduce home consumption[33] of an export earning commodity and also to aid in the war effort; and like most tax increases, was not reduced after the war. And, like all areas of commerce where the government becomes too heavy handed, a healthy black market rose to quench the thirst of the rationed consumer.

Not all distillers were part of the Scotch Whisky Association (SWA) and ignored their attempts to set a universal price. Due to the scarcity and demand bottles were often being retailed four times over what the SWA were

28. This order prohibited the manufacture of any spirits from cereals except under license from the Ministry.
29. It would not be until 1952 that exports would reach that level again.
30. As soon as all restrictions were lifted in 1959 grain production leapt to 44 million proof gallons – doubling four years later.
31. United Kingdom
32. Formed in 1917 from parts of the Wine and Spirits Association and later renamed The Scotch Whisky Association in 1942. This cut was in line with government guidelines.
33. Mainly it was felt that exports took priority but the government was mindful of excessive drinking in light of an expected invasion.

WHISKY SALE

£16 2s per Gallon Paid in Glasgow

KEEN BIDDING

Buyers from all over the country attended a sale of whisky and other spirits in Glasgow yesterday. Whisky was sold at the rate of 10,000 gallons per hour, and more than £100,000 per hour, and at the end of the sale the total purchases amounted to £320,000. The top price was £16 2s per gallon of over-proof whisky, and licensed dealers stated last night that it would be uneconomic to sell such spirit "over the bar."

"Judging by pre-war prices and the lower rate of taxation, we would require nearly 4s per 'nip' of such whisky," said one publican. "What must happen is that expensive whisky will be blended with cheaper lots already held in stock, thus reducing the retail price, or it will be made available at fantastic prices in luxury restaurants, hotels, and clubs."

The sale was held in the Crown Hall rooms of Messrs Morrison, M'Chlery, & Co., auctioneers, and Mr William M'Chlery disposed of the stocks on offer, nearly 25,000 gallons, in two hours and 40 minutes. The spirits were owned by the late Mr Edward Cronin, who traded under the name of Garvie & Co., Kingston Street, Glasgow. Some of the whisky is immature, and will be left in bond, but one hogshead sold is 45 years old.

Some of the largest purchases were made by London dealers. Manchester agents bought several lots. Edinburgh, Glasgow, and Falkirk were the most prominent Scottish centres which may have local stocks augmented, and other Scottish dealers who made successful bids came from Dumfries, Dunfermline, Ayr, Ardrossan, Wigtown, Greenock, Paisley, Musselburgh, Renfrew, Kirkcaldy, Aberdeen, and Fort William.

The Scotsman, 20 January 1944

recommending and neither were some companies adhering to restrictions on 'home' allocations. The SWA retaliated by banning wholesalers and retailers from receiving products from its members.

As mature stock was used demand, under normal trading circumstances, would have driven up the value of remaining stock. The government had installed an 'Excess Profit' tax which effectively penalised any company that could do well out of war (initially it had been introduced to prevent arms and fuel suppliers profiteering towards the end of WWI). The tax at 100% on any activity above pre-war level prohibited distillers from realising the true market value of their remaining stock. The scheme, initially, was a success and during his 1941 Budget, the then Chancellor of the Exchequer, Sir Kingsley Wood, stated that:

> "The yield of National Defence Contribution and Excess Profits Tax exceeded the estimate of £70m by no less than £26m. The large surplus is due mainly to the public-spirited manner in which many firms and companies have paid over the estimated tax due from them without waiting for the figures to be finally agreed."

Wherever a punishing tax is introduced (or at least one that tries to temper the natural trend of price fluctuation), someone who can find a way around it will do just that. Unscrupulous traders such as Jay Pomeroy (originally a London impresario, more concerned with Ballet than Blends) and, by association, Jimmy Barclay, found ways of buying companies with stock and then selling the shares at a small profit and the stock at market value. For instance, in the Autumn of 1941 book value for stock was around 3 or 4 shillings a gallon. By the end of the year brokers were asking £3-4 per gallon. More than a dozen companies were disposed of in this way and those that wriggled through the net made a lot of money (some of which was used after the war to buy distilleries)[34].

In 1943 an auction was held to sell the stocks of a recently deceased dealer[35]. 195 hogsheads from the estate of Samuel Coulter of Ross and Coulter Whisky Brokers, would, before the war, have fetched around £3,000. With buyers travelling from all over Britain, a bidding war broke out and the stock fetched over £110,000. The top price paid during the auction was 221s (shillings) a gallon. By February of 1944, just four months later, a similar auction saw 20 year old blended stock fetch 322s a gallon and remarkably not long after this a blend made in 1936 (but returned to wood) realised 410s (this equated to 90s a bottle). The SWA had recently set maximum prices for its members of 25 shillings 9 d (pence) for a standard bottle, and 27s 9d for the deluxe or better brands.

To try and help combat the profiteering on aged stocks of whisky the SWA began buying up everything it could at auction or on the open market[36]. The combined efforts of the SWA, DCL and the government, along with an industry that was in the main compliant helped to 'curb the illicit trade and to some extent conserved the rapidly falling stocks which would be vital for the post-war development of the industry[37]'. In the Autumn of 1943 the Pot Still Malt Distillers Association stated to the Ministry of Food:

34. For more on this incredible story the best and most thorough research I could find is here http://lightlypeated.org.uk (article 'The Two Jays')
35. News Chronicle October 1943
36. Ross Wilson "Scotch: Its History and Romance" Page 86
37. Moss & Hume "The Making of Scotch" page 164

"We have repeatedly... pointed out the extreme importance of our trade from a national point of view in the export markets of the world... With stocks as they already are, well below the danger point, my members visualise great difficulties ahead in the post-war period in regaining the ground they have lost in these export markets unless matters are so arranged that stocks to meet these export demands are built up at the earliest possible moment."

Companies that had relied on age statements as a way to convey quality began to struggle to meet their blending requirements due to mature stocks dwindling.

"As stocks [for Johnnie Walker] were being drawn down and not replaced, one of the issues to be dealt with was the use of age statements, both for Red Label in the USA (which still had an 8 year old declared age) and for Johnnie Walker Black Label. By 1944 the age statements had gone.[38]"

Most blends of the era were from spirit matured for circa four to five years. This meant that whilst maturing reserves from 1937-1939 were essential to continue products during the war it was becoming evident that a post-war industry would be in dire need of stock. This prompted Winston Churchill as Prime Minister in 1945 to say:

"On no account reduce the barley for whisky. This takes years to mature and is an invaluable export and dollar producer. Having regard to all our other difficulties about export, it would be most improvident not to preserve this characteristic British element of ascendency."

Exports and 'home' rationing had greatly changed the landscape of the Scotch whisky industry. The US was taking anywhere from 50% to 75% of all annual exports during the war years – at first to ease the burden on the finances on the exchequer. Later as Lend/Lease[39] was introduced by Roosevelt, shipping returning to the US having dropped its war time cargo was re-filled with, amongst other things, thousands of cases of Scotch whisky.

From 1946 exports of Scotch began to climb. The world markets, either from supply through the Empire, travelling troops (especially the American forces) or as trade to aid the war effort, had got the taste for Scotch and by 1950 total exports had doubled from 1946. Rationing and restrictions (and punitive taxes

---

38. "A Long Stride" Nick Morgan 2022
39. 'The Lend-Lease Act' was introduced by Roosevelt to allow the Allied countries obtain war materiel without paying up front.

on the home markets) were still affecting production and sales but by 1950, 97 distilleries were operating either part-time or fully (compared to 93 in 1939)[40]. Meanwhile dozens of smaller independents had been bought out and simply disappeared within the folds of the larger conglomerates.

The Distillers Company Ltd, already the largest distillers from their mergers including the great Buchanan-Dewar and John Walker merger in 1925, and later White Horse in 1927 and Wm Sanderson in 1937, continued their dominance with the purchase of A&A Crawford in 1944. With each buyout and merger several smaller, and competing brands would disappear. Although records are hard to find, no less than twenty smaller blenders and bottlers were bought up and their names discontinued during the war years[41].

With the ending of the war distillers began to look to the future but the growth was stunted by a world shortage of grain. Millions throughout Europe and Asia were displaced and many nations had little or no harvest due to the fighting. The combined rationing of grain (for a twelve month period between 1943-44 meant there was no spirit made in Scotland) and emphasis on maintaining exports left the industry desperately low on maturing stock to rebuild from. By the end of 1947 despite some distilleries being able to operate[42] (albeit at a much reduced level) the pre-war level of maturing stocks had almost halved to just under 80 million proof gallons[43]. The industry was particularly low on grain whisky and post WW2 saw the changing nature of blended whiskies. Pre-war blends had tended to be at least 50% malt (with a high percentage of Highland malt[44]) this was to slowly drop and would never return as a general trend.

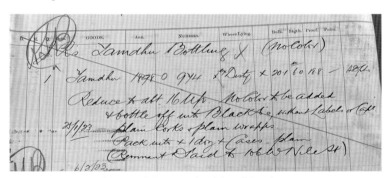

Robertson & Baxter Blend Scroll Book 1923

40. And a high of 161 in 1898 – a number never seen since.
41. This included: Glasgow Bonding Co Ltd, Alexander McGavin & Co Ltd, Peter Douglas & Co Ltd, J.S. & J Brown Ltd, Henry Simpson & Co Ltd, James McVey Ltd, Thomas Barr Ltd, William Hot & Sons Ltd, Gilmour Thomson & Co Ltd.
42. 70 malt and 6 grain distilleries in 1946
43. A level not seen since 1897
44. There was no official classification for 'Speyside' malt whisky until 2009 despite this blenders had been using the term 'Speyside' since at least the 1880s.

Tamdhu Distillery, previously closed for 20 years, was re-opened in 1947 by Highland Distillers, possibly to make use of grain allocations. Blair Athol and Tullibardine were restarted in 1949 and Pulteney, which was reconstructed, began again in 1951. In 1953 formal restrictions on distilling ended and Macallan began its expansion. Bladnoch was revived (having gone through a turbulent time during the war[45]) in '56 and Ben Nevis Distillery was bought out by Joseph Hobbs in 1955 from 'Long' John Macdonald Distillers.

Hobbs had a long and industrious career in the drinks industry[46]. Returning to the UK from Canada, having made a fortune and lost it, he set up the Associated Scottish Distillers to take advantage of the post-Prohibition burgeoning market in the US. In 1936 the firm bought Glenury Royal Distillery and then Glenlochy and Bruichladdich a year later. In 1938 the firm continued its purchases with Glenesk, Fettercairn and Benromach as well absorbing the blending firm of Train & Mcintyre.

The Associated Scottish Distillers, either over-extended or finding the war restraints stifling business, sold out to the all-encompassing Distillers Company Limited in 1953[47]. Working under a previous company name of Macnab Distillers, Hobbs immediately set out to rebuild. In 1955 he acquired the Ben Nevis Distillery. No doubt having ruffled feathers Hobbs found that buying grain spirit for his blends, almost entirely controlled by the SWA, difficult, and quickly established his own Coffey Still within the Ben Nevis Distillery.

Charles Doig, the renowned distillery architect and inventor who had designed Glen Elgin Distillery in 1900[48], stated that no new distillery would be built in the Highlands for fifty years. His prediction was one year out as Tullibardine broke the hiatus being completed in 1949. The distillery was converted from a brewery and fittingly designed by a new distillery architect; William Delmé-Evans[49].

This new distillery, along with an easing of grain and distilling restrictions saw a period of mass extensions in the industry. Three more distilleries would be built in the '50s; Glen Keith in '57, Lochside and Tormore in '58[50], but the

---

45. See http://lightlypeated.org.uk (article 'The Two Jays')
46. For more information read Iain Russell's excellent article "Joseph Hobbs' on www.scotchwhisky.com.
47. This brought into the DCL fold the distilleries of Montrose (later renamed Glenesk), Benromach, Glenury-Royal and Glenlochy. This acquisition also saw the end of several smaller blending names that were competitors to the large brands within the DCL.
48. Coming so soon after the Pattison crash, Glen Elgin closed just seven months later although would re-open in 1901. Doig is most famous for his Oriental style Pagoda roofs – an iconic image of Scottish Distilleries.
49. Who would go on to design Jura, Glenallachie and MacDuff. Delmè-Evans built Tullibardine to be gravity-fed.
50. Kinclaith Distillery was installed within Strathclyde Grain Distillery in '58 (closing in '75) and Strathmore Distillery within Cambus Grain Distillery was built the same year but operated for only one year.

decade would see many distilleries re-built, modernised and increased in capacity (and often all three).

As markets recovered and confidence grew, the industry stepped up its production of grain whisky. Between 1959 and 1966 production more than doubled from 41 million proof gallons to 90 million. Much of this was due to the construction of three new large grain distilleries. Invergordon was built in 1961, mainly to provide employment to the local community (hit hard by the closing of the Admiralty base). When opened Invergordon had the potential to add 4 million proof gallons a year but rapidly expanded just two years later with the addition of two additional Coffey Stills and a new potential of around 11 million gallons a year. Wm Grant & Sons, falling foul of supply issues from the DCL, built Girvan in 1963 on the West coast of Scotland near the town of the same name. Inver House Distillers also built Garnheath distillery in Airdrie in 1965. Combined these two additional distilleries could add a further 9 million proof gallons a year. Scottish Grain Distillers also invested heavily in new plant leading to the 90 million proof gallons distilled in 1966.

Quite how the industry survived the war years is really down to how one reads between the lines. A dip in quality, age and age statements and slightly shady practices were all part of the mix. The control and forward thinking of the Scotch Whisky Associations and its members (along with several other firms who saw the long-term advantages of their controls and measures) ensured the industry better weathered the Second World War (than it did from the First).

The large and traditional 'Home' market was punished in favour of getting the product overseas, and in particular to the US. Stocks, made in the two years before 1940, were used sparingly. We can only imagine the impact this period had on the rural communities as the distilleries lay dormant. Many of the warehouses were used for grain storage but not to any great extent. Conscription pulled the young men away and the remaining few were encouraged to find other local work. Despite assurances from the Churchill, and then Attlee governments, the small communities must have feared a similar fate as befell Campbeltown after The Great War[51].

Whichever way it is assessed, the larger firms came out fittest and an unknown, but not insignificant, number of small independent blending and bottling firms disappeared and with them their brands. Large brands took over the large markets and in particular the US became the focal point for the recovery of the industry. However, whenever an industry becomes heavily reliant on one market it becomes overly susceptible to changes within that

51. Between the end of the First World War and 1928 Campbeltown lost at least 17 distilleries. Much of this was due to a population loss and shift after the war.

WHISKY TRADE OPTIMISM
Hopes for an Early Restart of Distilling

THAT there is every likelihood of Scottish distilleries being given a quota of barley to enable them to resume distilling on a restricted scale early in the New Year is the view generally shared by prominent men associated with the industry on Speyside, home of the world-famous Highland malt whiskies.

A prominent North of Scotland distiller said yesterday that although so far no pronouncement has been made by the Ministry of Food, the Minister himself had not been unsympathetic to the appeal made to him on Thursday by a deputation consisting of North of Scotland M.P.s, along with representatives of the distilling industry.

Already, he said, barley was being dehydrated and malted for maltsters on behalf of brewers and quite a number of distilleries. Plants were being overhauled, and workers were being engaged at doing odd jobs round the distilleries in the hope of a restart. Once distillery workers were allowed to find remunerative employment elsewhere, it was difficult to get labour; but, he added, there was an optimistic view about a restart.

The Scotsman, October 1946]

market. As we shall see over the course of the next few decades, fashions, fads and economies will force the Scotch whisky industry into some uncertain times. At this point however, in the 1950s, with restrictions eased and a super-wealthy, growing population in the US desperate for its glass of Scotch, the industry expanded and distilled with gusto.

CHAPTER 3

FROM
NORWICH
TO
LOS ANGELES
TO
CAMPBELTOWN

"Independent bottlers play a huge part at Maltstock. And it has definitely grown over the years. I remember in the first years (2009 & 2010) we had distillery managers visit and there were some very memorable moments. But in the last seven to eight years there has definitely been much more independent bottlers that have hosted tastings – and these reps/companies tend to be whisky enthusiasts themselves. That's why it works. In the end (and in the beginning) whisky was always about the people! It is one of the things attendees really enjoy; having time to sit down and have a nice chat with the people that usually just pour them drams."

TEUN VAN WEL
Founding member of Maltstock

One of the themes that will run through this book, the contributions, stories and events, will be the generosity of those that work in and around the whisky industry. And equally as important, the gang that whisky attracts. Without this generosity (and a generous spirit of letting people find their feet) I doubt I, and many others, would have found our path or stayed the course. I can vividly recall the first tasting I hosted. Part way through I was trying to recall the name of someone I had met just moments ago and the harder I tried, the further away the name went. The tasting did not get much better from there either; stumbling over my notes and lacking any real, hands-on knowledge I realised that the audience were all each more capable of hosting this tasting than I was (not one person walked out, maybe the door was locked).

About a year prior to hosting my inaugural tastings I happened upon a young chap[52] working in a bar in a rather swanky hotel in Craigellachie. I was not a resident in said hotel but it had already gained a certain fame for its whisky bar which boasted, at the time, one of the largest assortments of whisky in Scotland. The Barman looked just old enough to be serving me alcohol and I plucked for one of the £2.50 malts (some were as much as £20 per dram). The Barman gave me the once over, me being slightly younger than the usual clientele that he was used to serving.

I could, at this point, lie and invent a whole host of small-talk before myself and the Barman hit it off. I could, but both Mark Watt and I are useless at small talk. Which is probably why we did hit it off, almost immediately. I think it was the fact that both of us were in an environment that was beyond our means, and yet here we were. I believe to this day, some twenty odd years later, neither of us still believe we should be amongst such grandness – but then, maybe we have each played a part in removing some of the stuffiness of the product.

Mark was a Dufftown native (well, Craigellachie at least) and had grown up with whisky in his blood. I've always felt Mark was like Obelix (from Astrix & Obelix), but rather than fall into a pot of magic potion he fell into a vat of whisky – and seems to have been superhuman ever since in his ability to drink it. Quite frankly Mark's story should be for another book but we will gain his insight later into the industry that he joined more or less around the same time as I.

I attended the next two Speyside Whisky Festivals and met with the publisher of the newly created Whisky Magazine. He suggested I get down to London for a job interview. The fact that a publisher would contemplate an entire magazine on Whisky was a real statement of the changing nature of the industry. In the late '90s the whisky industry (pretty much across the board)

---

52. He's 4 years my junior, hardly young.

was male dominated and certainly targeted towards men encroaching or past middle age. Tartan, twee and tins (the three T's of the Scotch whisky marketing departments) were still commonplace. Granted the industry had at least removed the dancing red-haired Scotsman[53] from the mainstream advertising but progressive it was not.

However, the newly created Whisky Magazine, whilst maintaining its glossy and unruffling approach, identified the change in wind. The fourth edition, printed not long before I joined, was centred upon 'Women in Whisky' and highlighted the long and varied contributions that women brought to the industry[54]. This was published around twenty-three years ago and feels odd mentioning now. I have never worked in or for a company that did not have a great mix – to the point of it not being a 'thing'. There has certainly been a welcome shift in the past twenty years of more roles being visible and a definite increase in production staff being women. My hope is that it is now not a 'thing' anymore and I, and all who I sail with, could not care who or what makes, bottles, markets, fills and serves my glass.

Whisky Magazine had a difficult tightrope to tread. In its infancy by far the greatest number of subscribers were within the industry. These readers wanted industry news, analysis and recognition. Whilst those reading as consumers and fans wanted information, releases, discovery and recommendations. The magazine wanted, naturally, to please as many readers as possible. Part of my role, along with the odd article, was to request bottles for sampling; contact the two reviewers to inform them exactly what was coming; ensure samples had been sent and had arrived; chase the reviewers for their tasting notes and scores; begin formatting for the next issue; chase the reviewers again; work on something else; chase the reviewers as deadline for print was days away and then finally collate the notes.

The two reviewers were, to begin with, Michael Jackson and Jim Murray. Michael was a fellow Yorkshireman (from Wetherby, although unlike me he liked Rugby League and not Union). He had found fame as a journalist of beer but began writing his Malt Whisky Companion in the late '90s. This was the first mainstream whisky guide that offered tasting notes and scores for whisky - it was by far the biggest selling whisky book of its time. Michael was a quiet, humble and kindly soul. He was encouraging to me and, whilst never the quickest at working, was always polite and gave freely of his time. Then there was Jim Murray.

To begin with Jim Murray and I hit it off. Jim had been a Fleet Street journalist and had followed his passion of whisky into becoming a full-time

---

53. Adelphi Distillery Co took great delight in reviving this as their logo.
54. There is much historical evidence to suggest that distilling (pre-industrialisation), was part and parcel of a woman's day to day life.

writer on the subject. Easily the most widely-travelled and knowledgeable on the subject he had built a solid following. I had read most of his whisky books and his writings had really got me into Bourbon and in particular Rye whisky. No doubt my praise and thanks for his guidance allowed for a harmonious start to the relationship. We hit it off to such an extent that Jim offered me a job as his researcher and PA. Essentially I was to manage his schedule, sample requests and tasting notes database. A timely intervention from my boss at Whisky Magazine paused my acceptance of the role. Consequently my relationship with Jim, rather abruptly, broke down.

Soon after Jim Murray was no longer a contributing editor for Whisky Magazine. [It was Jim that informed me I would never be an expert on whisky[55].] Instead Jim continued to publish books and attend festivals and tastings around the world (for a while). His Whisky Bible is published annually, and despite his prior decrying of writers giving scores, he scores all of the whiskies and announces annual winners for certain categories. Around 2015 he announced Crown Royal Harvest Rye the best whisky in the world and I'm not sure anyone has taken him seriously since. His name did start to trend again a few years back when his choice of possibly misogynistic language was called into question.

The industry was changing, rapidly. And whilst the big writers, names and personalities like Dave Broom, Charlie MacLean and Hans Offringa have enthusiastically embraced and encouraged this change. Others, and I believe Jim Murray to be one, have not embraced it. Perhaps clinging onto something they felt was theirs – a 'boys' club if you will. Thankfully, these harbourers of days long gone are very few and far between.

The highlight of my time with the magazine was undoubtedly organising and then taking part in what was termed the 'Best of the Best' tasting. Taking the fifty or so highest scoring whiskies from everything that had been reviewed up to that point and also inviting anyone and everyone the magazine felt would add to the event. The tasting was to be seven flights of whisky tasted over the best part of a day and each flight would have a theme. I had hand-picked my table which included Jamie Walker (owner of Adelphi) Ewan Gunn (at Cadenhead's at this point), Richard Joynson (then owner of Loch Fyne Whiskies), Bill Lumsden (Glenmorangie) and David Robertson (then Macallan). The whiskies we tasted were quite incredible but the highlight of the day was watching Bill and David try and guess their own whiskies when we had the 'Sherried Whiskies' flight (both were wrong – experts hey!) and also Richard giving every American whiskey a score of two out of ten with tasting

---

55. See opening line to Introduction. He was of course quite right.

notes that just repeated 'diesel and boiled potatoes'[56].

2001 saw the first Whisky Live event held in London. It was not the first single location whisky festival as there had been similar festivals in the US and Europe before this. Despite the growth in interest and readers there was an attitude of simply announce it and people would come. I was tasked with travelling around London to drop leaflets at stores and try and get tickets given away as promotions on local radio. The shops, bar a few, were not interested in giving out the leaflets and I'll wager most of what was left was binned and the radio stations could not have cared less. Most informed me that promotions like this take months of planning and cost a small fortune including ad campaigns. My budget for promotion was zero. Other than several pieces in the magazine there was very little promotion for the event and as such the event was poorly attended.

My time at Whisky Magazine, although enjoyable, was very brief; a combination of an unwillingness on my part to work on anything that wasn't whisky related and in part, as a scapegoat for the miserable attendance numbers of the first Whisky Live in London. Initially after leaving the magazine I attempted to start my own periodical that would catalogue Independent Bottlers – giving trade and consumers an insight into what was available and coming with independent reviews (and no scores). It was a good idea, I think, but several of the larger independent bottlers were not keen on sharing importer and retailer information and some never bothered to get back to me. The project died a swift death but did introduce me to quite a few companies.

Around this time I had met up with an old family friend who owned a publishing company and, as a whisky enthusiast, had had the idea of a printed updateable guide to whiskies. Similar in many ways to Michael Jackson's "Malt Whisky Companion" (ok, in too many ways[57]) this book, imaginatively titled "The Malt Whisky Guide", would be in a clip file where pages could be removed and inserted. The idea was that as new releases came and old whiskies were removed, the book could remain relevant without the need to buy a new book each year.

I had time, whilst working shifts at a Library, and since the publisher refused to pay the money a real writer demanded I was asked to write the book. I had the contacts, from my time at Whisky Magazine to ensure as many companies as possible were listed. The basic plan was to exclude all limited editions, market exclusives and independent bottlers. Even so the

---

56. When the American tasting was organised, one American attendee from a Bourbon distillery, when told that many of the whisky flights were all Scotch whiskies, commented: 'But they all taste the same to me'. Both countries make excellent and very different whisky. Fact. But Bourbon can never rival the diversity of flavour that Scotch can. Also fact.

57. Michael did not seem to mind – perhaps believing that imitation was the highest form of flattery – he even contributed the foreword.

book included well over one hundred malt whiskies which would arrive by an ever increasing bemused troop of couriers and postal workers. Eventually the small lounge that I shared with two other house mates was carefully arranged so that access to and from the armchairs could be managed without standing on a whisky. It was like a scene from a great heist – as if a whisky shop had been ransacked. I seem to recall that for several days I never left the armchair apart from obvious reasons. It was not the toughest gig I've ever had.

In order to feel I was competent enough about the distilling process I asked Stuart Thompson, then manager at Ardbeg, if I could come and learn the process 'hands on'. Stuart checked with head office and everything was ok'd and I headed back to Islay for just my second time. Working at Ardbeg in August was heavenly. The staff were typical to the Island in that I was immediately welcome and part of the team. The process part was of course not difficult to get to terms with (I was not there to learn what happened when things go wrong) so I spent most of the week with the warehouse crew filling and stowing casks in the traditional manner. By the time I had spent my time working there my clothes positively reeked of peat smoke (after all, they do it call it 'Peat Reek').

Whilst the book was fun it was, rather predictably, not a huge success. I'm not sure the publishers ever factored in the cost of shipping updates. Nor the incredible speed with which new whiskies and ranges were being launched. The number of pages quickly outgrew the small filo-fax style book and the initial large print run was hastily turned into a one-off paperback thereby defeating the purpose. I was left jobless, penniless and without much of a clue.

On a bit of a whim and a suggestion from a friend[58] in the industry I headed to the States in the hope of being a salesman or brand ambassador for Schieffelin & Somerset, importers of Diageo spirits. The meeting never happened and try as I may I could not find work in any industry. Down on my luck it appeared the only meaningful work I could possibly obtain was local government; i.e. the LAPD. I sailed through the first two written exams (apparently I was part of the one fifth who had English as their first language) and due to my degree I would, after basic training (and about six weeks walking the beat), be fast-tracked into pretty much any department I fancied. I had my eye on the fraud department or part of the business team. My final interview was scheduled for 11th September 2001. There are a few days in my life I will never forget, but none will come back to me as vivid as that day. It changed the world and redirected my life.

With all my options for work seemingly gone I was desperate when my publisher informed me that the Scotsman Hotel in Edinburgh was looking

---

58. John Glaser who was about to launch Compass Box Delicious Whisky.

for a bar manager for their specialist whisky bar. I found enough part-time work through family in California to afford a plane ticket home and with just about every cent I could muster headed to meet the manager of the hotel. Unfortunately during the last few weeks the board had met and decided that instead of a whisky bar they would open a second restaurant to ensure five star status. Much of the whisky was to be sold[59] off and the bar converted.

I was now at my lowest point and feeling very sorry for myself. Walking back along the Royal Mile I figured I would kill time before my coach departed to pop into a whisky shop at the bottom of the street near the Holyrood Palace called Wm Cadenhead's Ltd. I had made friends with a previous employee of theirs called Ewan Gunn who had since left to join Angus Dundee Distillers. I entered the shop and casually looked around (which, if anyone has ever visited, takes about three or four minutes to read the blackboard and look at the few whiskies actually visible). I remember striking up a conversation with the rather dapper chap working there.

"You used to work for Whisky Magazine."

"That's right." I replied.

"Are you looking for work?"

"Yes." And I explained what had happened with the Scotsman Hotel's bar.

"Pfft, silly decision." He exclaimed. "What do people want when they come to Edinburgh? Bagpipes, castles, the Tattoo and Whisky!" There was much emphasis on the last word. "Can you meet me in Glasgow in a week and we can discuss a job that is going?"

I didn't need asking twice. I believe in life you make much of your own luck but this chance meeting, for me at that time, was beyond propitious. The man I had casually chatted to was Neil Clapperton, Managing Director of J&A Mitchell, the parent company of Springbank Distillery and Wm Cadenhead's. After meeting Neil and some of the Cadenhead staff in Glasgow I was invited down to Campbeltown to meet the rest of the J&A Mitchell team before a job was offered.

Two things struck me on that first trip to the offices of J&A Mitchell. Firstly, I would try as hard as I could to never have to take the coach from Glasgow to Campbeltown again. Secondly, that evening I had dinner with the Company Secretary, a tall and friendly man called Stuart Campbell. At dinner he was very liberal with the wine (at least two bottles were finished, mostly by me) and before heading off he casually introduced me to the current Sales Manager of Springbank, a then young and ever hilarious Euan Mitchell (a touch shorter than Stuart).

---

59. Something I'll bet they regretted.

It was only the next morning, sporting a rather bruising hangover, that I realised Stuart and Euan had 'tag-teamed' me to see what I was like on a night out. The whisky industry is big in a way, but also quite small and as an employer J&A Mitchell could not afford to have someone that behaved 'differently' having taken a drink. To this day I still think that was incredibly prescient of them although not necessary for me. I am a soppy, tired drinker. I know my limits and then it's off to bed...[60]

---

60. I was especially lucky to get the job as the last employee, another Englishman, had recently made off with the company credit card – last seen somewhere in Thailand...

CHAPTER 4

The Whisky Loch

"We would not now be seeing such old releases from certain distilleries if it was not for independent bottlers. Certainly the independent bottlers are seen by the consumer with increasing respect which to me is well deserved. We were often told, or believed, that malt whisky was a robust drink only suited to hardy outdoor types. So in a sense the independent bottlers were a custodian of some of these brands and this sector."

ALAN WINCHESTER
Retired Master Distiller

We left the whisky industry after WWII frantically rebuilding in order to take advantage of a growing global demand for Scotch whisky. Formal restrictions (mainly the rationing of barley) were finally ended by the UK government in 1953 but in reality, by 1950, there were more distilleries operating than before the war. In 1960 the industry would reach 106 operating distilleries and this number would not noticeably change for decades. The Times Weekly would report in September 1963:

> "Each year since the war, exports of Scotch whisky have shown an increase and in 1962 they reached the highest ever figure of 30,069,705 proof gallons, a rise of 12.5% compared with 1961. As in previous years the bulk of these exports went to America... The European market has shown a spectacular upsurge over the past three years.

> "Blenders, who must in most cases buy their stocks of whisky several years before they will bottle it, are continuing to press distillers for greater production. In response to this pressure the distillers are installing additional equipment and, at the same time, using every method of extracting additional production from existing plant."

It does not take much of an economist to see that demand would greatly increase as restrictions were eased. Those able to secure stocks in the immediate post-war years made incredibly large margins when that stock was realised. This, in hindsight, was always likely to be the case. Between 1948 and 1958 production more than doubled and then more than doubled again by 1965. To put this into context, production during the two years before the war (when distillers scrambled to lay down stock in preparation for a prolonged period of hostilities[61]), were equal to what the industry made in one season in 1965-66. In the next year this went up by another fifteen per cent – and continued to climb.

In June 1960, Sam Bronfman, the enigmatic owner of Seagram's, said the following at the opening of the new Glen Keith-Glenlivet[62] Distillery:

> "It may well be that at present time more stocks of whisky are being produced and held than are necessary for the development of this industry. The era of shortage of whisky during and after the war produced inevitably considerable speculation in whisky stocks. This in turn forced up the prices and has encouraged a certain speculative element into our business, but the distiller who produces good sound

---

61. And having learned lessons from WWI.
62. Now known as Glen Keith and recently revived. Many of the distilleries local (and some not so local) to The Glenlivet suffixed their name to show proximity to the region and a perceived quality due to that locale.

whisky according to the highest standards of the industry and sells with dignity can surely look to the future with confidence. It needs a stout heart to brave the hazards and the ups and downs of the whisky business but quality and integrity will always win the day. Would it be true to say, that people generally are becoming more mature, more grown-up, perhaps more sophisticated, certainly more moderate in their outlook towards alcoholic beverages?"

This is a fascinating speech, and must have raised several eyebrows at the time. It is hard not to wonder how anyone hearing this must have reacted to the comments regarding 'people becoming more mature' and 'grown-up' in their drinking. No doubt this is a reference to changes in attitudes after 1945 as the war had seen a huge increase in the use of alcohol as a way of getting on with life[63].

There is no doubt, as Bronfman predicts, some companies had fallen foul of rising prices as we can see from the announcement in the Wine & Spirit Trade Record in January 1963:

"A fall in whisky prices was one of the causes of the failure of Alexander Davey (Holdings) Ltd., creditors of the company were told in London. The company, established in 1958 was formed to sell unmatured whisky to investors and also to export matured whisky either in bottles or in bulk... the prices of whisky fluctuated considerably and this caused a number of investors to request the company to purchase back their holdings, which the company did, sometimes for more than the prevailing market prices. During the past 18 months to two years the general trend had been for prices to fall. This was due according to Mr Davey to the emergence of brands of Scotch in the US that were not Scotch."

We'll get onto imitation Scotch later but Davey's company was not alone in getting out of step with regards to investment, and nor would this be limited to the early 1960s. But it is perhaps more incredible that Bronfman would suggest the industry was on course to oversupply on the very day that a new malt distillery was opened - and only the second built since the turn of the century. The problem facing the industry was one of maintaining stock and forecasting when certain brands required, or at least preferred an age statement. This, almost unique to the whisky industry will remain an issue – there is no choice but to wait it out[64]. Nick Morgan states in his book

---

63. For an incredible account of this read 'Stalingrad' by Anthony Beevor. The term 'drinking oneself to death' will haunt some of the passages.
64. And yes I am having a little pop at those industries that can 'solera' their products to suggest ages that are barely relevant to the contents.

"A Long Stride[65]":

> "Before the war the company [DCL] had had an ambition of achieving an average 10 year old age statement for Red Label and 15 (regardless of age statement) for Black Label... but the thought of achieving targets of this nature by even the 1960s seemed impossible."

It is possible that like so many great business visionaries, Bronfman was just ahead of the curve. There was an overriding confidence in the industry. And not just from within it, investors from several walks of life, and continually growing speculation from businesses and investors in the US, fed a surge in additional capacity and production. It would have been hard not to have got caught up with this fervour for stock. Exports doubled from the end of the war to 1950 and then doubled again just seven years later. By 1962 exports were six times greater than that of 1946. In monetary terms the value of Scotch as an export product went up 1000% in twenty years and nearly twice that by the end of the 1960s. In particular the industry had tried to catch up with grain production. As we saw distillers had preferred to make malt whisky during the war due to limited grain supplies and this fuelled investment and eventually overproduction. As surplus mature grain whisky became available prices dropped and confidence dissolved.

In many ways, this is the first 'Whisky Loch'. Until I began the research into this book I had believed that there was just one 'Whisky Loch'; whereas in reality, as everything is cyclical in business, the 'Loch' of the late 1960s was the first of several. Within the production departments of the Scotch whisky companies this would be referred to as the 'Seven Year Itch'.

With this oversupply came the introduction of cheaper products onto the market. In 1974 The Telegraph published an interview with Ellis Goodman, who was a director of Amalgamated Distilled Products:

> "With the excess production of grain whisky on the market between 1966 and until very recently it has been possible for substantial quantities of cheap blended Scotch to be exported to various territories for local bottling... this has led to various products under numerous labels (sometimes even under branded names), appearing on the shelves of retail outlets in important Scotch territories, side by side with the major international brands, but at substantially reduced prices. The public having bought these products and found that they are not only cheap as to price, but cheap as to quality, are

65. Page 232

turning away from 'real' Scotch, especially in Germany."

Becoming a highly-driven exported product and also now suffering with over supply the industry began trying avenues and/or increasing supply to what had previously been less important. This resulted in the growing market for the export of bulk blended and malt going overseas and the introduction of what the industry termed 'Cheapies'. These were blends of a younger age than established brands and being made up with a higher proportion of grain whisky (as this was in abundant supply). The Wine & Spirit Trade Record[66] (WSTR) noted:

"After the burnt fingers in grain whisky investment, especially by Germans and Swiss[67], in the 1960s (and for other reasons) the more attractive investment today is in malt whisky, the indispensable heart of any blend and the fastest growing section of the industry at the consumer purchasing end."

'Cheapies' were to become a greater problem for the industry from the 80s onwards, but like all of these developments, the trend has its roots much earlier. The Scotch industry was constantly struggling with investment due to the nature of how stock and profits were taxed[68]. Investment, in reality those able to buy new fillings (be they independent blenders, brokers or investors), were encouraged. But as with all investments there was an element of *buyer beware* as the WSTR noted in 1974:

"...to be deplored, are those who invest speculator's money in un-named, un-specified brands of whisky and take what can only be described as excessive charges, but a somewhat undesirable fringe of investor's, who will advise and invest in any sphere has grown up and are to be avoided in this the industry's hour of need to carry an increasingly heavy burden of financial investment. Malt is the particularly attractive field of investment, especially as there seems to be a shortage of mature malt emerging about 1974. In any event, the amount of new whisky which a blender himself fills is largely influenced by the prospect of selling any surplus he may hold at a profit. And towards the end of 1972 and the beginning of 1973 the prices of mature malt whisky firmed by as much as 20 per cent."

66. This was a UK monthly trade magazine that carried news and in-depth analysis of the wine and spirits trade. It was a fascinating resource for this book.
67. I have found no evidence to support this singling out of German and Swiss investors. It appears more likely that US investors were the main thrust.
68. This was eased in the mid 80s. Eventually banks would also lend against stock rather than company value.

There was a constant investment issue for the industry after the war. This is in no small part due to the very nature of the product; the ageing period for whisky providing an 'add value' period to anyone wishing to see a return. Coupled with the costs of building, maintaining and expanding distilleries:

> "Demand for five to six year old malts has again increased during the past year or so [1973-74], particularly for the better class malts. Much of this demand is due to the activities of speculators who buy to sell to customers. This artificial influence on prices was not indicative of a shortage of blending terms since the industry itself had been fairly realistic about production.[69]"

Islay Shaw, Group Distilleries Manager of IDV[70] replied:

> "The increase in demand is to some extent artificial. On average, the prices of six year old malts has gone up 30 per cent. Part of this increase is due to speculation. The supply and demand situation from the blenders does not justify the increase. Indeed, export sales have gone down by two per cent, so why should the prices go up? I came across a case recently of someone who had been sold a parcel of malt for £1.75 a proof gallon only to get £1.55 for it after he had held it for six months."

It is odd for us now to think of the industry being one of 'futures', seeing as it is now such a closed shop. But we need to recall that the industry was desperately trying to re-stock and re-supply markets after the punitive measures during the war. Invergordon Distillers, one of the few independent grain distillers, ramped up production due to the aforementioned scramble to lay down grain whisky. Again due to the nature of this industry (four to five years wait) production surpluses were not felt in the industry until either under or over production was well under way. 1966 was the first time this came to a head as brokering prices collapsed despite production remaining at near capacity[71].

It is incredible to think that some of this 1960s oversupply was still being traded as late as the last decade. As the cheapies grew, fringe operators realised the potential for this excess mature grain. New brands sprang up that bore no relationship in terms of cost to the actual cost of production. In 1968 a bottle was the equivalent of £4 (adjusted for 1973), whereas in 1973 a bottle was costing £2.40. This problem is still an issue today (albeit now a much smaller

---

69. WSTR
70. IDV, or International Distillers and Vintners was created through a merger of W&A Gilbey and United Wine Traders in 1962. Through an acquisition and then a takeover it became part of Grand Metropolitan which eventually became part of Diageo.
71. Despite the collapse in grain prices production in 1966 was 14% higher than that of 1965 and 1967 was 11% higher again.

one and less likely going forward with rising costs).

The 1960s also saw a boom in the export of bulk blended or bulk malt. Some markets like Japan and the USA had introduced taxes that made it considerably cheaper to ship bulk and bottle overseas[72]. Whilst, in hindsight this seems a very short-term and short-sighted solution, at the time the drive for the industry was production and export. Even Richard Paterson, writing in 2008[73] stated:

> "...one of the emerging markets for our bulk vatted malt business was Japan... There was a fear that the Japanese might copy Scotch so well that they would not want or need the real thing in the future... The Japanese distillers were purchasing bulk malt Scotch whisky to enhance their own blends[74]; almost all of which were drunk in Japan itself. Our critics naively thought that we should only be exporting *bottled* whisky to countries like Japan, but what they failed to realise was that this was simply not what the Japanese wanted. It [bulk malt exports] was a thriving business for everybody involved... this made the 1970s a boom time."

Paterson is at least right in that until the turn of the century Japanese whisky was really only consumed in Japan. In 1971 bulk malt exports totalled 3.3 million proof gallons. By 1978 that figure had reached 9.6 million proof gallons. During that period exports to Japan rose over ten times (in just one year from 1973-74 exports to Japan rose by 175% - the vast majority of which was bulk malt whisky). By 1979 6.4 million proof gallons were being exported to Japan who also did not lift import quotas against imported bottled Scotch until 1971 but retained discriminatory taxes on any Scotch bottled in Scotland until late 1987. It is hard to argue that, other than a purely financial step, the export of this amount of bulk malt was helpful for brand 'Scotch'. Serious questions would begin to be asked from around 2000 onwards as Japanese blends began to win numerous awards and was exported in growing numbers all over the world. A little case of reaping what you sow perhaps[75]?

Japan was only one market, and whilst easily the biggest, for bulk export, France, Germany, Belgium, the US, Spain & Italy and several other markets' growth were all skewed by large quantities of bulk blend or malt (and this practice has not gone away – there is still large quantities of bulk Scotch being exported to be bottled in foreign markets).

It would take years and even decades for some of these markets to switch

---

72. Since 2009 Scotch malt whisky must be bottled in Scotland.
73. "Goodness Nose"
74. This process if called 'admixing'.
75. Possibly due to the public outcry of this admixing, the Japanese whisky industry has suffered a damaging supply issue.

from the local distillates admixed with Scotch and branded as whisky[76] to actual Scotch. The damage of this short-term profit practice set the industry back – and in some markets blended Scotch whisky never dominated. Part of the issue was the very term 'whisky' and also the proliferation of the term Scotch. Prior to 1989, when 'Scotch' whisky was granted *Protection of Appellation* by the EEC (it had been attempted in 1958 by the Committee of Experts on Wines and Spirits but as there was so much disharmony amongst the members it was never resolved), there was nothing stopping markets from admixing or in some cases just labelling spirits (whether 20%abv[77] or 40%abv and over) as whisky. This of course watered-down, pun intended, the entire category and delayed many markets from getting a taste for Scotch.

The export of bulk was not ignored and many foresaw an issue for the industry. Bowing to public pressure (several MPs were bringing this matter up in Parliament) Seagram's and Hiram-Walker substantially cut their shipments of bulk malt whisky to Japan. The National Economic Development Committee, established towards the end of 1979 had reported that the sales of bulk Scotch was damaging to the industry.

There was even a call to boycott those brands that were responsible for large quantities of the export. Along with the two Canadian firms already mentioned, MP Dennis Canavan (who was part of the Committee) called out Whyte & Mackay, Stanley P. Morrison and Long John International as being responsible for 80 per cent of all bulk malt exported. Canavan commented:

> "This was going on to such an extent that the Japanese were now openly boasting that the highest selling single brand of whisky in the world did not originate in Scotland at all. The brand was Japanese and was called 'Old Suntory'."

This caused further friction between the Invergordon Distillers Co Ltd and other parts of the industry after a report by The Scottish Council of Development and Industry concluded that the industry would benefit in the long term if it abolished the export of all bulk Scotch. It proved to be too profitable at the time and even in the most recent review, in 2009, it was concluded that the practice had been going on for around a century and there were still economic advantages to continuing the export[78].

It is an important point to consider with regards to how the industry was beginning to view itself. These are the days when the Scotch whisky industry

76. The Scotch Whisky Association wanted a Europe-wide adoption of the UK's definition which was decreed in 1909 after the 'What is Whisky' question was raised.
77. Alcohol by volume
78. The three main points being; if it wasn't Scotch whisky fulfilling the demand it would be spirit from another country; some countries still maintained higher tax on imported bottled goods but not on bulk and if the export was banned some markets may have challenged the decision (as had happened with Tequila and the US).

regarded itself not just as Number One, but as being peerless. The industry was growing at an average of seven per cent compounded growth each year and revenue streams, wherever or however they were to be had, were paramount to feeding this growth.

There was considerable collateral damage to the industry, especially in markets like Germany, Belgium, Denmark and Canada (and many others) where the bulk Scotch export trade was propping up local brands that were admixed. In the late 1960s the SWA was reporting that the leading brand of 'whisky' in Germany was outselling the leading brand of Scotch. Canada had been admixing since the Prohibition days (and built its distilling industry at the same time). These instances of 'passing off'[79] kept the SWA busy and by the early 1990s over 100 hundred cases had been opened against what were considered indiscretions (and are still an issue).

It is strange to call out an industry for *selling* its products but at the time these 'sales' were just part of the growth. It does seem to go totally against the message of Scotch being a 'location' driven product. It is worth noting that in 1971 out of every 1,000 bottles of Scotch drunk in markets abroad only three were of single malt whisky bottled in Scotland[80]. This was hardly promoting Scotch in its greatest form nor Scotland as its heart and home.

By 1988 Japan had removed much of its tax against incoming Scotch bottled in Scotland (previously it had been as high as seven times the tax on Japanese made spirits) and introduced a uniformed tax on all spirits. This also coincided with greater Japanese involvement in Scotch whisky ownership[81].

The industry, despite the consolidations, amalgamations and closures described in Chapter Three was still heavily reliant on agents, independent blenders and brokers buying new fillings. A constant stream of advertisements in trade journals by Agents would offer distillery fillings - such as W P Lowrie (agents for Convalmore), Brodie Hepburn (Glen Mhor, Glen Albyn, Macduff and Tullibardine), Charles H Julian (Springbank) and James Boyle (Balvenie[82] and Glenfiddich in Ireland).

One such company, Peter J Russell was established in 1936 initially as a brokering firm. Surviving the war the original Peter passed away in 1956 and his son, also Peter, took over the firm and began looking to diversify.

"Our best days were in the late 1950s and early 1960s, when J&B took off in the States. Justerini & Brooks had no distilleries

---

79. I shall return to this in Chapter 12.
80. Richard Grindal letter to WSTR 1971
81. Nikka bought Ben Nevis from Whitbread Plc in 1989 and Morrison Bowmore were bought by Suntory in 1994. Much of this interest was to ensure continuity of supply. Interesting to note that in 1979 Tim Morrison claimed none of their malt was sold 'to those controversial Far Eastern Blenders' WSTR.
82. Interesting to note that this agency, advertising in the late 1950s used the name Balvenie-Glenlivet.

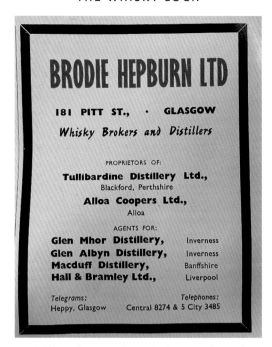

BRODIE HEPBURN LTD

181 PITT ST., • GLASGOW

Whisky Brokers and Distillers

PROPRIETORS OF:

Tullibardine Distillery Ltd.,
Blackford, Perthshire

Alloa Coopers Ltd.,
Alloa

AGENTS FOR:

Glen Mhor Distillery,	Inverness
Glen Albyn Distillery,	Inverness
Macduff Distillery,	Banffshire
Hall & Bramley Ltd.,	Liverpool

Telegrams: *Telephones:*
Heppy, Glasgow   Central 8274 & 5 City 3485

Ad from the Wine Spirit Trade Record 1964]

until they merged with Gilbey's in 1963, so had to go to the open market to buy their fillings.

The price rose. Feeling threatened, the mighty DCL attempted to pre-empt them by offering to exchange one cask of aged whisky for three casks of new make. The price rose even higher, and hordes of speculators here, in Europe and the US wanted to invest. We brokers were in sole position – I bought a huge warehouse in Dundee to house my stocks. But the day we took entry to the warehouse in May 1966, DCL stopped the exchanges and the market collapsed."

The brokers, like Peter J Russell, were an old boys club, often gathering to discuss the market and forecast for the future (amongst the canapes and drinks of course). Hector King, writing for the WSTR noted in 1974:

"...James Sword & Son Ltd[83], Glasgow, who are blenders and brokers, [run by] a very respected person by the name of Archie McQuattie... [would] see his cronies for lunch at the Kenilworth Hotel. The late James Barclay, who owned the hotel, started these Thursday lunches... [he would] come out of retirement to join the weekly get

83. The firm of J Sword & Co would be bought by Morrison Bowmore Distillers in 1984.

together. The firm of Bloch Brothers, now blenders, would have been classed years ago as brokers, and we have W P Lowrie & Co Ltd who are blenders first, but also brokers, bonders and coopers as well.

"Brokers were not an absolute necessity, but like so many other conveniences, you cannot do without them. Who will be the one to locate the 100 casks wanted in a blender's programme? No other than the man on the market – the broker.

"There is always an excess in fillings by holders, and the surpluses will find their way to the broker, a much better way of getting rid of unwanted stocks than peddling them yourself."

In the same article Marshall Clark, an investment broker noted:

"The art of broking is dependent on a large number of variable factors including the knowledge gained by personal contact of potential buyers and sellers. The broker is in constant touch with distillers and blenders and through them he channels each year millions of gallons of whisky of all ages and makes."

"These are family businesses who buy from the trade surplus whisky and in due course supply to the trade as enquiries appear. This business helps to take up the slack during lull periods and supply the demand coming from busy periods."

As Russell tells us (and King suggests) the best days for the brokers were behind them by the 1980s. Whilst the brokering side of the industry remained much longer than anyone anticipated, the main firms were either bought out or changed their business methods. Firms such as James Sword, Wm Lundie, James Boyle, Fraser Stuart, Irving Garrett, A B Grant, Douglas Hamilton, Hall & Bramley, Andrew MacDonald, Henry Wells, Hay & McLeod, W & S Strong & T G Paterson were all either bought out or closed by the 1980s. From the lists I could find, only R Sinclair (Belfast) are still operating (as a broker).

What changed in the industry to remove this once so required element? One of the main contributors was the ever-changing prices for mature stock. As these firms bought and maintained stock levels it became clear that a lot of money could be made by selling out when prices were high. Larger firms, perhaps not wishing to pick out individual parcels began simply buying out the smaller brokering firms to encompass their stock (and whatever brands came with them). Richard Paterson[84] hints at the

84. "Goodness Nose" page 64.

broker's demise:

> "...[one] way in which we obtained spirit was through the surviving brokers, who included Wilie Lundie, Hay & MacLeod and Andrew Wilson. This was always the last resort [to either buying new fillings or reciprocal trades], as it inevitably meant we incurred additional costs. At this time, my father was still in the broking business, but it was harder than ever to make a living."

As distillers began to more and more openly trade with each other the idea that brokers had previously acted as a firewall preventing certain stocks getting inflated prices was not maintained. It was suggested that if a large distiller suddenly made a demand for a certain make the market could easily adjust the price to maximise profits. By having an intermediary, the brokers felt, there was a certain protection against this. This was likely propaganda repeated by brokers – who were almost certainly ensuring that distillers paid a premium for any stock they were looking for.

As the overproduction of grain was a large contributing factor towards the whisky loch of the late 1960s, the second period of overproduction can be attributed to a combination of factors including, once again, an over-forecast for grain whisky. As has already been mentioned, the industry was experiencing an average of seven per cent compound growth year on year from 1946 onwards. Any industry doubling in size every ten years would struggle to survive. When coupled with a product that has to wait years to become legal this is difficult growth to manage.

In 1976 Invergordon Distillers Ltd produced a booklet called 'Observations On The Scotch Whisky Production Cycle'. In it the company argues that the industry will exceed its historical 7% compound growth and will instead reach 8.5% growth year on year. The industry had been maintaining maturing stocks at a high of 10 years' worth in 1967 (producing 164.8 million litres of alcohol) and retaining 1.6 billion litres of alcohol; and a low of 8 years' worth in 1974. In terms of consumption, in 1967, 165 million litres of alcohol were released from bond. By 1976 this had reached 327 million litres.

Invergordon had already increased its production capacity (from one Coffey Still when it was built in 1960 to three by 1963) and then added an additional, and much larger continuous still in 1978. The distillery had been one of the larger contributors to the grain rush in the late 1960s (and had done very well financially). Despite the price crash in grain whisky in 1968, Invergordon maintained steady production before deciding to go to full output in the early 70s. Grain whisky production jumped from 171 million litres of alcohol in 1968 to 272 million litres by 1974 (it wouldn't reach this figure again until 2006).

What was fuelling this mass production was not necessarily the growth in demand, but the growth in value. Whilst total stock released for consumption was growing at a healthy rate, the value of the goods was rising exponentially. If we look at the same period as above, 1967 to 1976, the value of exports rose from £107 million to £436 million[85].

With money pouring in the industry kept making more whisky. As new brands were developed, old brands redeveloped and new markets explored, each new salesperson or marketing manager promised yet greater market share, penetration and growth. By 1979 maturing stocks had hit the staggering figure of three billion litres of alcohol[86]. Annual consumption was 356 million litres. In any normal year since the war (even including its worst year of 1968) this ratio of maturing stock to consumption[87] was not a concern. But consumers and markets are fickle, and investors, shareholders and CEOs are easily spooked.

Due to oil price and supply issues coupled with a global economic decline the US market had already begun to shrink. There was a concerted drive to open new markets and ensure the Scotch whisky industry was not so heavily reliant on one market; but this did not prevent the US market remaining dominant. The US economy was no longer red hot and consumers had a growing choice of drinks to spend their money on. White spirits began to take ever larger parts of the spirits market. For the Scotch whisky industry it was a shock. White spirits were considerably cheaper to make and the brand owners were aggressively marketing these 'mixer' drinks to a new crowd; a crowd that did not want to drink the brand of their father's.

This forced the industry to sit up and take note of stock in a way they had not really done since 1898. By 1981 US consumption was down to 27% of total exports - US consumers, who would spend 2% of their total outgoings on spirits in the 1950s, halved this number by 1980. As Tom O'Hagan stated in The Scotsman in 1983:

> "We have just spent an anxious and gloomy weekend in Glenlivet with 50 per cent of the workforce of the Glenlivet Distillery expecting to be made redundant. After a year of being sustained by determined hopefulness, the whisky industry has sagged so dramatically that even such a giant as the mighty Glenlivet has been brought low.
>
> "As usual, reasons and scapegoats are being sought, and this time the culprits are said to be not only the fickle Americans for

---

85. To simplify this, between 1965 and 1976 exports rose by 120%. The value of these exports rose by over 400%.
86. Three times greater than the maturing stocks of 1964.
87. 8.5 years' worth.

daring to prefer white rum and vodka but also on some shabby entrepreneurs who are buying quality whisky to blend with poorer stuff to flood the markets and supermarkets with cheap blends to the detriment of more respectable, more expensive blends."

With so many distilleries closing[88], jobs lost and reinvestment needed, the industry lost its way. Brand owners refused, at first, to fight a price war with the glut of cheaper brands that appeared. Desperate for sales, companies bent over backwards to satisfy the demands of multiple retailers and importers. This was the catalyst to start the rush for 'own' brand blends. These began to appear everywhere and supermarkets and outlets would compete almost exclusively on price. This, naturally, was a double edged sword for the industry; how could it convince new drinkers that whisky was an inspired choice of drink, whilst at the same time seeing the poorly designed, poorly made and low-priced Scotch 'own' label offerings sat next to the premium 'brands'?

Stock released from warehouses reached a high of 418 million litres of alcohol in 1981. This number had taken just ten years to double from 1971 but in 1982 demand fell and stock released from the warehouses dropped by 17%[89]. Total production in 1979 had been 459 million litres of alcohol falling rapidly to just 240 million in 1983. Most remarkably perhaps is the drop in malt whisky production. In just four years, production fell from 204 million litres in 1979 to just 93 million litres in 1983. For grain whisky production it would take only ten years to return to the highs of the late 1970s. Malt whisky, however would not supersede the record high in 1974 (215 million litres) until 2008. This perhaps speaks more about the decline of blends (blended whiskies, on average, have a much higher percentage of grain whisky today than ever before[90]) and the current issues with malt whisky supply. 2016 was the first year since the war where malt whisky production was greater than grain whisky (in 2015 the industry broke the 4 billion litres of maturing alcohol mark for the first time).

In May of 1983 (the most infamous month and year for distillery closures) the WSTR ran a conversational piece to get to the bottom of what was going on. Reading now, almost forty years later, it is illuminating. When asked if the image of Scotch is well established, Clive Sims, Marketing Manager for John Walker & Sons Ltd:

88. The 1983 closures: Glen Albyn, Glen Mhor, Dallas Dhu, Port Ellen, St Magdalene, Glenury Royal, Glenugie, Lochside, Brora, Kinclaith, Convalmore, Millburn, Hillside, North Port, Banff, Glenlochy, North Port
89. The industry would not beat 1981's figures until 2007.
90. Many of the cheapest blends are as much as 95% grain whisky.

"Scotch drinkers are becoming Scotch drinkers at the age they always used to: 25 onwards. The difference now is that the younger drinkers are starting not with beer but with white spirits. Once they reach 25, they turn to Scotch for the same reason they always have; its image is masculine and mature."

Derek Hayward, Home Trade Director of White Horse Distillers, contradicted Sims:

"Yes, people are starting on spirits younger. But Scotch whisky has missed that opportunity. We've failed there as an industry. We've relied on the older, consistent drinker."

In spite of our picture
a few masculine prerogatives remain;
and, until the rise of Cutty Sark,
whisky drinking was one of them.
No longer.
Women love this elegant Scotch because
it is lighter in colour, softer in touch...
It is indeed the man's Scotch
that women prefer. CUTTY SARK
The man's Scotch that women prefer SCOTCH WHISKY

Image courtesy of British National Library

Jim McCourt, Director of Fine Fare, "Whisky isn't an easy taste for the younger generation. It's not always enjoyable at first taste!"

Suggested that this is because whisky is continually marketed as a drink that must be enjoyed neat, McCourt suggested that "...it might be a good idea to promote whisky specifically to the young as a cocktail base, or an easier long-drink with mixers or orange juice."

Hayward goes on

"It would be totally unacceptable to have an industry campaign to encourage young people to drink spirits. It's important when you consider that whisky has over 50 per cent of the spirits market that the industry maintains a responsible attitude."

These Managers make themselves an easy target for judgement by today's standards. I have included this not to ridicule but as an example of how whisky had lost its way in a world of choice and recession. The DCL, responsible for the vast majority of the distillery closures[91] was having a harder time than most. As the company was still run by the large blending houses being independent of each other, stock management was never consolidated. No-one realised, be it White Horse, Haig or Dewar's etc, what the other part of the company was laying down. This left the business massively overstocked when the recession hit (and also left them wide open for a takeover[92]).

It is worth noting Derek Hayward's parting shot from the article:

" ...if everything goes well, and we've got rid of the whisky loch, own label [prices] will presumably come up very much onto a level with the secondary prices, and whether an own label will sell against a secondary brand at the bottom end of the standard market is something we don't know yet."

Possibly, in the same way that the bulk export market has never gone away (and other than aiding to shift stock, has never greatly helped the Scotch whisky industry); the 'own' label and 'cheapie' brands that are in every supermarket, off-license and discount warehouse has never allowed Scotch to drag itself out of being considered a commodity or allowed the 'aged' nature of the product distinguish itself[93]. [A recent trip to Marks & Spencer demonstrated this – three products, all identical in size, alcohol content and price; one a flavoured white rum, the other a five year old brandy and the third an eight year old blended Scotch.]

Malt whisky, as a serious category, began to make a stir from the late 1960s. Glenfiddich, constrained by the DCL due to the success of their blend 'Grant's Stand Fast' (and behind the scenes disagreements), took the bold decision to begin promoting their malt brands with the same gusto and reverence all

---

91. Dr Alan Rutherford, who joined DCL in 1984 after most of the major closures was assured that the majority of these distilleries were mothballed rather than closed. The issue the DCL had was that most needed very large investments to continue running and the early to mid-80s was not a time for investing in decrepit distilleries.
92. For an amazing account of this read "Is Guinness Good For You?" By Peter Pugh.
93. It would take new thinking, a new generation of whisky lovers and new markets to change this...

other producers were giving their blends. It would be wrong to say that Wm Grants suddenly became a 'malt only' company as the Girvan grain distillery was built in 1963 to satisfy Wm Grant's own blended Scotch requirements (and later their gin Hendrick's).

There have always been malt whiskies available but the category had been considered too niche, or off-putting for a general push by any company. Even in the early 1970s Ivan Straker, Head of Glenlivet Distilleries stated:

"Suddenly the US [drinkers] have discovered that malt whisky is not the heavy, smoky, over-flavoured whisky they had thought. Already J&B Rare and Cutty Sark are coming to be thought 'a bit old-fashioned', and Dewar's and Chivas Regal are on the way to the top. The Americans always want something different, something else, and that something else will be The Glenlivet."

This quote is worthy of attention for two reasons; firstly, who has been telling the American consumer that malt whisky was 'heavy, smoky, over-flavoured' if not the Scotch whisky industry itself[94]? And secondly, the comments about Chivas Regal are prophetic when you consider that Glenlivet and Chivas will be synonymous with each other just a few years later after Seagram's bought The Glenlivet Distilleries Co Ltd.

The Italian market seemed to get the taste for malt whisky first as Nick Morgan states in his book "A Long Stride"[95]:

"...challenging the Walker brands were the increasingly popular single malts, for which Italy was probably the largest market in the world, particularly 5 year old Glen Grant, which experienced huge growth in the late 1970s and early 1980s, and Glenlivet 12 year old, launched by Seagram in 1985..."

In 1981 Glen Grant, which had begun selling its Five Years Old expression in the early 1970s, controlled 70% of the Italian malt market (this was 160,000 cases – remarkably double the amount of The Glenlivet being sold to the US at the same time). The product was introduced by an Armando Giovanetti who began a heavy marketing campaign in the clubs and bars where the younger drinker was hanging out. By any means necessary[96] Giovanetti got huge coverage and market penetration. This malt whisky was being drunk 'long' with mixers. Italy was succeeding where other markets could not.

At the same time that the Glen Grant was picking up for the younger Italian

---

94. The American Business Week, perhaps simply lifting from the WSTR piece, suggested "To most drinkers, straight malt whisky conjures up an image of a heavy, smoky concoction served in brandy snifters.'
95. Page 241.
96. It is rumoured that 'bribes' were the most popular means.

drinkers, there was a similar move within Italy towards more expensive aged malt and blended whiskies as reported in the WSTR in May 1981:

> "This move to the more expensive and more traditional types of Scotch whisky conflicts paradoxically with the trend at the same time towards cheaper, sometimes low-strength, whiskies, indicating that different attitudes are being adopted towards both price and 'quality' and that less faith is being placed in the long-established brands."

It was very hard for the larger companies to acknowledge the role malt whisky was playing in the market. It wasn't so much that brand owners were clinging onto their blends (as even today malt whisky sales are still only a fraction of what blended sales are) it was more an inability to see that the two could live side by side.

In 1980 Terry Brooke of the DCL, the largest owners of malt whisky distilleries, stated in the WSTR:

> "We have never wanted to boost one malt, and the only advertising you will see is where a malt whisky is shown alongside a blended whisky as part of the complete range.[97]"

It would take the undeniable success of Glenfiddich and then DCL's own Cardhu for the company to realise the potential of malt whisky. In 1988 they released the Six Classic Malts[98] which was a huge success with bars and retailers. Although even the mighty DCL were hamstrung with regards to the 'Regions' of Scotland (not owning a Campbeltown malt[99] and creating a region, so to speak, with Talisker), the Six Classics was the gateway for numerous whisky drinkers that had never discovered malt whisky before.

Macallan, who had a long history of promoting their single malt, had an odd arrangement with Gordon & MacPhail. In 1981 Macallan released a 1938 expression, although admitted it was from the warehouses of G&M; William Phillips, then Managing Director of Macallan-Glenlivet Distillery stated:

> "If Gordon & MacPhail had stocks of '38, we have stocks of the next vintage which will follow on from that, then they perhaps of the next one. We are working in combination. To release a 'vintage' year, we have to have enough available to ensure quality."

97. Very similar to a statement made to me twenty-two years later.
98. I believe that originally this was the Seven Classic Malts (Blair Athol being the seventh) but was reduced to six when released as full bottles. The Seven Classic Malts miniature packs can still be found in auctions.
99. Rumour has it that Springbank has received numerous offers from willing buyers in the past fifty or so years.

Cardhu Highland Malt Whisky

Why it may not be your kind of whisky

CARDHU is malt whisky—the very essence of most good blends. It is a rich, single whisky that is pot-distilled, and matured in oak casks for at least 8 years.

Cardhu is 5° higher proof than usual whiskies and considerably richer in flavour. Naturally, it has limited appeal. It compares with ordinary whiskies as cognac compares with brandy. Thus, it is only for the palate that likes its whisky neat or with just a drop of water.

A brief history of this new whisky that is over eight years old

Set among the purple hills above the river Spey, the Cardhu distillery is a self-contained community devoted to the art of pot-distilling. Johnnie Walker, who own the distillery, take most of its yield for their Red Label blend. For some years however, they have kept a reserve and now are able to bottle a little of it. They call it Cardhu Highland Malt Whisky.

Why it is rare

Because Cardhu requires at least eight years to mature, very little of it is available at one time. In fact, only 5,000 cases can be released each year. Not much when compared with the total annual production of Scotch—over 50 million cases.

Why every bottle has a number

And to make sure that no more than this amount is released, the people who distil Cardhu number each bottle to indicate the year it left the distillery and the batch from which it came. This enables them to keep a careful check on every single bottle of Cardhu. And lets you know exactly the year of your bottle's release to the world.

How to get it

Because so little Cardhu is released, it is not easy to find. If your search is unrewarded, please write to John Walker & Sons Limited, Kilmarnock, Scotland.

Image courtesy of British National Library

The conditions of sale were changed in 1972, forbidding the bottling of The Macallan as a named single malt other than for the owners Macallan-Glenlivet Ltd[100]. This is one of the more peculiar chapters in the whisky industry but demonstrated that there was a period when distillers were not just working with independent bottlers but were advertising the fact. This, of course, was a time when no distillery could use its entire output for single malt expressions.

100. I go into this in more detail in Chapter 12.

It would be wrong to paint the 'malt scene' as all plain-sailing. Between 1980 and 1981 the malts sector in the UK dropped by 40 per cent[101]. The MD of Glenlivet bemoaned the reversal of four years' worth of growth. Duly the company gave more attention to its Queen Anne blend. 1981 also saw the supermarkets, fighting off eager sales people with burgeoning stocks, began bottling 'own label' malts to go with their blends. Rather than diminish in market share and reach parity in price as Derek Hayward had hoped for, these 'own label' products grew in popularity and shelf space.

It can be reasonably argued that these aged, and quite often, high quality own label malts were a means of helping introduce the next generation of drinker to discover the category. And in a time of overproduction, it was possibly a better sales route than exporting in bulk for foreign markets to admix. The real issue, however, was price, as the WSTR noted in May 1981:

> "There are a number of whiskies on the market which did not exist or were unheard of two or three years ago but which are now doing phenomenal business and grabbing astonishing chunks of market-share.

> "These are the 'cheapies'... with often mawkishly absurd names; they do very well in off-licenses and supermarkets, not just because they are cheap, but because, in fact, they tend to be extremely good whiskies.

> "Which is where the whisky lake comes in. The large companies have obviously been finding stocks building up as demand slackens so the sensible thing has been to slap another label across the bottle and sell at a close-to-the-bone margin."

Even today when mature stocks (and this is not referring to whisky with 'great' age) command such high prices from bottlers, there is still an enormous prevalence and plethora of 'own' label malts and blends. It is clearly the case that large buyers can command these bottlings (perhaps rewarding the supplier with greater market penetration through their outlets) and that producers would rather work through these channels than allow this stock into the open market.

Previous events like mergers and acquisitions no longer have the same effect on the industry where stock was often off-loaded to recoup investment. It was hoped, within the independent bottling community, that the vast acquisition of Beam by Suntory (completed in 2013 and costing $16billion) would require liquidations of stock. This may have happened but did not trickle

101. WSTR Nov 1982

down to the IBs. Nor did the takeover of Benriach Distilleries Co by Brown-Forman (in 2016 costing £281million) release any great quantities of stock. The list of buyouts and mergers is long and with each one the net appears to get tighter around the strings controlling the release of spirit into the wild.

It is hard to collectively sum up the industry's attitude to the growth in independent bottlers. In all probability, concerned with their own growth, and taking a leaf out of the book already written by the existing bottlers, the industry sat back and watched the IBs from afar. Slow, initially, to change their habits, good quantities of stock continued to find their way onto the market. One larger firm was still selling considerable volumes until recently through the few remaining brokers. When asked why they did not trade or find brand avenues for this stock they simply replied 'it's just easier this way'.

In reality, it was the noise that independents made that changed the game. Had it remained an underground, and mainly continental demand, the distilling enterprises may have never bothered to change their practices. What wasn't anticipated, or at least, what took the large blending brands by surprise, was the incredible explosion of, noticeably, younger drinkers with a thirst for malts, and equally, for knowledge of the industry. Suddenly practices that were deemed perfectly fine before for off-loading stock came under the scrutiny of directors, marketers and the demanding consumer.

Even today it seems odd that the larger firms will continue to supply supermarket 'own' labels but not enter into negotiations with independent bottlers. As if somehow supplying IBs direct is worse; or more detrimental to brand 'Scotch'[102]. The continued supply of bulk malt to export markets for admixing is also supposedly more favourable than allowing a new, brash and youthful blender create noise with interesting and well-thought out blends. It seems to me at least, a case of 'thanks for the ground-breaking work, we'll take it from here'.

From the conditions placed upon the industry during WWII; through market spats; over-forecasting and outside influences, a vast and incredibly interesting lake of whisky was filled (and added to) from the late 1960s through to late 1990s. The Scotch whisky industry, unsure exactly how to remedy the situation turned to every avenue to offload stock and relieve cashflow problems. This unique set of circumstances has led to the creation and proliferation of the independent bottler. Even some of the decisions on re-using wood would have a knock-on effect for decades later when these over-aged (by industry standards) whiskies became highly revered; many of which were independent bottlings. Whiskies which, had it not been for the malt whisky movement, would have never seen the light of day.

---

102. Last time I checked, no supermarket 'own label' malt was ever represented at a whisky festival. I don't think I've ever had a tasting with Mr Lidl...

If, for nothing else, IBs can be thanked for helping to shake an aged and stuck-in-the-mud industry into believing that all categories of Scotch were worthy of backing. And yes, they should all give themselves a big pat on the back; the independent bottlers I mean.

CHAPTER 5

CAMPBELTOWN; WHISKY AND GHOSTS

"While official bottlings from distillery owners may be considered to be the backbone of the whisky industry, at least in terms of volume and overall value, it is often the independent bottlers that the whisky enthusiasts get their kicks from. Most of the time these companies, relieved of the accountants and shareholders that the larger players suffer, will release expressions that enthuse the whisky connoisseur. The importance of these mavericks for the whisky category is hard to exaggerate."

INGVAR RONDE
Publisher of The Malt Whisky Yearbook

One of my first tasks with Cadenhead's, due to some already organised tastings, was to set off around the UK to existing retail customers to gauge opinion and feelings towards the brands and bottlings. Despite offering whiskies from around 120 different distilleries (many of which were closed), sales were falling. My trip included visiting the Lincoln Whisky Shop, The Wee Dram in Bakewell (run by Adrian and Alison Murray), The Wright Wine Co in Skipton (run by Julian Kaye) as well as the two UK Cadenhead shops at the time; one off Covent Garden in London (now in Marylebone) and back to the scene of my fortuitous encounter on the Royal Mile in Edinburgh.

Cadenhead's, up until a few years before I joined, had built up a reputation of excellent bottlings coupled with no nonsense packaging. The mid 1980s and 1990s had seen a move towards tall, green bottles and at first brown labels and then screen printed bottles with small cream labels. The cartons were solid black and robust. I joined just after they had introduced black tubes with rather garish silver logos repeated all over it. The bottles were still the common tall ones but now clear (to better show the colour of the whisky) and the labels were mainly black with very small writing. The overall impression was a mangled mess and this was hammered home everywhere I went. Each and every retailer informed me that the packaging change had seriously damaged the retail sales and product placement[103]. Even staff and customers in the two Cadenhead shops reeled at the packaging.

Upon my return I wrote up my report. The market, whilst experiencing new competitors, was still growing and Cadenhead's was evidently missing a trick by persisting with an appearance that was clearly turning customers away. My report was met with a simple 'Well we're not changing the packaging.'

One of my next tasks saw me return to Whisky Live, this time manning the Cadenhead stand. I was delighted when Michael Jackson stopped by to chat and have a dram of the Banff that we were pouring. A young man behind him said:

"Excuse me, can you please autograph your book for me?"

Michael took out his book signing pen (he always carried a specific pen for signing his books with) and turned around.

"Er, sorry, not you, I meant the man behind you." The gentleman said motioning over Michael's shoulder to me. Michael looked down and realised the speaker was holding a copy of my "Malt Whisky Guide" and flashed me a look as if to say 'you young pretender'. I have never been so proud and embarrassed in equal measures.

---

103. Under the guidance of Mark Watt many years later, Cadenhead's would return to a much more familiar style of packaging and product which would result in sales figures the company had never got close to experiencing before.

Part of the role allowed me a period of time to work at Springbank Distillery. Springbank was famous for controlling every part of the distilling process from floor maltings[104] through to maturing every single cask in their own warehouses. No other distillery could boast this and whenever I had the chance I would put the office phone on 'forward' and walk the few hundred yards from the Cadenhead office (once a wine bar) to the distillery. There is something quite magical about walking through the malting floors as the freshly steeped barley slowly begins to stir into life. Springbank, despite having gone through a slight modernisation a couple of decades earlier, was still like a time warp. Things were done the old fashioned way as, along with the floor maltings, there was a peat fired kiln and a partly direct fired still. Springbank, and Cadenhead bottlings were also all bottled on site. There was usually something going on and someone to have a blether with which eased the boredom of the office work.

I'm not sure I was living in Campbeltown at its greatest period. The RAF had long pulled out of nearby Machrihanish and the Jaegar factory and purpose built call centre were both now distant memories. After the Local Council, J&A Mitchell were the largest single employer with over fifty employees. Vestas, the wind turbine company from Denmark, had employed a number of locals which eased some of the pressures on local employment. It was certainly a culture shock having moved from Los Angeles to the 'wee toon', as it is referred to. Shops, and really there was only a couple, closed early on Wednesdays and I don't believe there was a single espresso coffee maker for miles (granted this was before the recent coffee boom).

Campbeltown is really unrecognisable now from what it was like twenty years ago. The High Street boasts several restaurants and espresso machines are an easy spot. Even Cadenhead's and Springbank are unrecognisable from my time there. Eaglesomes, which had been a sandwich and wine shop, is now an excellent whisky shop for Cadenhead's. Springbank distillery now has a visitor centre/shop and the new Washback Bar is serving the hordes of tourists that make their way each year. The annual Campbeltown Whisky Festival is also a must-visit for most malt whisky fans.

One thing that was striking about Campbeltown from the first day I ever set foot were the ghosts of distilleries past. It was a weekly occurrence when, having told someone in the town what I did, they would suggest a number of distilleries that had come and gone. Anything from twenty to fifty distilleries was continually guessed at. Surprisingly I found that despite all of these ghostly shells strewn about the place there was scant information on what had come and gone. Most of the historical writings were from a local Postman

---

104. The floor maltings had been re-born by a previous manager, John McDougal in the late 80s. For more information read his book 'Wort, Worms & Washbacks, Memoirs from the Stillhouse'.

called Angus Martin who I happened to meet. He had long thought about a book on the history of the distilleries but had never got round to it. Enter onto the Whisky History writing scene, me; young, fresh and willing to give it a go.

I won't bore you with the full details of my research (or for some, the lack of it). I am not an historian (and even if I was, everyone has to start somewhere) but I tried every nook and cranny I thought to uncover the region's history. I held a tasting for the local Rotary group and asked all present if they had any information whether they could share it. Hoping for shopping bags filled with ancient ledgers, letters, labels and receipts to come pouring in I received nothing. I scoured through the archive of the Campbeltown Courier without much joy. Reaching out to Diageo with their supposedly world-class Archive I was informed there was nothing suitable and was denied access. I reached out to a notable whisky historian who also effectively shrugged his shoulders (if you can do that in an email) to say he could not help.

The book got off to the worst possible start when having enquired with my boss (staff never spoke to Hedley Wright, the owner of J&A Mitchell, directly) whether I could get assistance, I was informed that alas Mr Wright was too busy to help. It was quite a surprise when a few weeks later Hedley turned up with some maps under his arm and a pre-written history of the family firm. Sadly, however, that was all I got and I realised that anyone looking for a more in-depth history of J&A Mitchell would be disappointed. Similarly, as Richard Joynson pointed out to me, Campbeltown was the 'who dunnit' of the whisky world. Why did so many distilleries close? And so many at a similar time. My research led me to believe there was no *one* reason. No guilty party with the smoking gun and the book could not be written and read like a thriller. On the contrary the lack of evidence caused the book to be padded out with anecdotal evidence and re-printed information.

I was initially living in a tiny one bedroom apartment above the hairdressers adjacent to the Cadenhead office. This did mean a two second walk to work but it was like living in an ice-box; it was time to move. Around this time accommodation was ridiculously cheap in Campbeltown. I eventually bought, for £26,500, a four double-bedroom ground floor flat that had been built on the site of the old Dalintober Distillery. Out of the front it looked onto the Mussel Ebb[105] and, just about, the harbour. At the rear it was no more than thirty yards from Glen Scotia Distillery. Less than four hundred yards away was the old Benmore Distillery where my, now, wife worked for a local businessman (the distillery buildings being part used for offices and partly as a bus depot and workshop). The flat was concrete and brick with severe damp issues. It would

---

105. This was a piece of reclaimed land that had previously been used for the dumping of effluence, entrails and excrement. Must have been a joyful place.

smell of mash whenever Glen Scotia was mashing and the carpets would get wet whenever it rained. Eventually I ripped out all of the carpets and applied liquid bitumen to all of the floors. Having never sealed floors before I made the rookie mistake of painting myself into one of the corners. It took me several hours to chisel my ruined socks out of the bitumen and even longer to remove it from the soles of my feet. I also had to replace the brand new hallway carpet. I vowed to never use the horrid stuff again.

Around this time Springbank began to catch up with supply. The warehouses had been bled fairly dry by an aggressive sales campaign a decade earlier, coupled with sales of casks to the general public (which had been a roaring success but was a short term cash solution) and a lack of production. Euan Mitchell, Springbank's Sales Manager, would often joke that he had a harder job refusing stock to a market than selling it to one. Springbank was effectively withdrawn from 'multiple' outlets (like supermarkets) and efforts were made to work with suitable import partners that would be sensitive and long-term minded. With a slow catch up of supply a new sales person was hired and Kate Wright joined the company. Kate was tri-lingual and a returning Campbeltown native. Euan and Kate would continually have to deal with a misconception that there was a family link to the company (either through the company name of J&A Mitchell or the owner Hedley Wright). Neither would have to worry about it too long as both would depart within the next few years.[106]

My work with Cadenhead's sent me all over Europe and one trip to the States. Cadenhead's had the same US importer as Springbank – a company based in California called Preiss Imports. I had been with Cadenhead's for a while and had received no communication from Preiss - nothing about sales or the market. Eventually I was told to head out to help them attend Whisky Fest New York. I was excited (this time flying to the US with a credit card[107]) as had never been to New York before. I was also going to fly over to California and see my mother and brother who I had not seen for several years and then fly back to New York for a big wine and spirits show to see if I could better understand the market (and try and seek a new importer if necessary). Whisky Fest turned out to be one of the worst festivals I had ever attended (and over twenty years on is still one of the worst). The show was too short and folk were just there to get their money's worth. From opening until closing it was just a sea of glasses asking to be filled. The punters did not care what they

---

106. Euan went to Arran Distillers where he is now their longest serving (and dare I say it, most successful) MD and Kate went to Glenfarclas Distillery.
107. I had previously flown to San Francisco for Whisky Magazine who refused to give me a credit card, and I had none of my own. Upon checking into the hotel I was informed that without a credit card I could not stay (I had only cash). Thankfully my mother who lived in LA came to the rescue. I vowed to never ask anyone to travel for me without suitable credit facilities.

were drinking just so long as it was from the oldest or most expensive bottle on the table. Preiss Imports were also one of the rudest importers I had ever encountered and other than the show I was left to my own devices the entire time I was in New York. Suffice to say that Cadenhead's pulled out of the US market and only returned with a radically different team and new importer more than a decade later.

I headed back to the Spirit of Speyside Festival, this time with a brand to promote and a bit more of a story to tell. Heading back to the Craigellachie Hotel's Quaich Bar, I noticed that J&A Mitchell had a bottle in the locked cabinet[108] - at the time this was a bottle of the 1919 Springbank[109]. A quick phone call and the expensive and very limited whisky was being withdrawn by the barman (no longer Mark Watt who was now working for the Scotch Malt Whisky Society in Edinburgh). There was a silence in the bar as this whisky was (very) carefully poured out for me. I would say stunned silence but old whisky had yet to reach such emotional levels within society. The whisky was surprisingly fresh for something made eighty years ago. It was low in abv (37.8% - illegal by today's standards) as it had aged for 50 years before being bottled. This was by no means a life-changing dram but I could see someone next to me take a keen interest, and as I have always felt a dram shared is a better drinking experience, I offered the remainder of the dram to this gentleman. Taken aback, he did not pass by the offer and I'm very glad he did not as Hans Offringa[110] and I have been friends ever since.

Cadenhead's first international shop (the first addition to the shops since the opening of the London store in 1995) was in Köln, Germany and had been established about two months before I joined by Markus Müller and Gregor Nacke. The two young men amazed me with their passion and dedication to what was a fledgling industry. They both saw the potential of the market and put their lives and futures into the brand. I attended the first few Whisky Fairs in Limburg with them and several other shows including Berlin and InterWhisky in Frankfurt. Sales, at this time, were hard work. Markus, working part-time, would deal with trying to repair the damage done to existing retailers by the creation of the Cadenhead shop. The retailers found it difficult to understand how buying from a shop could still be competitive for them. Without their support the enterprise would not survive. Gregor remained in full time employment to ensure he and Markus had an income.

It therefore came as a great shock to me, and an even bigger shock to

---

108. This was a small cabinet for producers and supporters of the hotel. Several of the local distillers had bottle spaces.
109. This was £12,000 a bottle at the time. Now valued over £180,000.
110. Now a highly-regarded author of several whisky-related books.

Markus and Gregor when an agreement was made to allow a second shop in Germany, in Berlin, to go ahead. I had the dubious honour of informing Gregor in Limburg before the Whisky Fair. He rightfully did not take the news well. I felt terrible. I really felt that the sacrifices and hard work the two had put in was ignored.

The second Cadenhead shop was opened sometime in 2003 and I flew over for the opening. As I had a day to kill until the evening tasting I was invited to a different part of Berlin where Bar Madonna was situated. This was owned and run by Lars 'Jack' Wiebers and Karsten Kirmse. It is a proper beer drinking, whisky tasting and football watching bar in the Kreuzberg area of Berlin. Lars and myself hit it off having a similar sense of humour and before long we were raising ridiculous toasts whilst drinking shots of Apfel Korn[111]. This was of course never going to end well. At about six pm I was bundled into a taxi and headed to the new shop to open it and host the evenings tasting. I was in no state to do either. Having arrived at the new shop I headed in through the front door, said hello to the owner and then surreptitiously exited through a side door and back into the same taxi that I had just arrived in. Taken by surprise, the taxi driver said something along the lines of 'Alles ok?' to which I thrust some money and the key card of my hotel into his hand. I have only

111. Which I have never been able to drink since.

one more memory of the evening, and that was of turning off my mobile phone and unplugging the hotel phone before collapsing fully clothed on the bed[112]. Not my finest hour and to this day it is still the only tasting I have ever missed when hosting.

112. To Klaus Pinkernell, the owner of the Berlin Cadenhead shop, I of course apologised profusely, blamed Lars Wiebers and also sent a bottle of 1967 Glenfarclas as an additional *entschuldigung*.

CHAPTER 6

"*Where do you get your casks?*"

"Whilst, understandably, distillers and blenders concentrated on consistency of blends, independent bottlers kept the single malt flame alive and also started the flicker of single grains. This dedication to celebrate the uniqueness of not just a distillery but a single cask helped bring malts back to the attention of whisky lovers; their contribution to the industry is profound."

MARK DAVIDSON
Manager Royal Mile Whiskies

The most frequently asked question, to any independent bottler, is where they get their supply of whisky. Why would distillers sell you their whisky to compete with themselves? Why can you not just call up a distiller and buy casks?

In his 1992 Book 'The Spirit of Whisky' Richard Grindal states:

"For many years distilleries, in addition to laying down stocks of their malt whisky to bottle when it is mature, have 'filled' casks not only for the blending companies but for whisky merchants. The whisky merchants may have used the whisky to produce their own blends or they may have bottled it as single malts, using the name of the distillery but on their own labels. Until recently the number of single malts put on sale by these 'independent bottlers' was relatively small and the volume of their sales insignificant. With the rapidly growing interest in Scotch malt whisky the picture has changed. Independent bottlers like Gordon & MacPhail of Elgin and Cadenhead's whisky shop of Edinburgh are now putting on the market a wide range of single malts, many at different ages, a large proportion of which are not bottled for sale by the distilleries themselves."

Picture courtesy of Photographer Guus Pauka and Marcel van Gils

Certainly, until quite recently, independent bottlers were the expensive choice for a whisky drinker. Twenty years ago a ten year old official malt whisky was likely to be around the £20 mark whereas an independent bottling could be £30 plus[113]. As bottlers and not producers they had to educate the average consumer in order to explain the discrepancy. 'Higher duty due to higher alcohol', 'no chill-filtration', 'single cask as opposed to vatted', 'limited bottlings' and so on was repeated ad nauseum to build up awareness. The two areas that seemed to confuse customers the most was firstly; why would a distiller sell you their good casks and secondly, why bottle at 'cask strength'.

To tackle the first point we need to understand how the market works. At the time of writing, blended and blended malt Scotch whisky still account for around 88% of all Scotch whisky sold around the world. Of the 1.24 billion bottles sold, single malt sales accounted for around 14 million bottles (in 1992 when Richard Grindal wrote his book the malt whisky percentage was likely around 3% of total sales). To create a blend you need ingredients (different distillates) and even the largest of distillers (Diageo, Beam-Suntory and Pernod Ricard) do not rely solely on their own inventory of distillates for the recipe or make-up of their blends. This means that each production cycle the distillers trade stock to ensure that future blending programs have sufficient quantities of different malt (and grain) whiskies. This requires clever people to forecast what stock the company will require in the future (remembering that the youngest age Scotch can be bottled at is three years old[114]). Invariably forecasters will try to slightly oversubscribe what they feel the company will need as it is far easier to shift unwanted stock than to try and buy mature stock to fill a gap.

This results in a cross section of a distiller's warehouses containing whisky from all over the industry (and this has been going on for as long as anyone can remember). Blends are then produced and surplus or unwanted parcels are sold on; often to alleviate cashflow or simply make space for incoming parcels of mature whisky or new distillate. It is therefore frequently the case that distillers are not even selling on their own makes - although as the spirit is often sold to them in tankers they are responsible for the wood used for maturation. [This did result in one difficult scenario where a cask of whisky was given the number '1' as it was the first one laid down in that particular warehouse. When the bottler applied this cask number they were then informed that the owners of the distillery had the 'real' cask number '1' and would be grateful if the bottler changed their label...]

This is why in the early 2000s Macallan was able to release a large series

---

113. I apologise profusely for the UK-centric pricing and analysis here.
114. And many blends have age statements.

of ex-Bourbon (American oak) matured whisky[115] despite, supposedly, never filling Macallan into anything other than ex-Sherry. This was called, rather confusingly, the 'Fine Oak' series, and created a mini furore with Macallan purists – personally, I loved them.

SCOTCH WHISKY OPENING PRICES 1980										
	p per original proof gallon	p per litre of alcohol		p per original proof gallon	p per litre of alcohol		p per original proof gallon	p per litre of alcohol	p per original proof gallon	p per litre of alcohol
Grain			**Campbeltown**			Dufftown-Glenlivet	275	106		
Caledonian	116.78	45	Glen Scotia	275	106	Edradour	NP	NP	Inchmurrin	270	104
Cambus	116.78	45	Longrow	NP	NP	Fettercairn	270	104	Isle of Jura	NP	NP
Cameronbridge	116.78	45	Springbank	275	106	Glen Ablyn	275	106	Knockando	270	104
Carsebridge	114.18	44	**Highland malt**			Glenallachie	NP	NP	Knockdhu	270	104
Dumbarton	116.78	45	Aberfeldy	275	106	Glenburgie-Glenlivet	275	106	Ledaig	*	*
Garnheath	116.78	45	Aberlour-Glenlivet	275	106	Glencadam	270	104	Linkwood	275	106
Girvan	116.78	45	Allt-a'Bhainne	275	106	Glencraig-Glenlivet	275	106	Lochnagar	275	106
Invergordon	116.78	45	Ardmore	*	*	Glenfonach	*	*	Lochside	272	105
North British	116.78	45	Auchroisk	270	104	Glendullan	275	106	Longmorn	278	107
North of Scotland	NP	NP	Aultmore	275	106	Glen Elgin	275	106	Macallan-Glenlivet	278	107
Port Dundas	114.18	44	Balblair	270	104	Glenfarcas-Glenlivet	275	106	Macduff	278	107
Strathclyde	116.78	45	Balmenach	275	106	Glenfiddich	278	107	Miltonduff-Glenlivet	272	105
Lowland malt			Balvenie	275	106	Glengarioch	272	105	Mortlach	275	106
Auchentoshan	272	105	Banff	270	104	Glenglassaugh	270	104	Mosstowie-Glenlivet	275	106
Bladnoch	267	103	Benriach	272	105	Glengoyne	270	104	Oban	270	104
Glen Flagler	NP	NP	Benrinnes	275	106	Glen Grant	278	107	Ord	275	106
Glenkinchie	270	104	Benromach	270	104	Glen Keith	275	106	Pittyvaich-Glenlivet	275	106
Inverleven	270	104	Ben Wyvis	272	105	Glenlivet, The	278	107	Pulteney	270	104
Ladyburn	270	104	Blair Athol	275	106	Glenlochy	270	104	Rhosdu	270	104
Linlithgow	267	103	Braes of Glenlivet	275	106	Glenlossie	275	106	Royal Brackla	270	104
Littlemill	270	104	Brechin	270	104	Glen Mhor	275	106	Scapa	270	104
Lomond	270	104	Caperdonich	272	105	Glenmorangie	NP	NP	Speyburn	270	104
Rosebank	275	106	Cardow	275	106	Glen Moray-Glenlivet	275	106	Strathisla	275	106
Islay malt			Clynelish	275	106	Glenrothes-Glenlivet	275	106	Strathmill	270	104
Ardbeg			Coleburn	270	104	Glen Spey	270	104	Talisker	280	108
Bowmore	275	106	Convalmore	270	104	Glentauchers	275	106	Tamdhu-Glenlivet	275	106
Bruichladdich	275	106	Cragganmore	275	106	Glenturret	272	105	Tamnavulin-Glenlivet	272	105
Bunnahabhain	275	106	Craigellachie	275	106	Glenugie	*	*	Teaninich	275	106
Caol Ila	275	106	Dailuaine	275	106	Glenury Royal	270	104	Tomatin	267.3	103
Lagavulin	280	108	Dallas Dhu	270	104	Highland Park	275	106	Tomintoul-Glenlivet	270	104
Laphroaig	280	108	Dalmore	272	105	Hillside	270	104	Tormore	*	*
Port Ellen			Dalwhinnie	270	104	Imperial	275	106	Tullibardine	272	105
	280	108	Deanston	272	105	Inchgower	275	106	NP price not publicised		
									*Price not yet available.		

Wine Spirit Trade Record 1980. It was common practice to print the opening prices for distillate at the beginning of each production year.

[As an aside I remember being invited on the Classic Malts Cruise one year by Diageo. This was a few days sailing from Oban to Islay and onto Skye and included sleeping on the boat (a first for me). It was a fantastic trip but notable for a few reasons. Firstly I had my first and only, so far, boating accident. The sailor of the yacht I was on tried to get close to Lagavulin, too close. Motoring in at around 2 knots the boat hit a rock and stopped instantly. Now just over two miles an hour doesn't sound a lot but when you are stopped suddenly it is quite a shock. I was topside, next to the opening to the stairs, but not for long. Down I went with an almighty thud. Although I did not appear injured I felt pretty stupid (as one does when they go for a tumble), sadly I had mild concussion and had to miss the boat trip to Skye (not as sick as the skipper though who scuba dived to assess the damage and came back up as pale as I have ever seen anyone – not a simple fix then).

115. Having bought stock back from companies it had supplied spirit with.

I also remember having a few drinks with part of the marketing team from Diageo. These were predominantly desk jockeys that went around telling the distilleries how their produce should be marketed. I recall boldly stating to one of them that if they were to let me loose in their warehouses I would guarantee a £1 million profit in the first year. The reply was something along the lines of 'Diageo is a blending company. The company turns over £13 billion each year, the trouble that you could cause in search of your £1 million profit would not be worth the hassle. And Diageo will never bottle single cask whiskies.' I have no doubt I would have caused mayhem – would've been the greatest year of my life though. Oh, and Diageo very much bottled single casks not long after that chat. Their 'Manager's Choice' series (a single cask selected by each distillery manager) was released with wildly varying retail prices. I'm glad I had not been involved – my personal preference of whisky bottled for drinking (i.e. affordable) would have not sat well.]

The large blending houses work from 'indicative samples' – that is, should they be considering casks of a parcel of say twenty, rather than take a sample from every single one, they will take a few samples as an indication of what to expect from all of them. From these samples they will then create their blend using grain whisky (often from just two grain distilleries, sometimes even one) as the base and malt whiskies as the dressing. It is a touch harsh on grain whisky to call it neutral but for the most part it is the malt whisky that adds the real punch/kick/complexity to blended Scotch. Grain whisky (until recently) therefore makes up approximately 60% of all new spirit laid down in a year (remembering that it must be the same age or older than the age statement on the label – no corners cut).

The skill of the blender, apart from making something a mass market will want to drink, is the ability to put together a blend that barely changes from batch to batch. Even when it comes to single malts a blender will look to mix batches of wood types (for instance, Sherry and Bourbon) and even slight differences in age (ensuring that any age statement is adhered to) in order to create consistency. Glenfiddich is possibly the best example of this ability to maintain a homogenous taste – pick up a Glenfiddich 12yo bottled 20 years ago and one bottled this year and you will only notice very subtle differences. That is the skill of the blender.

All of this explanation is to try and dispel a myth that all of the casks made available to independent bottlers are somehow inferior or rejected by blenders. 'Why would they sell their best whisky to other companies to earn recognition and reward?' In many cases there is little to no knowledge about the quality of the whisky being sold. The companies selling the casks are often oblivious to the contents – it is simply surplus stock on the spreadsheet. That means what they are selling and trading could be anything from absolute

Images courtesy of thewhiskyvault.com

stinkers to incredible gems. The numbers of casks we are talking about negates the possibility of a quality control measure being put in place. One trade alone that I was privy to, saw the sale of several £million of 1973 & '74 Invergordon (as per the over production by Invergordon previously mentioned). It is highly unlikely that a single cask of this had even been opened before the first samples were requested. It had sat for over thirty years just patiently maturing, untouched and, barring legal and compliant records, completely forgotten about.

I recall being on the Malts Advocate course at Royal Lochnagar with then Manager Mike Nicholson. The distillery had a duty paid cask for sampling from and this happened to be a first fill ex-Sherry butt. I forget the age, but that is not important, what was relevant was that Mike suggested this cask was too heavy for the blenders – it didn't fit the part of the blends that Royal Lochnagar was supposed to fill. For myself, and the other writers on the course that weekend, it was a heavenly dram and still one of the finest Royal Lochnagar whiskies I have ever tasted[116].

Obviously I am simplifying the process here and each and every blending house will have a slightly different set up and approach. I am trying to explain how casks can get overlooked and then made available. What was certainly interesting was noticing that parcels of whisky would often be made available that were situated in similar locations. And as business decisions were made within the industry this could sometimes have a massive knock-on effect to supply for the independent bottlers. One such decision was the sale of the Broxburn site, owned by Glenmorangie Plc, to Diageo in 2008. The site was Glenmorangie's blending[117] and bottling headquarters and no doubt the sale was part of Moët Hennessy's strategy to premiumise the business having bought Glenmorangie Plc in 2004 (which included Glen Moray and Ardbeg). Up until the sale large amounts of whisky that I was buying were housed at the Broxburn warehouses. Once the sale went through this stopped – it caused a fairly seismic shift in the availability of stock.

Similarly, decisions made by companies to lay down stock for future projects can also lead to stock being made available. Drambuie, the most famous whisky liqueur, had long planned an age statement expression and launched the 15 year old in 2011. The stocks laid down for the premium bottlings were not insignificant and rumour has it that this greatly overextended its finances. Sales of the 15 year old liqueur were not significant and this put the company in trouble. Large quantities of quite excellent whisky were made

---

116. My offer of purchasing it, as clearly Diageo did not require it, again fell on deaf ears (this seems to be a theme).
117. Some of you, like me, will fondly remember the blend B.N.J. or Bailie Nicol Jarvie. It was one of the greatest bargains in the whisky world. Sadly discontinued in 2014.

available which greatly benefitted those with capital and eventually the century-old, family-owned business was bought by Wm Grant & Sons in 2014.

Independent bottlers also had a golden period of buying casks that had been bought privately. Arran, Springbank and Bruichladdich (and there were several more distilleries that had sold small parcels in their past) became available as they matured. As these distilleries did not sell or trade their distillate with other companies for stock to blend, this was the only way IBs could get access to these whiskies. I once asked Euan Mitchell, Managing Director of Arran Distillery what he felt about the number of independent bottlings of Arran whisky that were on the market.

> "For the most part it is not a problem." He stated. "Sure, it is annoying when a bottler beats us to an age statement but we realise that these cask sales were crucial to the creation and independence of the distillery when we started. It would be a bit churlish of us to now bemoan the fact that they are being bottled. And, at the end of the day, it is all Arran spirit that we distilled and put into wood. Some IBs re-rack into different wood and we shouldn't be held accountable for that. Our only main concern is when a bottler thinks it is fine to continually bottle one Arran after another. This, we feel, is riding, a little too hard, off the back of our marketing and brand reputation."

Other opportunities arose when one large distiller laid down stock for a series of premium blends that due to trade arrangements were then cancelled – this saw a huge number of excellent aged blends (in wood) hit the market[118] and also large parcels of aged malts that were now surplus to requirement including Glenrothes, Ben Nevis and Ardmore [interesting to note that up until that point Ben Nevis was not considered one of the more sought after malts. With the independent bottlings came a renewed interest as drinkers recognised the quality of the spirit].

As the 2010s continued it became more and more evident that stock was being offered 'subject to first refusal from the owner of the distillery'. This meant that stock on the open market was first offered back to the original distiller. It is quite clear that these agreements, although not always strictly adhered to, caused a big dent in available stock. Producers began to seriously control the amount of their whisky being available for bottling. At this time many distillery makes simply disappeared from lists of stock being offered.

In recent times there has been a slight shift in thinking and strategy with regards to supply. A few of the new independent distilleries have begun to

---

118. My personal favourite was the parcel of 1980 blended whisky.

openly embrace the fact that IBs can present their output in a novel way and often to different markets. Ardnamurchan, Glasgow and Annandale Distilleries have all had successful partnerships with independent bottlers or have offered bulk. In this respect they have taken a greater interest in what is bottled and how it is presented. There has also been a shift in one of the larger distillers, realising they were not prepared to represent all of their own distilleries, to release stock directly to allow IBs to show their malts. How long this continues remains to be seen but it is refreshing that a large company acknowledged and appreciated the work of IBs.

One company outside all of this is Gordon & MacPhail. As Scotland's largest independent bottler and also one of its oldest, it has had a long history of buying and laying down distillate in wood of its own choosing, and in their own warehouses. This makes them a unique company and their story deserving of exclusion from this account (and worthy of their own book). The vast majority of all independent bottlers and bottlings is spirit bought in wood and quite often matured for, the most part, in the original warehouse it was deposited.

This does raise the question; why are some companies approved for supply and not others? Why can Gordon & MacPhail buy new fillings to lay down for decades and bottle, and in most cases, using the distillery name on the labels, but you or I cannot? Firstly, the answer is we are in the era of the 'scramble for stock'. We are back to the 1940s where distillers are overtly concerned they do not have enough aged stock to fulfil brand requirements. Secondly we are in a period of premiumisation not seen before. Aged stocks now carry such value, profit and kudos to distillers that, not only are they not releasing these from their warehouses, but they are actively trading and re-purchasing stock they previously sold.

That explains the mature aging stock conundrum – but as far as new fillings go this is mostly due to the change in the industry outlined in Chapter Four. The agents are gone; the brokers have all but gone and distillers simply don't offer filling contracts like they used to. This is likely due to the nature of new fillings business. Unless you have warehousing space, access to enough wood and means of filling and storing, you are not going to be a viable option to any distiller selling you spirit. It is one thing to buy and bottle a cask, it is quite a different operation to organise tanker loads of spirit each year.

⁎   ⁎   ⁎

Angus MacRaild

It was out of this industry practice of openly selling, trading and brokering that independent bottling, as we know it today, would eventually emerge. An independent, third party market might have been curious and at times irksome to the mainstream, blending oriented Scotch whisky industry, but it served a clear purpose within the wider framework of the industry and how Scotch whisky was bought, sold, traded and - eventually - consumed.

It was an evolutionary process and what we term and understand as 'independent' bottlings today, were not at all common before the 1960s. A good example is Gordon & MacPhail. The earliest releases known from Gordon & MacPhail, and what we understand about their early practice as a whisky merchant, would be termed 'licensed bottling', as opposed to independent bottling. They would be purchasing fillings from the distilleries and selling them under semi-official distillery sanctioned labels. They still do this today and you can see examples of Linkwood, Mortlach, Glen Grant and Macallan (as Speymalt) all released by Gordon & MacPhail. It wasn't until 1968, when they launched their Connoisseur's Choice range, that they began to offer fully 'independent' bottlings in the sense we would understand today. The same could be said of Wm Cadenhead Ltd, who only began to offer what we would technically term independent bottlings in the 1960s. Prior to that their focus was much more heavily upon blended Scotch products and occasionally rum as well. This is not to detract from either company's history, or their significant contribution to the promotion of malt whisky, but rather to help clarify our understanding of what independent bottling is and how it stands apart from the numerous, and undeniably confusing, world of Scotch whisky products and practices.

Indeed, it can be hard to look at the vast web of commercial whisky bottlings throughout the 20th century prior to the 1960s and discern what is 'official' versus what is 'independent'. There were many small batch blends bottled by, or for, breweries for example, which to us today might look like a form of early independent bottling. These existed often because numerous larger breweries had pubs or tap rooms and they saw a market for selling Scotch whisky; better, commercially, to sell your own than a big brand. In that sense these types of bottling were more of a forerunner of a supermarket own label bottlings that you can commonly find.

The true 'pre-cursors' to independent bottling would have been those of shippers and merchants. From the 1950s onwards bottlings of named single malts did start to appear more frequently and would have been available through wine merchants and grocers. Notable names from this period were Christopher & Co, a London-based fine wine merchant and shipper, which released a number of bottlings of Glenlivet, notably including some at higher or cask strength - a practice well ahead of its time. Similarly, the wine merchant and shipper Averys of Bristol began to bottle single malts under its own livery. The labels featured prominent detail about these stocks being matured in 'their own Spanish oak Sherry casks'; as an importer and merchant of Sherry during an era when the drink enjoyed far more widespread popularity in the UK, this is a great insight into the symbiosis between these two drinks. It also reveals that these kinds of firms (along with the aforementioned breweries) were speculators in bonded Scotch Whisky - 'investors' you might say . There were a number of exquisite single malts released by Averys from the 1960s and into the 1970s, most of which will fetch four figure sums at auction today.

However, when looking at this 'pre-cursor' world of proto-independent bottlings, one of the most important names is Berry Brothers. An ancient family wine merchant located in the heart of St James in London, this was a business perfectly positioned to develop a practice that to us today looks very much like independent bottling as we understand it.

Berry Brother's customers throughout the 19th century would have noted the declining availability of Cognac due to the phylloxera blight in French vineyards; French misfortune inevitably became Scotch whisky's opportunity. As a seller of fine wines, Berry's had the physical premises and a customer base with sufficient depth of pocket and appetite to buy Scotch Whisky. Like Averys, it was also an importer and merchant of sherry, able to fill their own casks with Scotch whisky and retail the mature contents directly to customers from their own warehouses – a business model most whisky shops and bottlers can only fantasise about today.

There are price lists from Berry Brothers that date back to the late 19th century, listing named single malts, proprietary blends and blended malt bottlings, at a variety of ages and strengths. This is arguably some of the earliest examples of what we would term 'independent' bottling. The bottled evidence becomes a little better from the 1920s and 1930s onwards, where you can see a number of fascinating old bottlings by Berry Brothers under their own livery. One great example being an 8 year old Talisker bottled in the 1930s.

These are just some early key examples, there is also a wealth of obscure and now extremely rare examples of named, unofficial single malts bottled by, or for, hotels, small grocers and private individuals. There's also other early and important names whose output contributed to the fledgling independent bottling scene and are well worth exploring: Robert Watson of Aberdeen, Douglas Murdoch and Campbell Hope & King of Elgin are three important ones. We can be certain that the remaining existing record is but a small fragment of what was bottled throughout the earlier decades of the 20th century. Scotch w hisky thrived *because it was subject to a culture of consumption and drinking - there are far more surviving examples of bottled Cognac from the 19th and 20th centuries, given cultural attitudes to Cognac (informed by those drinkers and practices of fine wine etc who would cellar their drink) – therefore the great Scotch whisky 'archive' was more often than not destroyed in the act of enjoyment.*

Like many aspects of Scotch Whisky, when viewed in retrospect it is easy to see how things evolved from one point to the next. Although independent bottling was not a recognised concept until relatively recently, it has been practiced in partial, or haphazard forms for well over a century now. It was simultaneously a response to, and an influence upon, enthusiasm in Scotch whisky that sought to go beyond the more standard or commonly available products and desired something different, more robust and - more often than not - a single malt bottled in natural form.

∗　　∗　　∗

CHAPTER 7

OFF THE PENINSULAR; SURVIVAL OF THE FITTEST

"My initial contact with independent bottlers came when I visited my first whisky show, Whiskymessen in Denmark. I remember that there was a huge variety of whiskies from Douglas Laing and I then discovered The Bottlers and Adelphi. I found it very interesting to find whisky from, for me, unknown distilleries and also to find different cask maturations from well-known distilleries that they don't bottle themselves. I went to Limburg for the first time in 2006 and have returned every year. There I came in contact with Samaroli, Moon Import and local German bottlers. I have always found IBs to be extra special as they are the ones that break boundaries and dare to do something different. There is so much new and fun whisky still to discover and the journey will never end."

MAGNUS FAGERSTRÖM
SMWS Country Manager, Sweden

My two great pleasures in the offices of Cadenhead's were delivery day for samples and the selecting of the casks. Strangely, I was not in charge of selecting which casks we asked for samples from for buying, nor from those we owned and warehoused for bottling. Regardless each box arrived, either from a broker or distillery, containing hidden treasures where often I was the first person to taste them. It was a glorious time to be a bottler as samples of Littlemill, St Magdalene, Dallas Dhu and Rosebank would arrive along with a Mortlach, Macallan or Ben Nevis. Prices were fairly straight across the board and always calculated on either an OLA (original litres of alcohol) or RLA (re-gauged[119] litres of alcohol) – often dependent upon age; as a general rule, whisky up to around ten years was sold on OLA and older was RLA.

The first cask selection I was involved in was in the form of a panel that consisted of myself, Frank McHardy, Euan Mitchell and a couple other colleagues. No-one seemed that fussed about being on the panel and before long I was alone in selecting the casks for each bottling. It was very encouraging that the management never second guessed me in my cask selections. If I felt a cask wasn't good enough, regardless of age, name or rarity, the company did not bottle it. I guess they felt as I was the one on the road representing these whiskies I would have to explain if any were duds (and not everything I selected was appreciated quite as much by everyone who bought them).

You may remember from my opening salvo in the Introduction that I don't believe there are whisky 'experts'. Not when it comes to your odyssey or enjoyment. Similarly I don't believe there are any special palates out there with regards to selecting casks. I'll refer to this more later but I very much see cask selection as just part and parcel of the enjoyment of Scotch. I will admit though that certain markets have a preference in general to certain types of whisky and one learns to distinguish which casks will appeal with broader markets and those that are market specific. One trip with Cadenhead's saw me travel from Copenhagen to Malmo (where I performed a tasting for the Mayor[120]), then onto Stockholm before Borlänge in the North. In Borlänge I hosted a tasting for around 150 of the locals (they apologised for the small turnout but there was an important ice hockey game on the same night). I had hand-picked six whiskies and included the obligatory Islay to end the night (a 15 year old Caol Ila from memory). At the end of the evening, as is my preference, I like to find out people's favourites. Caol Ila was almost unanimously the

---

119. This is the process of dipping a cask to calculate the contents. It is an ancient technology using a dip rod, ullage tables and hydrometers.
120. I asked him why the duty on alcohol was so high in Sweden. He replied that Sweden had a big problem with drinking. Looking around the calm and serene city of Malmo at about midnight I suggested to him that he needs to see any UK city about the same time and rethink what he views as a 'big problem'.

winner. I should have just brought six heavily peated whiskies with me and brought the house down[121].

My tour then took me across country to Oslo where I met with the most peculiar importer; House of Cognac, owned and run by Jon Bertelsen. He and I went for lunch in a very swanky restaurant where he spent about 15 minutes poking at an expensive plate of food and ordering several even more expensive Springbank's for us to drink. Having had a small heart attack at seeing the cost of everything I asked him why he had not touched his food. 'Oh, I've already had lunch and am also meeting someone else in a few hours for another meal.' To be honest it was only really a courtesy visit as Norway was a near impossible market to sell Cadenhead products to at this time[122]. Pretty soon I was on an overnight ferry taking me back to Copenhagen. I made the acquaintance of two Dutch truck drivers who were no strangers to this journey and they in turn introduced me to a pear cider called Kopparberg. A few too many of these[123] and I was awoken believing I was at my port of exit. I hurriedly dressed and disembarked into a cold and wet morning with barely a soul around. As the ship departed I began to wonder why so few people had disembarked and why the ship would leave its final destination so quickly. It didn't take me long to realise I had disembarked in Helsingborg, Sweden and not Copenhagen. A rookie error and just a couple hours on a train to remedy the situation.

On one particular Monday morning the postal worker delivered a large box of samples. I regret that I was not foresighted enough to have archived every sample and cask I had the privilege of tasting – in much the same way as locals never saw fit to record the distilleries on their doorstep, I never thought too much about recording what I tasted in a methodical manner. I do recall however, that there were several samples of St Magdalene whisky from 1983, the year the distillery was closed. Enclosed, usually, with the samples would be a price list and details of each cask (emails were just beginning to take off at this point, things were still sent by fax and post). The St Magdalene were in hogsheads and the seller was asking for £1.35 per year per RLA. This meant that an 18 year old hogshead of St Magdalene with about 90 litres of alcohol (at cask strength of mid-high 50s% that would yield approximately 230 bottles) would cost around £2,200. Just writing this now seems ridiculous to me, but that was the case. That would result in a bottle retailing for around £50-60 including all taxes and margins[124].

---

121. Scandinavians are by far the most peat-centric whisky markets.
122. Norway and Sweden both have state-owned monopolies that sell alcohol; Vinmonopolet and Systembolaget.
123. Which I have also never been able to drink since.
124. Context here is difficult as St Magdalene is so rare. The last bottles to go for general retail, albeit much older than eighteen, were well over £800 per bottle.

Whilst I cannot state, from the twenty or so that I have tasted, that St Magdalene was a top-quality single malt (which may have contributed to its demise), I added these casks to the list of those that I would like the company to buy only to have my recommendation rebuffed. The reason being that the previous ones bought had been £1.30 per year RLA and by buying these it would set a dangerous precedent. At this time there was much more concern over bulk costs rather than desirability of or any future increase in value. Much of this was a hangover from a much earlier period when malt prices were routinely announced at the beginning of each distilling season. My protestations that they weren't making any more St Magdalene[125] and that these were good, fell on deaf ears.

The 'whisky festival' was still a relatively new concept and many international markets were experiencing their first. Around 2003 I headed off to Austria for the first whisky festival in Vienna. The importer there, a company called Potstill, had a near monopoly on many independent bottlers and distillers in Austria so the fair was well attended from an industry viewpoint. It was, in contrast, almost completely bereft of general public[126]. This was just as well, as on the night before opening there had been a get together with a 'bring a bottle' table. This was quite the collection and many of us (that is at least those in their 20s and 30s) duly tucked in to the fantastic array of whiskies on offer (I can vaguely recall that a bottle of Redbreast 15 year old was emptied). The first session of the festival was notable not just for its lack of attendees but also a plethora of empty stands as much needed, and restorative, sleep was being taken in the hotel[127].

By the second evening Andrew Hart (then working for Hart Bros) and I decided to head off to find a different bar from the hotel. A few streets over we found what looked like an old fashioned 'speak-easy'. In hindsight the oversized and grizzled bouncer should have signalled it was not what we were looking for but in we went regardless.

The 'speak-easy' was about the size of a fairly generous living room. In one corner was a small bar, in two other corners were comfortable seats and small tables and in the middle was a pole on a slightly raised stage. The seven or eight other patrons were very large men in fur-lined coats, with gold dripping off anywhere it could; and with them were several young ladies dressed rather inappropriately for the winter weather outdoors. Andrew and I realised, fairly quickly, that we had made a mistake. However, with a bouncer of equal size

125. The distillery, in Linlithgow, is now a rather mixed appearance block of flats.
126. I think, very much like the initial Whisky Live in London, there had been an attitude of 'Build it and they will come' a la 'Field of Dreams'.
127. Not me, I hasten to add...

and menace manning the door on the inside we figured this was not a joint where one could casually walk in and out on a whim. So we ordered a beer... that cost 25€, each. Deciding to stay at the bar, rather than sit with the large men in their coats, the atmosphere was icy and closing fast. One of the large men grunted in what we could only think was Russian (but just as likely Belarusian or similar) and one of the companions, looking about as enthralled as a trapped tiger in a performing circus began an uninspiring, yet watchable, fling about the pole in the middle of the room.

Andrew and I are simple folk really. We like the home life, roaring fires, a good dram, a book, family – you get the picture. We're not thrill seekers. And this moment in this weird little bar with its deathly quiet atmosphere and severely overpriced, and poor quality, beer was not what we had in mind for the evening. We had both been nursing our 'king's ransom' bottles until, mid-way through the dance (which now featured less clothing than at the beginning), one of the larger, and older fur-wearing gentlemen said to us "You like?" At which point, and quite frankly from nowhere it seemed, another of those six foot high and wide, long coat wearing, face like a bulldog chewing a wasp, henchman appeared at the bar, next to us. It became apparent that should a certain amount of money change hands, and this was posed not really as a question but an eventuality, then the girl dancing, now sporting a summer pirate's outfit (eye patch and not much else), would be accompanying us.

This put Andrew and I in a slight dilemma as between us we only had enough money for about another beer, and not much else. I am kidding of course; the dilemma we had was getting out of there. And quickly. Our beers quickly disappeared and thankfully so did we back to the familiarity of the hotel. I'm pretty sure we both looked at least once to make sure we were not followed.

Around this time, and out of the blue, Cadenhead's had contact from a company in Russia looking to import. The Russian market was very strange with brokers acting on behalf of importers. One such broker was an ex-KGB (are all Russians ex-government?) officer called Alexander Russkikh (pronounced 'Russky' - I swear I am not making this up). He visited the team in Campbeltown along with the importer and we took them to the best restaurant in the town, The White Hart, for lasagne and chips. Their first order from us was quite sizeable (over £50k) and I flew out the following February to attend a large wine & spirits expo in Moscow.

After a dreadful flight, hair-raising landing (it appears Russians, at least at that time, would vacate their seats the moment the wheels touched down, despite the plane still going well over one hundred miles an hour) and clearing Soviet-style customs, Alexander greeted me in the airport. His first words seemed very odd to me:

"David, please do not use the prostitutes in the hotel." I am sure these were wise words to a seasoned traveller but rather confused me. After a three hour journey to go about twenty miles, we arrived at the hotel and having got my room key I realised why Alexander had said what he had. A young lady that had been in the lobby followed me to the lift and entered as I did.

"You need company?" she said.

"Ah, no. Thanks, I'm fine." I replied.

And that was that. If it hadn't had been for Alexander's incredibly pertinent council, who knows what might have happened...[128]

The Moscow trip was fascinating and freezing in equal measures. Although it had been technically colder in Borlänge, Sweden when I visited, Moscow was around -18 degrees C and hurt to breathe in[129]. I witnessed a man, shortly after he exited a bus, slip in ice and land heavily on his back. Not a soul went to his aid. I made a mental note to watch my step. I did fancy, as is my wont on my travels, to taste the local distillate; Russia of course means Vodka. I found a stall at the side of a road near the hotel selling bottles of a brand I had never heard of and bought a bottle (I seem to recall that everything back then was bought in $US). The bottle came in a brown paper bag which I buried into my jacket. I then turned, immediately finding a bit of iced pavement and flipped, landing heavily on my back. Again, not a soul came to my help, and more importantly the wetness I could feel was from the ice, and not the vodka. When I mentioned this strange lack of public concern to Alexander he suggested that people were afraid it would be a scam and they would have their wallets taken. People seemed very afraid of each other in Moscow. The Vodka was vile and was left almost full for the cleaning crew when I departed.

The importer took all of the agents/sales people out for dinner on the Friday & Saturday night. The first night was to the second best restaurant in Moscow and on the Saturday night we went to the best restaurant; I cannot remember the name of either although one of them had something to do with a boar. As I dined on caviar, foie gras and Chateaubriand, washed down with some outstanding Spanish and Portuguese wines I could not help but think back to the lasagne and chips we had served up just a few months prior in Campbeltown.

---

128. Alexander did tell me, although possibly apocryphal, that a businessman had taken a women to his room, had a drink with her and awoke to find all of his possessions gone. I doubt that was anyone I knew...

129. It was so cold that two of the Portuguese wine reps were rushed to A&E with respiratory issues after a walking tour of Red Square. They had come ill-prepared for 'Major Winter'.

On the Sunday night, which happened to be 14ᵗʰ February, I and another rep called Dennis Billecart (from the Champagne House Billecart-Salmon) were left to our own devices. Hungry, we set out for dinner, and it being Valentine's Day (which appeared to be quite a big deal in Russia) the restaurants were all romantically themed. After finding a suitable establishment, we were looked upon with great suspicion when we asked for a table for two. The service, frankly, was appalling, despite Dennis ordering a bottle of his own rosé Champagne at well over $150. We realised that the staff had assumed we were a couple and also realised that Russia was a bit behind the West (or at least the UK and France) when it came to acceptance of sexual preference. Dennis, being a bit of a self-professed *enfant terrible*, played up to it and I could not help but giggle. The service then got much worse.

Finally after what was a very quick and rudely served dinner, clearly the staff wanting rid of their suspected two unusual patrons, we left, only to be confronted by the owner who blocked our exit.

"You did not leave a tip!" He proclaimed eyeballing each of us in turn.

"But darling, the service was terrible." Dennis replied in a lilting French accent. I did not think now was time to continue the charade. "You do not leave until you pay the staff." Demanded the owner.

"Fine. But we could at least have a smile from you." Dennis said looking at the staff who had all congregated around us.

"There are no smiles for you in Moscow." The owner said with more than a hint of menace.

Dennis finally took the hint and $50 later we were out on the street. I cannot admit to enjoying my time in Moscow. The city had an edge and general unease that pervaded into almost everything. I had travelled there only six months after the dreadful bombing of one of the underground Metro stations by Chechen rebels and had therefore promised my girlfriend that I would not visit the magnificent underground stations (which I still regret to this day). It was incredible though to be walking through the Red Square knowing some of the history that had taken place and a tour of the quite enormous city, seeing the seven large buildings (the Seven Sisters) that dominate the skyline.

I was extremely fortuitous to be working for J&A Mitchell in the years[130] that they built Glengyle Distillery. Not many people can say that they have watched a distillery being born from announcement through to production and I would often wander up to the site (which was the original site of Glengyle Distillery closed in 1925) to watch machinery and plant being installed. Strangely the

130. 2003-2004

trademark 'Glengyle' belonged to Loch Lomond Distillers Ltd[131] and due to some dispute J&A Mitchell decided to call the distillate 'Kilkerran' (the original name of Campbeltown). The stills were from Ben Wyvis Distillery (where Frank McHardy, Springbank Manager and Manager of the Glengyle project, had previously worked) and I watched them being installed. One day when I wandered up the stills were firing away and Frank McHardy called me over:

> "David, try this. This is the first distillate from Glengyle Distillery. You're the writer, tell me what you taste." Frank said handing me a glass of new-make that he had just withdrawn from the Spirit Safe[132].

I took the glass realising the momentousness of the occasion. I, David Stirk, a young, fairly imbecilic, care-free, uncouth and definitely without grace, pretender in the whisky world was about to be the first person in the world to try Glengyle (aka Kilkerran) spirit. No-one can ever take this away from me. This was a seminal moment. A once-in-a-lifetime occasion. One to tell the grandkids.

I took a large swig... and swiftly spat it out. It was revolting. Frank and the distillery worker next to him[133] roared with laughter. Sensing my confusion, Frank took the glass back and explained:

> "You have to run the distillery a few times to work through the cobwebs; the saw dust and copper sulphate etc. It won't taste good until we've done that."

I nodded in understanding – I guess it is why the first time you use your kettle it has that weird taste. However, it does not excuse the fact that I was the first person ever to taste Glengyle distillate. And that I shall carry with me always.

It had always been hinted by the Cadenhead management that I could one day work remotely. Not being a Campbeltown native the distance and time involved to get anywhere began to take its toll. As you will remember from my first trip I had resolved to never take the coach from Glasgow to Campbeltown again. My options (with no ferry services at the time) were only lifts (and thank you Kate and Euan for the many lifts[134]) and the Campbeltown-Glasgow 'flyer'. At the time I had no issue with flying at all and quite enjoyed the thirty minute

131. They acquired this with Glen Scotia after the purchase of Bloch Bros.
132. Someone needs to rename these beautiful copper cages that show the new-make disgorging from the stills. 'Safe' they are not as never seem locked and I seem to be constantly given glasses of liquid drawn directly from them.
133. James or Callum, I can't remember which.
134. And especially Kate who saved my life, and hers, when on returning to Campbeltown one Sunday in her mini (an original one) a truck decided it would take our side of the road around a bend. Kate managed to instantly divert into a side dirt road. An almost certain tragedy was diverted.

flight that used about 1/50th of the largest runway in Europe at Machrihanish, just outside of Campbeltown, and flew over Arran (so low it felt like you could reach out and stroke a sheep on the mountain tops) to Glasgow. These flights were great because you could see straight out through the cockpit (the plane could probably seat twelve, including the two pilots) but also sometimes a little hairy as were often used as the training flights for newly licensed pilots. The flights were often cancelled which meant an overnight stay in Glasgow which was never frowned upon by me.

I had always desired to be a Brand Ambassador for a major company. Travelling and taking the story of Scotch around the world seemed a romantic and exciting role. Most of my work for Cadenhead's had been doing that and I thoroughly enjoyed it. These jobs, although growing in number, were still few and far between – companies often preferred to send marketing or PR staff to festivals along with a token manager or blender. Many of those sent, the likes of Jim McEwan or Richard Patterson, excelled in this role. They not only brought the drink to the show but a personality, warmth and experience to the tasting or evening. Companies and brands wanted in on this and I wanted to be a part of it. I had a few interviews; one with Angus Dundee was interesting (where I was continually accused of looking 'too young'). In reality I had no intention of working for Angus Dundee after a story I had heard from one of their ex-Salesmen. He told me of an encounter in one of the Baltic countries. On discussing the terms for an order of blended Scotch whisky the buyer, sat behind a large Bond-baddie-style desk, asked for a price that was below the minimum available to the salesman. Upon hearing the minimum price re-confirmed the buyer opened a drawer, retrieved a revolver, placed it on the desk and repeated the price he wanted to pay. Suffice to say the salesman agreed, got out of Dodge and never went back. That was enough for me to know I was not a suitable candidate but interviews are always good and meant an overnighter in Glasgow.

Another interview was with Morrison Bowmore Distillers where I would be selling everything from Midori to Bowmore (I proclaimed defeat in my ability to represent Midori & Mandarine). Another interview was with John Dewar & Sons (recently acquired by Bacardi in 1998). Dewar's were looking for a US Brand Ambassador[135]. I had quite a bit going for me, not least my US Passport that avoided any issues with Visa's and Green Cards etc. The role, however, involved travelling throughout the US to mostly big universities to entertain the student body and/or professors. The idea of night after night being amongst Frat parties did not appeal to me in the slightest. I turned down the job.

---

135. As if I was somehow stalking him, Ewan Gunn had, since leaving Cadenhead's in 2000 been with Angus Dundee and then joined John Dewar & Sons in 2004 taking the position I had turned down. Since 2011 he has been with Diageo.

Eventually however, having mentioned to Stewart Laing, one of two brothers that owned and ran Douglas Laing & Co Ltd, I was job hunting he invited me to their offices in Glasgow's West End for an interview. The role, as it was described to me, was to increase the single cask sales in the European market. This seemed ideal as with Cadenhead's I had concentrated on Europe and had not been involved in the other two big markets; North America and Asia. I moved to Cambuslang in the Spring of 2004 and shared an office with a young lady from Dufftown that I already knew from her days as a Glenfiddich tour guide (and as one of Mark Watt's closest friends); Susan Webster[136]. Douglas Laing was a far more impressive outfit than Cadenhead's. Fred Laing, who was responsible for much of the advertising, marketing and presentation drive, was more acutely aware of what customers wanted. The packaging and company positioning was considerably more professional and I learned a great deal about how a progressive bottling company could be run. Stewart, who was more involved with the commercial side of the business, developed markets in parts of the world I had not thought possible. The company, albeit old fashioned in a way, was also wide spread, well set and forward thinking.

I had brought with me a few suppliers and customers that were of some use to Douglas Laing. It was quite clear though, at least to me, that the company would be split at some point in the future and that left my sales often getting bogged down in a slight tug of ownership. Sometime in September one of the suppliers sent me a sample of 1969 Strathisla that had spent its life maturing in an ex-Sherry butt. I knew it was good, excellent in fact, but Strathisla was hardly a 'big name' malt and despite its age and quality would not fly off the shelves. The sample was turned down by Fred Laing as the company had sufficient stock from that distillery. A day later I flew off to Stockholm to help Douglas Laing's importers attend the Stockholm Beer & Whisky Festival. Over the long weekend, and amongst pouring out dram after dram, I decided that I would buy the cask of Strathisla. The sample was from a supplier I knew and had been offered to me directly. At that moment I decided to strike out on my own.

Looking back on this decision now it was the kind of decision a young, brash and (probably) foolish twenty-nine year old would make. I realised I had good basics of the process and a great enough passion for the product and industry that would carry me far but I was still very green. Had it not been for the likes of Jamie Walker at Adelphi, Andrew Symington at Signatory and John Glaser at Compass Box showing me that it could be done, I would not

---

136. We would spend at least one afternoon a week trying to make the other cry with laughter. I'm not sure poor Fred, who's office was next door, really approved. Susan if you are reading this, I apologise for my myth busting details about Christmas and Elvis and also for my George W. Bush impressions.

have made that phone call to secure the cask of Strathisla.

In 2013 Douglas Laing & Co Ltd did split, Fred Laing taking the name Douglas Laing & Co Ltd and Stewart Laing operating under the name Hunter Laing & Co Ltd. Both have gone on to be bigger companies than the original and now own and operate their own distilleries.

CHAPTER 8

Golden age
or just lucky?

"I've always been interested in this magic spirit since I got acquainted with the collection of old bottles my grandfather had. I was lucky enough to get to work with The Whisky Exchange and there I discovered more independent bottlers. I was able to taste old Samaroli's, Intertrade, Moon, Sestante and rare casks from many others. One that really stands out was a Bowmore distilled in 1966 and bottled for Jack Wiebers in his 'Old Train Line' series. This whisky set me off on a quest to find other whiskies that tasted like that. IBs continue to fuel my interest in discovering all of the different nuances of each distillery and from different production eras. They also challenge stereotypes; for instance one absolutely mind-boggling dram was an eight year old Glen Garioch distilled in 1971 and bottled by Samaroli. Eight year old whisky is not 'supposed' to have that much complexity and flavour."

DIEGO LANZA
Senior Whisky Specialist, Bonhams

One of the great draws that the independent bottling sector has for young start-ups, and I am living proof, is that there are no remarkable skills required for entry. I am not meaning here to diminish the work I, and others, have put in to make their enterprises a success. I simply mean all you need is a few factors (money and suppliers) and a clear understanding of when a whisky is ripe for bottling (or not). This is why, and I shall come on to this in far greater detail later, the IB sector of the industry has exploded. To take on the building of a distillery is, well, nearly infinitely more difficult. That story is for someone else to tell but the money, time, knowledge and other hurdles make it only for the very, very few. Independent bottling, on the other hand, is for the many.

In the 1970s through to the late 1990s, spirit, mature and otherwise, was readily available. You could pick up the phone to any broker, blender or distiller and buy from whatever was available. For supply it truly was a golden period. The vast aged stocks that were taking up valuable real estate in warehouses was sold with gratitude to anyone that could use it. The likes of Cadenhead's, Gordon & MacPhail and later Signatory could pick and choose filling their warehouses with incredible whiskies. There was almost no cache on make or age.

Now, of course, this just seems remarkable but at the time malt whisky was a novelty. Closed distilleries were not much more than a reminder that markets go up and down or that consumer behaviour/tastes can be fickle. Bulging warehouses reminded distillers that the forecasters were occasionally wrong. So to look back on this period and think of it as a great time to be an IB is more than rose-tinted thinking. Selling these premium malts at this time was a hard task. Demand was low, consumer knowledge and understanding was not like today and the public's acceptance of prices even slightly above what was standard offerings made anything out of the ordinary a difficult thing to shift.

The UK was quite slow to realise that the large stocks of maturing whisky was such a treasure. The large conglomerates and blending houses were still so insistent on the bulk trade of blends that the gold mine they were sitting on was just a hangover of overproduction and needed shifting. Like with most things that taste exceptional, it is often the Italians who are the first to take notice. Samaroli[137] may have the right to the title of 'foremost' in the Italian market and certainly his bottlings are now some of the most sought after and highly regarded of any independent bottlings.

Without meaning to, Samaroli was demonstrating to the blending houses that what they had was worth some inspection. There was simply no attention

---

137. See the entry in the list at the end of this book.

paid to what Sarmaroli or Cadenhead's or Gordon & MacPhail was doing. Too much of a novelty to the larger companies looking for ways to increase their blend's market share. There were those, in particular at Glenfiddich, Macallan and Glenfarclas, who were banging a drum for malt whisky:

> "To mix blended whisky with whatever is quite acceptable; to mix anything with malt whisky, other that perhaps a drop of the Highland Spring water, is nothing short of sacrilege. After all, unlike blended whisky, malt whiskies are produced by craftsmen, working deep in the glens, using traditional skills handed down from generation to generation.

> "... the [malt whisky] consumer is looking not only for a malt which he knows, recognises and can pronounce the name of, but also one that his peer group will identify and be impressed by.

> "It has been a major historical failure of the malt whisky industry, to educate the consumer that each distillery produces a unique spirit and that there are eighty plus distilleries producing single malt whisky for sale.[138]"

The quote, taken from the Wine & Spirit Trade Record (November 1985) so perfectly sums up where the industry has been and where it was heading. Firstly, the insistence of the industry to tell consumers how to enjoy their drink and then how the same industry is failing to educate consumers on the incredible variety within the category. A few years prior to this Ian Coombs, Chairman of Long John International stated:

> "I do like to think there is a place for single malts, but I'd like to see them competing with Cognac as an after-dinner drink, not with blends. I believe that if people start their Scotch drinking with malt, they might turn away from it all together, because it's a different taste, and a connoisseur's drink."

And David Connell, Managing Director of John Walker & Sons said:

> "The industry is structured to sell blended Scotch whisky. Anything which promotes the idea that malt whisky is superior must be damaging."

The Journals and Press of the time continually led with pieces extolling the virtues, demand and popularity of single malts but as can been seen from the two quotes above, there was a real issue within companies to understand

---

138. Mark Elliott, Brand Manager for Glenfarclas at Saccone & Speed.

their place. Both quotes suggest that the casual drinker would either be turned away from the drink or turned away from blended whisky if single malts were allowed greater exposure.

The fickle consumer was sending the producers mixed messages. As we saw in Chapter Four, malts were continually rising year on year (although remaining a small percentage of total consumption), especially in markets like Italy and the UK, but as John Burns, Marketing Manager for International Distillers, pointed out in March 1981:

> "1980 was a poor year for malts in the UK, with a drop of up to 30 per cent... This year we're looking forward to a better performance for Bruichladdich... Promoting malt whisky involves carefully controlled graduated moves because if growth comes too quickly, then doubts are cast upon the credibility of the product in the future. One has to keep within the feasible bounds of production capacity and maintenance of quality."

It is clear that distilling companies were thinking of single malts very much in the same vein as blends; bulk, bulk, bulk. The idea, around this time, that single malts could be offered in a more targeted and focused manner was alien to their business mantra. And thus what Cadenhead's, Samaroli and later Signatory was doing barely registered on anyone's radar. Andrew Symington, who started Signatory Vintage in 1988, states quite openly that at the time he started you could buy mature stocks from any distiller. Some were very glad to get stock off of their books. Samaroli is also on record stating that he would visit Scotland several times a year to nose and taste casks and cask samples selecting whatever he wanted. Gordon Wright recalls the buyers for Oddbins visiting at least once a year to select their bottlings for each season.

I have already recalled my story about asking Diageo to let me loose in their warehouses to bottle extraordinary casks of whisky (and guaranteed them a first year profit of £1million). And I'd like to dispel a little myth here; independent bottlers do not get to roam around warehouses picking the casks they like (unless it is their own warehouse and they own the casks). Those days ended a long time ago. Diageo of course, or at least the employees I had presented my case to, were not interested. It is therefore the double whammy of not only the ability, or rather freedom, to pick and choose casks - coupled with the fact the choice was from vast mature stocks that were of little interest to the owners; that created the 'Golden Era' of independent bottling.

I think it is important to make one point about this and I return to my opening point in my introduction about being an 'expert' on whisky. Whilst there is no doubt that for choice and selection the 70s-90s was a golden period, I'm fairly confident that the exceptional bottlings we now pay £000s for would have been selected by you and I. What I'm trying to delicately suggest is that there is no 'nose' or 'palate' that singles out any one person as better suited to selecting a single cask bottling. I have hosted countless tastings and warehouse tours and seen enough consensus of opinion from the near novice to the hardened, whisky in their veins, veteran afficionado. My admiration for the likes of Silvano Samaroli, Donald Hart or Andrew Symington is not that I believe their nose or palate is superior to mine - nor their ability to select a cask, it is because they were doing it at a time when few else were. It is that they all discovered something they found fantastic, looked around and realised that few were offering this to the public, put their might behind it and offered it up. They all very much rescued incredible whiskies from being blended into total obscurity. All of those incredible closed distilleries are remembered by the work of the pioneers of this industry.

Were it possible to gain access to the distilling and filling ledgers of all of the distilleries and distilling companies over the past 60 years we could see exactly how casks became available. As I've already noted, some locations (and ergo some intermediaries or suppliers) were a greater source of supply than others to the IBs. Along with this was a trend or a 'seam' of certain makes from certain years. This has resulted in enthusiasts declaring that a certain make from a certain year was legendary (think '67 for Ardbeg or '73 for Glengoyne). Without wanting to get into an argument over whether there are Vintage years for Scotch, it is clear, as outlined in Chapter Four, that some years had greater production than others [greater production therefore resulting in oversupply and thus IBs getting a slice of the cake].

Whereas in Samaroli's period casks could be selected from a particular 'seam', nowadays, with the proliferation of IBs, we get to see a much fuller picture of a distillery's annual output (good and bad). We can take the recent resurgence in Ben Nevis whisky as an example. What was previously a distillery that appeared to purely exist to provide Nikka with fillings, is now highly sought after due to a very substantial and quality-driven 'seam' of casks from the mid 1990s. With so many of these casks being bottled, and often from one production period, the consumer can get an incredible insight into the distillery character. Prior to these being bottled the distillery (much to the lament of its late manager and greatly-missed John 'Colin' Ross) was not much more than a rare West-highland distillery. Now, with interest never greater, the distillery is struggling to satisfy demand.

It is interesting to note that Samaroli began to decry the lack of quality in the cask samples he was being offered (this is around twenty years ago).

"I assisted the 'birth' of single malts and now [see] the 'death' of single malts'.[139]

As Samaroli had originally got into whisky through the blends he was importing (and claimed were exceptional) he returned to using the casks available to create his 'No-age Series' vatted and blended whiskies. I think Samaroli would have got on very well with John Glaser and thoroughly approved of Compass Box.

What Samaroli would think of the modern industry is anyone's guess. He would barely recognise the malt whisky sector and, likely, would not be an independent bottler today. He was the right man, at the right time; able to roam around warehouses selecting casks the likes of which we may never see again.

139. "Collecting Scotch Whisky" Emmanuel Dron

CHAPTER 9

BUSINESS PLAN? IS 'SURVIVE' SUFFICIENT?

"As a specialist retailer we find our customers are on a journey of discovery. This often starts with trying a dram of something easily accessible. As their interest grows they discover more distillery own bottlings. Independent bottlers give us the opportunity to help lead people further down that path by showing often a different face of these distilleries and then often introducing them to new distilleries. Watching as their passion grows for these wonderful liquid treasures is the most rewarding thing we do."

MATTHEW MCFADYEN
Good Spirits Co, Glasgow

Without a single clue of the legalities, restrictions or protocol, I registered The Creative Whisky Co Ltd and bought the cask of Strathisla 1969. It cost the princely sum of £15,000 and it took a loan from my Dad to buy (he had matched my £10,000 investment made from selling my flat in Campbeltown[140]). I had enough money to also buy a small barrel of Tomatin 1976 (which tasted like blueberry muffins). The name of the company was an 'off the cuff' decision believing I could come up with something better later. I had not been a fan of the tenuously linked Scottish names like Murray McDavid or James MacArthur; I was also loathe to put my name on the label (Stirk means a young bullock or heifer – still used in the cattle trade today). I also came up with the brand name by simply stating 'I need a name that tells the customer that the product is exclusive and is a malt'. Therefore Exclusive Malts was born. No multi-million pound PR executives needed to make the logo walk forwards...

I should state at this point that I don't believe my company, nor my journey is any more remarkable than many other independent companies listed and referred to throughout the book. Indeed, many of these company's stories would make a far more interesting read. My intention is to show 'a' journey and give, albeit in a small way, an understanding of the process.

I had recently made the acquaintance of Alan Gordon who was the Finance Director at Duncan Taylor Scotch Whisky Ltd. The firm began as an independent bottler when a parcel of whisky was made available by an American entrepreneur called Abe Rosenberg around 2002. It had been offered around the industry and J&A Mitchell had made an offer on the parcel of Springbank within the collection which was not accepted (ignoring the incredible old stocks of rare whiskies from the 1960s like Bowmore, Kinclaith, Port Ellen, Ladyburn and Macallan). I can only imagine what it would have been like for Cadenhead's had they bought the entire parcel.

I reached out to Alan to see if he could help me bottle the cask and he duly moved it, bottled it and shipped it for me. Lars Wiebers agreed to take half of the Strathisla outturn (bottled with his Auld Distillers Collection label) and even paid 50% up front which gave me enough capital to pay Duncan Taylor for their services. 'This is child's play I thought...' I then had the good fortune to be in London for the sale of a business called Old Red Lion Blending where all stocks were to be bought with blind bids[141]. Whilst in London I called in to see an old friend, John Glaser, who had also gone out on his own four years previously. His company, Compass Box, was beginning to make some waves with incredible marketing and equally impressive blends. I filled John into

---

140. I was lucky to sell - the entire block of flats are now condemned. I hope whoever bought the flat from me did not lose out though.
141. I managed to buy, with incredibly limited funds, only one cask; a 1975 Balblair for the princely sum of £1,500.

all of the details of my business thus far (which took about two minutes).

"So you've got your WOWGR then." John asked.

"My what?"

"Your WOWGR. Your licence to hold casks of whisky duty suspended in bonded warehouses."

Ah. I did not. After our chat I contacted Alan who assured me that I had not broken any laws as the goods had been transferred to Duncan Taylor, bottled and dispatched by them. He suggested that I hurriedly apply for my licence which I did and within a few days a lovely rep from HMRC came out to the small office in the house I was renting to check the business for approval. Despite some resignations about operating without one, I received my licence just a few days later. Again I thought, this is a breeze.

I believe to be a great independent bottler you need two things; time and money. I had neither of these and cannot claim that my early bottlings were knock-out whiskies[142]. I was able to bottle the Strathisla '69, Tomatin '76 and Balblair '75 (whiskies that most IB's could only dream of now) but as funds were so limited I was not able to take advantage of stock around me. I recall when I started in 2005 that one broker told me I had missed the boat 'Gone are the days of the Port Ellen's, Dallas Dhu's and Brora's. You've started at the worst possible time'[143]. What he failed to maybe see was the growth in demand for independent bottlings would counter the fact that many closed distilleries were no longer available.

I was lucky to be buying direct from a large distiller at this time and whilst there were caveats on the age and some makes available to me (limited supply for instance of the company's own malts) I was able to get a wide array of young whiskies to make each bottling interesting. Around this time casks would cost approximately £700-800 for a ten year old. I recall one of the casks I purchased arriving at the bottling hall empty. Bone dry to be honest. I immediately called up the supply team. The cask was replaced but I was informed that this was part and parcel of buying bulk Scotch; the next cask that was light or empty would not be replaced. This taught me a valuable lesson when it came to costing although the shock of leaking casks would haunt me, well, continually.

The deal with the distiller had required, as soon as I paid for any casks, to move them to a different warehouse. As I was on good terms with the

---

142. As this is Jan Kok's favourite story about me, I have to mention that very early on I tried recruiting Whisky Import Nederland to import my whiskies into the Dutch market. Upon receipt of my samples Jan (and Marcel) were thoroughly unimpressed. In 2009 I tried again and very quickly became one of their largest suppliers.

143. He was right though, I never did manage to get a cask of Port Ellen, Dallas Dhu or Brora.

warehousing team at another large distilling group, and this being the days when space was not so much of a premium, I was able to move the casks to their warehouses. This arrangement was very convenient as the warehouses were very close to the company that were contract bottling for me. The arrangement continued allowing me to buy parcels of around a dozen casks at a time until one day I got an email from the suppliers asking me to come in for a meeting. Assuming I was simply asked in to meet the new supply manager I was shocked to be accused of selling my stock to the company receiving the casks. 'If we wanted to supply them we have agreements in place.' I was told. I was allowed to carry through the final order and then that was it. No more supply. It was, frankly, a ruse - at no point had I ever dreamt of contacting the warehousing company about selling casks. Buying yes, but selling no.

I was distraught to say the least. My ability to buy and bottle inexpensive young whisky vanished. To a certain extent though, considering how little time and money I had, it had allowed Creative Whisky to get off the ground. During the early part of the venture I was surviving from the sales to Germany (through Jack Wiebers Whisky World), Japan (3Rivers), Denmark (QualityWorld) and some limited sales to UK shops. In April 2006, the end of our first financial year, my accountant informed me I had made a profit of around £45,000 and owed the tax man £7,000. This came as a complete shock. £45,000 might sound like a lot, but I had not paid myself a penny during the year, nor had I much in the way of expenses. I now owned a few casks and just about enough cash in the bank to pay the taxman (which thankfully was not due until the following January). I realised I had foolishly included every bottle, cork, capsule and carton in my end of year stock. These were worth almost nothing to anyone else and skewed my end of year stock figures.

Other than any independent bottler having direct relationships with distillers there were only about four brokers buying and selling casks. One of them who I had met in my Cadenhead days was Andrew Wilson. Andrew was always talking about retiring and about the good old days. His business harked back to the '70s and he would often grumble about how little stock was available and the prices[144]. An incredibly loving husband his wife's health issues took all of his time and energy.

In October 2005 I managed to buy a butt of 1982 St Magdalene for £8,000[145]. It was as rough as an elephant's trunk so I re-racked it into a fresh ex-Port pipe. I waited for several months and tried it – still rougher than a bricklayer's palm. I had no choice - I had to sell it on. Thankfully I got my money back and was

---

144. He would be shocked to see how things have gone.
145. I'm not trying to make anyone sick with these prices, it is what it is. If you really want to be sick, I bought a 1971 Teaninich for £2,800 in the same month – no one was interested in Teaninich.

intrigued when I saw it on the shelves of a whisky shop a few months later in the livery of a different bottler. Just goes to show that one man's poison...[146]

2006 was a terrible year for the company (I am still surprised it did not go under). Money was incredibly tight and whilst there was stock available the market had yet to take off. 2007 was mildly better but I had begun wondering if I could provide for my family (my daughter was born in 2006) remaining as an independent bottler. Money began to be a real worry for us and despite my wife working full time, I had to find additional work and began my training to become an English secondary school teacher. Looking back, this is the most stressful year of my life; juggling training, whilst being a full-time teacher, and also trying to hold together the skeleton of The Creative Whisky Co.

In February of 2008 I concluded a deal to supply a chain of three stores in Moscow with several casks. The profit from this order was nearly what I was earning in a year as a teacher in training and I tossed in the towel, deciding to instead concentrate on the Creative Whisky Co. Looking back on this period now, afraid of letters from the bank about your mortgage, or your card being declined for petrol, it was a great spur of motivation.

Strangely, despite a world recession brought on by the banking crisis, 2008 changed everything for the business. In August of that year I was sent a list of casks that included casks of '76 Glenlivet, '83 Coleburn, '80 Tamdhu, '80 Macallan and '75 Laphroaig among others. The entire list was around £200k and pushed me to my absolute limits in what funds I, and my family, could gather. By pre-selling some of the best casks I was able to secure the parcel and I can still vividly remember the drive from my house, I was then living in Wrexham, to the bond in Glasgow to collect the samples from all of the casks. They were all bought blind, as was the practice. At the security booth two boxes of 50cl samples were waiting for me and I quickly signed for them and began putting them in the boot of my car. The cheery guard had already taken a cheeky look.

"There's some good whisky in there." He said, nodding to me as the second box was deposited. I nodded back in agreement as if I knew, although I had not a clue what they were like. Generally someone nosing around a box of samples worth every penny I could muster was not going to sway me, but it bode well. I drove out of sight of the bond and at the nearest chance to pullover without attracting too much suspicion I opened the boot and began to look through the samples.

As an independent bottler, and certainly before I had my own warehouse, this was the most exciting and nerve racking moment. Before, like my time with Cadenhead's, when cask samples had been sent, the fear of

---

146. This is an example of *Caveat Emptor* – for all those thinking about investing in mature stocks, has this whisky been passed from pillar to post? Why is it for sale?

disappointment or thrill of success was far removed (not to mention the fact that it was not my money, nor did my pay check depend upon it). It is gambling, as much as any business venture is, but the thrill of finding a cache of stellar casks was a huge high. And this stash was, and remains, the greatest batch of mixed, aged malt whiskies that I have ever seen (I should add 'affordable', as the parcel that started Duncan Taylor was more incredible but exponentially more expensive).

I, and a friend, flew off to Berlin to show Jack Wiebers some of the samples we had. Jack, as my first customer, biggest purchaser of own-label bottlings and also of my Exclusive Malts series, received preferential treatment. The flight from Liverpool to Berlin takes just over two hours and I boarded feeling fine. Strangely though, as soon as the plane started moving and the flight team began their safety speech, I began to get a cold sweat. My friend noticed my discomfort. "Dave, you look green." I was in real trouble.

After what seemed like the cruel slowing of time to a snail's pace, we took off and as the cold sweat poured down my head and through my body I watched and waited, in ever more discomfort, for that blasted seat belt sign to go off. 'Ping!' – I was off like a rocket and barely made it. Everything inside of me came out (I guess thankfully, just orally). I'm sure at one point I saw my soul fly out, stop, look at me and depart shaking its head.

Again, after what felt like an eternity my heaving stopped and I realised there was a bit of commotion outside the door. I heard a knocking but, realising the carnage of the scene inside the cramped toilet, I knew I couldn't open the door.

"It's the Captain here, are you ok."

"Yes." I spat more than spoke. "I'll be out in a bit."

The Captain was having none of it and a few minutes later I heard over the PA system.

"Ladies and Gentlemen, if you could all please use the toilet in the rear of the plane. We have a slight issue in the forward toilet. Please note we will begin our landing procedure in about twenty minutes."

TWENTY MINUTES?! I needed about three weeks to get presentable, and maybe another week to recover. I scrambled around doing my best with the meagre tissues and spurts of water from the tap. I looked in the mirror (that I had just 'tried to' clean). It was me, but it was like someone had put a grey imprint of me on a pillow-case. I was exhausted. Then it dawned on me, I had to get back to my seat – about halfway down the plane – with everyone facing forward.

There is a golfing phrase which describes the moment after realising a ball you have hit is now lost and you have to walk back to where you were before to hit another ball. It is known as 'The Walk of Shame'. I now had to undertake the greatest ever walk of shame. Known only to people who have been locked out of their hotel room naked, or had to walk into a local hardware store for help because they have just locked their two year old daughter in the car[147].

Had I known what impact the smell of the toilet would have on the first few rows once I opened the door, I think I would have just made the pilot land with me in there. There were gasps of horror, eyes watered and I think I made a small girl cry. Trying my hardest, my absolute hardest, to not make eye-contact with anyone, I walked, as quickly as my hollow body would allow, back to my seat. My 'mate' was hardly comforting.

Between fits of hysterics all he could manage was: "God, you look like shit. And you stink."

Looking back, I am certain this entire affair was caused by a Prawn sandwich. I've never had one since. And I think they retired the plane...

The only disappointments in the entire parcel, for me, were the two old Laphroaig's from 1975. Barely above 40% in alcohol I thought they were too soft and unlike 'Laphroaig'. I felt sure I would be pilloried for bottling them. Both of these went to Jack Wiebers and, to show how little I know about such things, he loved them and they scored very well and were very well received.

I don't think it is an exaggeration to say that that parcel of whisky changed my business. I was able to sell a few more casks, bottled in my 'coloured bird series' and from this was able to buy a smaller parcel that included the likes of Glenkinchie '78 (bottled in the Old Train Line Series by Jack Wiebers), some Banff '74 & '75 among others.

One other notable parcel that I was offered around this time was valued in the region of £3.5million. It consisted mainly of Speyside and Highland malts, the oldest, a Tomintoul from 1966 to the youngest being around eight years of age. Buying the lot was clearly out of the question but I could cherry pick. I tried for a bank loan as the UK Government had launched the Small Business Loan Backing Scheme (the government, in order to help small businesses, would back 90% of the loan from a financial provider). My bank at the time, NatWest, agreed to lend me £125k and I went through the list of stock to see what I could get.

Picking out some '70s Jura, '60 & '70s Ben Nevis and several others I made my order and contacted the bank to set up a meeting to sign for the loan. On meeting the bank manager again he had some bad news. Apparently one of their team in the Edinburgh office had decided that there was no future in the Scotch whisky industry and they would not release the funds (remembering that their exposure was 10%). I was apoplectic. I have had many occasions to lose my temper with bankers but this was beyond any rational understanding.

147. Don't ask.

Again I was reminded that to be a great bottler you needed 'Time & Money' and I was still fighting for both. Thankfully I was able to buy a few of the casks and this included two of the best I have ever managed to bottle; the Tomintoul '66 and Ben Nevis '68. I managed to acquire two of the '68 Ben Nevis and learnt a valuable lesson when I came to bottle them. As I mentioned before, casks are bought on either OLA or RLA. Casks of this age will always be sold on RLA (regauged) and herein lies a slight problem. Regauging requires a modicum of skill and a slight bit more of concentration, care and willingness. It was known that certain warehouses were, shall we say, a touch slapdash with their regauging efforts and both Ben Nevis casks were well below what was sold. Protestations often fell on deaf ears (why would a very large warehouse get into a fight about missing litres of alcohol when they can blame things like 'loss in transit' or 'bottling loss' as they did in this case). Trying to explain to my customer who has already promised their customers a certain number of bottles that they were now getting about half of what was promised can cause accusations of dishonesty (for example 'have you sold half of the cask to someone else') but it is what it is. The problem is that as a bottler you calculate the sales price on expected bottles from the cask which can cause you a massive headache when the cask is 'light'.

Both the Tomintoul '66 (well, half of the butt[148]) and one of the Ben Nevis '68, along with an '88 Laphroaig, were bottled as a five year anniversary of Creative Whisky. A bit grand really, but the whiskies were too good to just simply release.

As the business grew I began to fully realise that old phrase 'you are only as strong as your weakest link'. I was having great difficulty with the bottling side of the business as was still reliant on using another company to bottle for me. This meant a huge amount of paperwork to move a cask, or get a sample, or duty pay a bottle. With every single process incurring a fee I would regularly fill three or four lever-arch folders a year with invoices just from the contract bottlers. One year I calculated that I had spent over £50k in bottling services and as I grew the problems grew. Wrong casks were re-racked, wrong labels applied, incorrect strengths taken, labels lost and so on[149]. It was time to make a change.

I began the process of looking for a warehouse in late 2009. The Scotch Whisky Association as part of the new Scotch Whisky Regulations released in 2009 had determined that all single malt Scotch whisky must be bottled in Scotland which meant a warehouse had to be found north of the border. I

---

148. Butts are often split between markets and customers.
149. Just to reinforce this point, the first six casks that we bottled at the new warehouse all had to have tiny stickers cut and stuck over labels already printed as the strengths were so much lower than what we had been told by the dispatching warehouse.

avoided all the major cities and areas to keep funds reasonable and eventually found a small lock-up in Stevenston, North Ayrshire that was owned and run by the local council. This was the easy part.

Unlike today, where everything is applied for online with swish fill-out forms, I had to write to HMRC[150]. I shan't bore you with the full details but will recount a number of phone calls and trials. One such call went something like this:

HMRC	"Mr Stirk, I have some queries about your warehouse proposal. We understand that you intend to bring in bulk whisky in casks?"
Me	"That's right."
HMRC	"But we also note you are not a distillery so how are you going to mature your whisky?"
Me	"I'm sorry, I don't understand the question. Whisky matures in a cask and yes I am intending to move casks I own into the warehouse in order to bottle."
HMRC	"Ah but you can't mature casks in your warehouse."
Me	"Again, sorry, I don't understand. I am not making whisky, I am bringing in whisky to bottle."
HMRC	"Yes, HMRC has no problem with you bottling bulk whisky, but you cannot mature your whisky in the warehouse."
Me	"But technically I cannot stop the whisky maturing as every second that goes by with the whisky in the cask the whisky is maturing?"
HMRC	"Yes, so you will not be allowed to mature the whisky in the warehouse."
Me	"Well I am assuming you are not asking me to transfer every single cask into a plastic drum upon entry into my warehouse and therefore I cannot stop maturation occurring. What do you propose I do?"
HMRC	"That is not for us to say. I am just informing you that you cannot mature whisky in your warehouse."

150. Her Majesty's Revenue & Custom.

Another conversation:

HMRC	"You've stated that you would like to re-rack casks for a finishing period sometimes before bottling."
Me	"Yes, that's right."
HMRC	"How long will this process take?"
Me	"It takes about 10 minutes to transfer the whisky from one cask to another."
HMRC	"No, sorry, I meant how long is this 'finishing' period?"
Me	"Well, until the whisky is ready to bottle."
HMRC	"We really need a specific amount of time."
Me	"But there is no such legislation. It could be weeks, months maybe years – it is impossible to give it a definite period of time."
HMRC	"We are going to put in the notes three months."
Me	"But three months might not be sufficient amount of time for the finishing period?"
HMRC	"No, you misunderstand, you have three months from bringing in the cask to dispatching the goods."

This went on and on until the final straw for me was the first visit by HMRC (this is now a year later) at the warehouse in Stevenston and one of the reps informed me:

> "We do not like businesses' like yours – too much room for fraud to be committed."

Luckily I had brought along my friend Alan Hall as he would be running the warehouse[151]. He sensed my anger and frustration and put his hand on my arm to make sure I kept my tongue.

At this point I realised that I was getting nowhere. Ridiculous obstacles were continually being put in my way and I felt my only course of action was to seek help from my local MP. Luckily, and by pure happenchance, my MP was Lord Kenneth Clarke; a very long in the tooth, professional politician who

---

151. I was living in South Nottinghamshire at this point.

had, amongst many other roles, been in charge of the Treasury. I explained, in a few minutes, the barriers to trade that had been placed in front of me and Lord Clarke frowned and reassured me that the Treasuries' job was not to stifle business. A couple of weeks later I was sent a letter that Lord Clarke had sent to the then Chair of the Treasury and his reply. Essentially the pair both concluded that what was happening was against government guidelines and specifically highlighted the nonsense about 'maturing' casks of whisky and time for 'finishing'.

I informed the reps that I had been dealing with in the HMRC office in Glasgow about the letter. Naturally they had neither heard nor seen of any such letter and wanted to see my proof which I duly provided[152]. With [a lot] more toing and froing I was eventually approved to open a Trade Facility Warehouse. This was part one. Part two was to get a Movement Guarantee[153] and this meant getting a bank involved.

After the fiasco with the bank NatWest I had moved to HSBC and arranged a meeting with my 'Business Development Manager[154]', a spotty-faced oik, that had recently left school and was no-doubt still living at home. At first I was informed that HSBC did not provide Movement Guarantees. When I showed him that HSBC was on a pre-approved list by HMRC (which he at first refuted) I eventually (and many months later) got a note through the post that guaranteed the duty on importing commercial vehicles. The spotty oik, adamant that this was the correct guarantee, only began seeking the correct forms when I managed to get HMRC to send me a letter stating that the bank's form was incorrect (rather infuriatingly, HMRC would not send me a blank Movement Guarantee form as it was an agreement between the finance provider and themselves).

Eventually, and only after insisting the bank change my 'Business Development Manager' to someone who was not obtuse, did the correct form come through for signing. Almost two years after I had started the process, I finally got the keys which would allow me to begin bottling my whisky. One last story from this debacle: I had very recently taken on my first employee who had previously worked as a plumber. We had driven the near six hour journey from South Nottinghamshire to the warehouse to get the keys and begin setting up the warehouse. The rental manager from the local council was waiting for us and the second he handed over the keys swiftly got into his car and raced out of the estate. 'That's odd' we both thought and began getting things ready. We turned on the water at the mains (outside) and then

---

152. And to my great annoyance never got back.
153. This is an indemnity against loss of duty due to any number of reasons such as fire, theft, negligence or simply disappearing in transit.
154. 'Development Prevention Manager' might have been a better description.

turned on the tap within the warehouse (water being quite important to bottling operations). Nothing came out and yet we could hear the water coming through the pipes. We then noticed a flood coming off the roof of the small internal office. Looking up we saw a very small version of the Bellagio Hotel fountain display as no less than six leaks sprayed water all over the warehouse and nearly flooding the office and all of the brand new equipment. Having an ex-plumber on site paid dividends.

Coincidentally, it was around this time that my hair fell out.

CHAPTER 10

Compass Box and the road least travelled

"The history of Scotch whisky's rise to world dominance too often focuses on the distillers, where it was the merchants who sat between them and the drinkers that really developed its relationship with the world. The grocers and blenders whose names dominate the mainstream are but one part, with the work of independent bottlers rarely documented; despite their importance in the creation of many of the whisky brands that we know today."

BILLY ABBOTT
Author of "The Philosophy of Whisky"

Personal investment (and I don't mean monetary) is hard for an independent bottler to convey. If you don't make the whisky, in most cases don't fill the cask and in several cases don't actually bottle the whisky[155], what attachment, investment or personal account can a bottle of whisky possess? This is something I struggled with throughout my time bottling as Creative Whisky – it is also the reason I never entered any of my bottlings for awards. My feeling was always 'what are you rewarding me for?' I didn't make the distillate, didn't fill the casks – is this award simply for ensuring this cask did not become

155. Many bottlers will never even see the cask they have bought and bottled from.

John Glaser

anonymous in a mass blend?

When I meet with John Glaser, creator of Compass Box, we talk about this. Independent bottling can be an impersonal journey. How can someone bring across any emotional attachment to a product that they had barely any contact with.

"That word, emotion, is still super important to me. That was the key thing that gave me confidence – I felt I could create a brand that would connect with people." John says.

Although I have known John for over twenty years, I am ashamed to admit that this is the first time I have visited his offices and blending room in West London. Many of his bottlings are arranged in a glass cabinet just as you enter. Hedonism, John's first bottling is bottom right and I recall the launch of this at the Speyside Whisky Festival.

"That's right." John confirms. "I recently went up to Speyside with James Saxon (one of Compass Box's 'Whisky Makers') and I told James how on the 22nd October 2000 I was sat in the Highlander Inn hand numbering as many cases as I could fit in my car at the time."

If you wanted to sum up John and Compass Box, then Hedonism, the first release is a good start. At a time when no one was drinking or interested in grain whisky John decided to launch one as his opening act. And, as if that task was not hard enough, John had blended it using two different distilleries.

"It was my dad who pushed me towards doing something a touch more noticeable than what was considered a traditional blend. I was desperate to

get a blend into the market as Compass Box was trying to convince, or rather win over, two key markets; the malt whisky drinker, or whisky connoisseur and the high-end bar. Hedonism was just 250 bottles and we didn't sell out in our first year. I was selling it bottle by bottle and I remember thinking it was a big deal when Royal Mile Whiskies ordered two cases!"

As with most start-up success, twenty years on it is easy to think John hit the ground running. But the reality of these underfunded[156], stock-driven companies is that it can take years and years before any light emerges from the end of the tunnel.

"I think it was in our second year when I had the first moment of feeling we were getting somewhere, albeit not financially. Whisky Magazine had awarded us 'Innovator of the Year' and it meant a lot to me that Michael Jackson presented me with the award."

The award helped get the company recognition; adding to an existing importer in Denmark[157], Compass Box began to export to Germany and the Netherlands. A lunch with Thierry Benitah, owner of La Maison du Whisky in Paris, opened the French market – one that was especially important to John.

"I said to Thierry that I knew he had a large portfolio of products and I didn't want to be just another company on the books. Perhaps rather flippantly I said that I would only be a supplier if one day Compass Box would be an important one. We will likely never be the largest by volume, but I like to think that La Maison has us closest to their hearts."

And 'heart' is what is key to Compass Box. I mention to John that I always felt the French market was ideally suited to what he was trying to do. Traditionally a big blend market, the French have always appreciated a total package when it comes to anything hedonistic. John recalls one of the first Whisky Live's in Paris when he was told by an attendee "John, you are an artiste." John said he just glowed – it was all he needed to hear.

Like my Glenlivet moment, John's epiphany with Scotch whisky came whilst working for Johnnie Walker. He had previously wanted to be a wine maker but having been persuaded to get more into the business of wine, and obtaining a business degree, the closest work he could find was in the Scotch whisky industry. A trip to Scotland with the Johnnie Walker sales team encompassed a visit to all of the Classic Malts distilleries. This resulted in a 10am, straight from the cask, drinking experience at Talisker Distillery that put wine firmly to the back of John's thinking.

Throughout John's time with Johnnie Walker the blended category for Scotch whisky was flat. Despite working on new brands like 'Swing' and 'Gold' John felt that blended whisky was ripe for a shake-up.

---

156. John started Compass Box with £50,000.
157. Qualityworld, who also imported my products at the time. The company dissolved a few years later.

"Later on in that same trip I was with Maureen Robinson[158] watching her explain how these grains and malts are combined to create a brand. I realised that just about anything was possible – there was no limit to the creativity here." With a lighthouse beam now permanently flashing this idea, John's hive mind was feverishly at work. Believing that Diageo, being by far the largest player in the Scotch blended market, should be at the forefront of a new wave of brands; independently minded and run, free to express a personality and difference to what the industry was offering. In a move akin to Tom Cruise's character in 'Jerry Maguire', John wrote up a new business plan; one with creativity and independence at its heart – a plan that asked the largest company to shelve the establishment rules and explore the category.

John's plan predictably fell on deaf ears[159], though unlike Jerry Maguire, he was not fired. The germ, once planted would not stop going round and round in John's head. A holiday, not long after, on the Island of Eleuthera, was the moment when John realised that this idea was going to happen.

"I distinctly remember turning to my wife and simply saying 'I can do this. I have the experience of retail and wholesale, and marketing. I had been working with Maureen and Jim Beveridge[160] I can blend these whiskies myself'. I remember Amy just looking at me and said 'So do it'. So I resigned."

That was in January 2000. In the twenty or so years that Compass Box has been around the industry has changed dramatically and many of the stereotypes and misconceptions have slowly eroded. John was very keen to remove age statements from his products – not wanting to be constrained - as so many brands are. This was not so easy in the early days when Compass Box was up against old whisky being readily available and bottled – and old single malt whisky at that. It took a lot of guts; as I joke with John, perhaps it was ten per cent inspiration, eighty per cent perspiration and ten per cent insanity.

"Naivety, perhaps more than insanity." John says laughing. "I like being set apart – that we stand out. We're not trying to take over the world, or anything for that matter, but the fact that we have inspired a few companies perhaps with the fun we have with our labels and always offering something compelling and delicious."

A big turning point for the company was the launch of Peat Monster which was originally intended as an exclusive to Park Avenue Liquors in New York[161]. This was just the fourth creation launched after Hedonism, Asyla and then Eleuthera (created due to the owner of Milroys asking for a blended malt[162]) and

---

158. Diageo's Master Blender. Maureen recently retired after 45 years in the industry. She is generally regarded as one of the finest blender's the industry has ever had.
159. Good to know it is not just my idea's that Diageo don't like.
160. Dr Jim Beveridge OBE was also a highly respected Master Blender at Diageo.
161. This year marks the 20th Anniversary of Peat Monster.
162. And named after the island where John decided to take the plunge.

was a huge success. Thankfully for John, Park Avenue saw no reason it could not be sold across the world, and it became a worldwide release, and success.

What I find truly remarkable is that in the twenty plus years that the industry has watched Compass Box grow (the company has released one hundred different brands and now bottles over 300,000 bottles a year) there has been no real impostor or imitator. Larger companies have taken notice of the sector, for instance Monkey Shoulder from Wm Grants (now an international phenomenon) and some independents such as Douglas Laing's Regional Malts and the SMWS's spin off J.G. Thomson are brands that would sit side by side with Compass Box on a retailer's shelf. Unlike the other parts of the independent bottling world, there is really no 'Compass Box Two'.

"It is a lot harder now than when you and I started." John states. "Just getting access to stock is harder. I was so lucky that I was working with Maureen Robinson. Once I had been promised supply by Turnbull Hutton[163] I asked him how I should proceed to which he said, just go talk to Maureen. And for years afterwards I would sit with Maureen looking at stock and tasting cask samples and blending with her. It's now so complicated to do what we do. Just simply getting access to the stock will be a large hurdle. We were both lucky with our timing."

Lucky. There is that word again. It is such a large part of the independent side of this industry and the industry, I believe, is poorer because of the boundaries and hurdles it self-perpetuates. However, to claim that Compass Box was just a lucky accident (and I am hoping to dissuade you the reader from this idea, not John) - a chance meeting, or somehow providence – is to suggest that Ayrton Senna was lucky his dad took him go-carting. Talent will out itself. The industry, despite its barriers, hurdles and staidness found John and he, like all good entrepreneurs, saw that something was missing.

What is clear from the success of Compass Box is that the Scotch whisky market is open to all its nuances. Never before, in its 400 plus year history has the consumer been more knowledgeable, had greater choice and demanded greater information than the period right now. The driving force behind this has been the independent sector – whisky lovers, first and foremost, providing the growing customer base with what they want. A speed to adapt and flex at the slightest whim, and well, because they can.

I shall return to this theme in the last chapter, but possibly Compass Box has offered a chance to the industry to support independence and independent bottlers. Here is a business model with no brand overlap or interference, no marketing department getting annoyed[164] by infringement, no embarrassment at products being superior or inferior carrying a distillery name. The personal

---

163. Diageo's Director of Scottish Operations. In his later years he became Raith Rovers Chairman.
164. Jealous perhaps...

attachment and investment is a private one – only Compass Box can take credit for their whisky and any awards won are theirs and theirs alone.

"You have to be pretty bold, in a world of single malt enthusiasts, to bottle and promote blends. But above and beyond all the marketing, all of the packaging and any press coverage, this magical drink has to do just one thing; call you back to the glass. If it fails to do that then the product has failed. That is really our mission statement at Company Box."

And herein lies John's success; his brands and bottlings have an uncanny ability to want you to return to them, talk about them and share them. His choice, in 2000, to return the industry to the world of boutique blending, which no doubt got sniggered at in some corners of the whisky world, has been proven a pioneering path. John looked at the whisky roads ahead of him and wondered what was lying down the overgrown, untended and forgotten about lane. What he found was a world of creativity just waiting to be discovered.

CHAPTER 11

ARMCHAIR BOTTLER NO MORE

"The industry by and large had its blended brands and had no desire to muddy the waters by talking about the ingredients. They didn't even want anyone visiting their distilleries. It was the superlative casks chosen to show off these distilleries, and the smaller scale businesses that made bottling single casks worthwhile, that made their name for the big companies. And still today, without IB's continued good works, my gantry wouldn't be half as rich. Want a Ben Nevis? Either buy some Nikka or look for an IB, because it's more available from them than the distillery. Go looking online for Balmenach and you'll be dropped at the page for their gin. Go looking for it on a gantry and you'll only find indies."

FRANK MURPHY
Pot Still, Glasgow

I had zero knowledge of how to run a warehouse and, if possible, even less of what the bottling process was. Turning to friends within the industry, Adelphi, who had just opened their own warehouse, offered to train me on the ins and outs of warehouse management. They had recently employed Gordon Hamilton who had worked for several years with Glenmorangie and he took me under his wing and showed me the ropes. Whilst there was not a lot to the process of emptying a cask, passing through a light paper filter and filling into bottles - the real task was recording every last drop of alcohol that passed through the warehouse. HMRC were interested to know about average losses, processes, samples, re-racks and re-gauges. Everything came with a list of procedures and methods of recording. It is testament to this incredible industry that a company would go out of their way to train a competitor[165].

With the keys of the warehouse came the very first cask. Records and memory are hazy and I'm not sure why but over the winter the warehouse had one solitary cask in it. Alan Hall was managing the warehouse as I was still living in South Nottinghamshire. I did not realise the stress that this put on him, living about thirty minutes from the warehouse, he spent his Christmas concerned about the cask of 1984 Tamdhu sat on its own in the corner of the warehouse.

165. I remain a friend and ardent supporter of all that Adelphi, and now Ardnamurchan, do.

Eventually other casks arrived and the warehouse, this time without leaks, began to bottle whisky. Occasionally we would have visits although this was rare; being far from anywhere other than maybe the ferry to Arran. On one particular summers' day we had a visit from a few of Alan's ex-colleagues. I had completely forgotten that on the same day a film-crew from Germany was also arriving to shoot a short piece about independent bottlers. I was assured by the 'Director'[166] that the additional guests would not be a problem. My polo shirt stating 'The Creative Whisky Co Ltd' was a problem however[167], and it appeared the only solution was to borrow the sound man's shirt. He was a fair bit smaller than me, and already beginning to feel ridiculous, and now looking ridiculous, we began doing our little pieces to camera.

The 'visitors' thought all of this was brilliant and began to join in, voluntarily, and involuntarily. This wore down, with a lack of any alacrity, the mood of the boom operator, who could hear everything the visitors were saying, and the director who was likely already tired of making this documentary. The resulting piece still exists on YouTube somewhere and, like most people watching themselves back on film, it is excruciating but funny to look back at.

The six hour car journeys to and from the warehouse began to take their toll and the easy decision was taken to relocate. Stevenston, not being a place anyone chooses to raise a family, was ignored and we settled on a small village called Thornhill due to its road links, excellent school and village feel. We would spend the day bottling and I would spend the evenings and weekends doing the paperwork[168]. We lasted just a couple years at the Stevenston site before finding an old farm steading in Thornhill and moved everything down the road. Now instead of a three hour round trip each day it was just a couple of minutes.

The new warehouse was definitely closer but came with its own set of unique issues. Firstly, being an old farm steading meant that it was damp (very damp) and at times extremely cold. This is absolutely fine for the warehousing of casks but disastrous when trying to bottle whisky. Just a few degrees difference in temperature between the bottles and the liquid results in condensation on the glass before labelling. The damp also wreaked havoc with anything card or paper based. Secondly the buildings were too low for any fork lift trucks and everything had to be pulled over uneven ground using pallet trucks. One large order heading to the US had to be relabelled (apparently, or at least according to the US authorities, the 75cl we had put on the bottles would not

---

166. This has to be the loosest sense of the word.
167. Something to do with French regulations about advertising alcohol companies?!
168. The paperwork is a fairly significant task and in true HMRC form, they cannot advise you how to do it, only tell you when you've done it wrong. My first six months of files had to be re-written due to an error in recording received litres of alcohol.

Alan Hall in our 'not-fit for purpose' bottling room.

be understood by the American consumer used to 750ml). In on my own, to undertake this task, I began trying to move the lightly wrapped pallet. A small crack in the rough concrete floor brought the pallet truck to a grinding halt and 80 cases of whisky fell on top of me. Dazed and slightly bashed up I was amazed to find only two bottles of whisky had smashed. The warehouse was certainly serving a purpose but would not be fit much longer.

I had by this stage found distributors for Denmark, Netherlands, Taiwan & Sweden. Russia never bought from me again after 2009 when the Russian banks stopped lending import businesses money. Jack Wiebers was still importing good quantities into Germany and was also supplying Switzerland for me and I was still exporting to 3Rivers in Japan. At that time just about everything being bottled was divided between these markets.

In 2008 I introduced a new range of single cask bottlings called The Exclusive Casks. These were all casks that had been re-racked; taken from their original cask (be it often an old barrel, hogshead or butt) and put into virgin oak (American or European) or an ex-Sherry hogshead and so on. These were not the first casks that I had finished as several had been used in the Exclusive Malts since I began bottling in 2005 (a Laphroaig in Sauternes was one particular success) but there had been a growing resistance to the idea of 'finished' whiskies at the time. With the plethora of official and independent finishes now it seems ridiculous that that was the case but The Exclusive Casks was my way of separating those that had been through a finishing process - so if any consumer was not happy with the idea they could ignore them. I think the fact that the first four releases were all Islay whiskies helped them sell and this range never struggled afterwards.

I was a big fan of virgin oak as it took around three months for the cask to make an impact, both on the colour and on the flavour and once emptied the casks were excellent for a second use for twelve months or more. Inevitably these did not always go well, but just like the St Magdalene there was always somewhere else these casks could go; one man's perfume...

I have always found it necessary to explain the reasoning behind cask finishing. In almost all cases, and I mean 99%, it is because the aged whisky has not matured properly in the original cask it was filled into. There is absolutely no logical reason to take a perfectly good whisky and empty into a very expensive additional cask for an additional maturation period. Don't be fooled otherwise. Does this mean that finished whisky is the industry conning you the consumer. Absolutely not. Often you are drinking an exceptional whisky without even realising it has been 'finished' or vatted/blended and returned to a specific type of cask for a final marrying period. Whisky is good if you like it, what has happened to it on its journey is just information for you to read whilst you enjoy the whisky.

One aspect of independent bottling that always hurt was the leaking cask. I've already described the cask that arrived bone dry and the half-empty Ben Nevis '68, but leaking and empty casks would continue to haunt me. Any bottler that buys parcels of young whisky takes their chance that the cask has not shed its load – it only takes a drip, just a few a minute, to empty a cask in a week or two. Therefore it was often the case that until the cask arrived at the warehouse no real clue of content was known. It is one of those cruel twists of fate that for every cask that yielded a good amount, four or five would be disappointing. Re-gauges were rarely accurate.

Two casks stick out in particular. I had the very good fortune to have been able to buy £20,000 worth of 1996 Laphroaig at approximately £1,500/cask (this was around late 2005). I kept some of these so as not to bottle too many too quickly and in 2017 I moved the very last one to bottle as a 21 year old. This cask was now worth several times what had been paid originally. At least it would have been had it not arrived devoid of any liquid. A small leak in the head of the cask had slowly added to the Angel's Share. I had also bought a parcel of Clynelish 1997 and had kept one of these back to bottle as a twenty year old. Again this cask, which had cost around £3,000 when bought was now worth considerably more and the outturn was not as expected. Instead of the 270+ bottles I was expecting it yielded just 52 bottles at a cask strength of 44.6%. A yield so low I divided all of the bottles amongst the staff. If I ever get to heaven those 'Angel's' have got some explaining to do.

Every purchase to a greater or lesser extent is a risk but by far the greatest risk is buying older whisky. Since around 2007/8 samples were rarely sent out for casks that were for sale. This meant that a 30 or 40 year old whisky was often being bought blind and that could be a very large five figure sum for an unknown. Often I would find that some of these older whiskies, especially with a low alcohol content, could have quite an inviting nose and even a nice palate but for me if the finish was unconvincing – in other words either off-putting or simply would disappear – the cask was no good and this happened on a number of occasions.

As a bottler, especially as a small one, you are only really as good as your last bottling and you always have to remember that at some point in the future you are likely to be presenting this whisky to an audience. I don't have much of a poker face and on the few occasions I have got it wrong am unable to argue with anyone who points this out. I always stated that if anyone was not happy with a bottle of whisky they purchased I would replace it. I believe this only happened twice; once where someone complained that the whisky oxidised too quickly[169] and the second was due to a customer finding a fly in their bottle (this was not so much of a complaint as the customer admitted to simply removing the fly and drinking the whisky regardless, but we sent another bottle just for good will). Speaking of flies, we received an order of glass bottles from a supplier on the continent and began bottling with them. Part way through the bottling we noticed a fly in the bottle, and the next one, and then found that almost every single bottle had a tiny fly at the bottom. If this was a form of sabotage the saboteur had gone to extraordinary lengths.

My travel at this time was limited to trips to the Netherlands[170] and occasional journeys to Denmark, Belgium and Sweden. I make no apologies that my favourite markets to travel to are the Netherlands and Sweden[171]. I had begun telling jokes in my tastings back in my Cadenhead days as found regurgitating facts and figures about distilleries to be not just boring for the poor souls listening but I got bored too. With the advent of internet search engines everything is at one's fingertips and facts and figures are only ever interesting if surprising. This did result, after one tasting for Kruts Karport

169. This was an Imperial from an ex-Sherry hogshead which I swapped for something else – and then very much enjoyed drinking it.
170. One of my first trips to the Netherlands coincided with the Icelandic eruption of Eyjafjallajökull which grounded all of the flights. I took the channel tunnel.
171. And must apologise that I have yet to visit Japan and Taiwan.

in Copenhagen, being told by a rather elderly participator that I had 'offered great whiskies, but appalling jokes'. That is criticism I can live with.

The beauty of being an independent bottler and hosting tastings is that you know you will not please everyone in the crowd. Someone won't like the 'Sherried' whiskies; someone won't like the peaty ones and so on. It is therefore not the job of the host to even try and convince anyone what they will and won't like (remembering that no one is an expert on what you like). And unlike those Brand Ambassadors who represent just one or two brands (and for me they are much harder workers with a much harder task, than any of the independent 'Ambassadors') the story of each distillery or company is again not all that important.

I recall going to a tasting at the Stockholm Beer and Whisky Festival with a group of Danes I had befriended. There is no need to mention the company, but all of us had paid to attend a 'Masterclass' with the chief blender who had travelled quite a distance. Whilst the host was interesting and full of facts, the crowd grew ever more restless as they watched with despair their drams slowly evaporate from the glasses in front of them. Nearly the entire two hour time slot was up before we quickly worked through the expensive whiskies in front of us. If you are going to host a tasting, start with a dram, then talk about it.

Back L-R: Lars, Lennart, Kim Seated L-R: Jesper, Anders, Peter

Hosting a tasting is a very personal thing - I was struck early on how different the likes of Michael Jackson, Charlie MacLean and Richard Paterson would approach them. Each were entertaining but were also 'themselves'. As part of the new breed of ambassador (if you'll allow me such a description) that did not have the decades of experience and stories to fall back on, entertaining the crowd with other people's stories or jokes was the answer.

This only ever came to be a problem once, and in the most unlikely of settings. Whilst on a trip to the US I attended one of the largest Highland gatherings in the world in Orange County. Surrounded by 'Scottish-Americans' (or Americans as I call them) all claiming heritage with one clan or another, I was to host two tastings. The first went so well that a couple people bought tickets for the second one (despite being informed that the whiskies and jokes would be the same). I had got in the habit, due to my accent, of beginning tastings with a joke that ridiculed the English in some way. I felt that was 'ploughing the field' to allow a mickey-take of the Scots, Irish and Welsh as the tasting went along. The first joke got a roar of approval, particularly to two bearded, kilt-wearing attendees. I then explained:

> "...that the first distillates running of those small stills in the Highlands centuries ago, had two incredible side-effects for those that drink it. Firstly, it gave the drinker a warmth from within, which in the Highlands is a rare treat. The second side-effect was that the more they drank, the more attractive the opposite sex became. Which in the Highlands was also a rare treat."

At this point the two large, bearded, kilt-wearing men who had roared with laughter at my first joke, stood up, gave me the 'V' sign[172] with their fingers and stormed out. They tried complaining to the organiser (about what I'm not sure) who had thankfully been in attendance and asked them why the first joke was ok but the second wasn't. Ah well, you can please some people most of the time but bearded, kilt-wearing Karen's... you haven't got a chance.

I loved touring the Netherlands in particular. A small but populous country that has laws preventing supermarkets selling liquor resulting in wine and spirit shops (otherwise known as Slijterij) often being independent and family owned. This generally meant an interest in whisky by the owner and a keen customer base that were on friendly terms with all of the staff.

I was not a coffee drinker until I began touring the Netherlands and quickly realised that everywhere you went you would be offered one. To say no, is the equivalent of refusing a cup of tea in Ireland – it's just bad manners. I therefore

---

172. I'm not sure they fully understood the history of this sign as it is English in origin and mainly used towards the French.

began drinking it and slowly weaned myself from adding sugar[173]. I have a caffeine intolerance and I recall on one trip I was staying in a large hotel not far from my importers HQ. After a long day visiting customers, which meant several cups of coffee, we drove the longish (there aren't any truly long road trips in the Netherlands) journey back to the hotel. By the time we arrived I was desperate for the toilet. I quickly checked in and headed off to my hotel room. And walked, and walked, and walked. The place was like a convention centre. Eventually, and now cross-legged, I placed my key-card on the lock. Red light. I tried again; red light again. In near tears I retraced my steps, as fast, but as gingerly as possible and made it to the lobby toilets before an ambulance (and a needle and thread) were necessary. Note to self, if there is a toilet available, just use it.

It is remarkable how much the industry has changed in such a small space of time. From just a handful of wine & spirits retailers stocking more than a dozen or so whiskies in the 80s, whisky specialists and whisky-exclusive shops are now found in most major cities and sometimes in the most unlikely of places[174]. I have always tried to be as supportive to the distributors and retailers as possible. The retailers in particular are the boots on the ground, the ultimate ambassadors. They spend more time with the end consumer than any company representative and are far more acutely aware of what customers want. To get the product on the shelves takes importers and distributors that also understand their part in the process. To aid this, I never sold my product direct to consumers and tried to engage with retailers in understanding what was selling and what wasn't. Things had become complicated as a couple of companies were selling casks direct to the public with just a small margin per cask. This resulted in many retailers, bars and whisky clubs cutting out the independent bottler, and often the importer or distributor - buying casks which they had bottled for their own stores. With good supply and growing demand this only causes a little friction but as prices rise the traditional routes to market, where a margin is made by the bottler, the importer/distributor and the retailer, begin to get strained.

Independent bottlers, without direct supply, are mostly reliant on what the market has to offer. In my first five or six years cash was the problem and old whiskies were abundant. Then around 2011 there was a dearth of old whiskies but an abundance of young whiskies around the eight to twelve year old age group. This meant a rethink of strategy and I released the Exclusive Range;

173. I still drink what the Dutch refer to as 'kinder-coffee' – coffee for children, as I like either a cappuccino or latte.
174. For instance my nearest town, Dumfries, has the most wonderful retailer T B Watson.

single cask whiskies and bottled at 45.8%[175]. Because of the good supply price these were keenly priced on the market and I had huge success in the Netherlands in particular. Sadly, almost as soon as the reasonably priced young whiskies arrived they disappeared and the range was short lived.

I had been trying for some time to break into the States but without any luck. The independent bottling scene was still a strange one for US consumers. Gordon & MacPhail were available and some specialists had Signatory. Previously the US had been quite a good market prior to the late 1990s and early 2000s but for some reason the sector had gone quiet. I tried calling every importer in California I could find and contacted all those that I knew had history with independent bottlers. Most were completely uninterested and those that did show any interest wanted me to pay for the clearing of customs and profit on the goods before they were sold.

We were visited by two buyers from a small Californian retail chain called K&L Wines who selected a number of casks for bottling and were bringing them into the US through an importer called ImpEx Beverages based in San Francisco. I had never heard of them and asked the buyers from K&L if they minded my contacting ImpEx about importing my range (as K&L were only interested in single cask exclusives for their shops[176]).

175. We made an error with the first series bottling at 45% and finding some of the whiskies went cloudy.
176. I have to admit, and on behalf of several other bottlers, that customers only wanting their own selected casks, and not the ones you have bottled in your range, is rather irritating. In this instance, it was a means to an end.

Contact was made and a meeting set up. I flew to LA to see my family and then headed up to San Francisco. The offices, as so many are in small and mid-sized companies in the US, were unassuming and spoke of a business more concerned with trading than impressing anyone. I met Sam Filmus, owner of ImpEx and Chris Uhde (Sam's right hand man and a director of the distribution company JVS[177]).

With pleasantries done we discussed the samples I had brought and what could be achieved. Candidly I asked Sam how much he was seeking to bring in each year.

"Maybe three or four shipments a year, with five or six casks in each shipment." Sam replied.

Frankly I could have hugged him. My two fears were that it would be such small fries as to never make any economic sense (remembering that I had to have all new packaging and bottles due to the US law of 75cl bottles) or that he would be similar to some of the other importers who I had contacted that began by talking about container loads. Neither of which I could have done.

The first range included some great whiskies including Littlemill '88, Glenlivet '76, Mortlach '95 and Clynelish '97. This was in early 2012 and the order was just shy of £60k[178]. Together and with quite a bit of travelling we expanded the sales and the US became my largest market. It was not easy though and was completely alien to everything I had been accustomed to. Reps and salespeople would often queue to see the buyer or buyer(s), generally in a specific part of the shop (usually in a corner) and the buyer would go through the samples of each whisky.

That is not that different from the rest of the world. But, here is where it differs; firstly the buyer is, almost always, on some sort of power trip. You are taking up their precious time, they are already overstocked, your whiskies (or products) are always too expensive, their customers don't understand independent bottlers ("Why is your Glenlivet 1976 more expensive than the 21 year old Glenlivet?"), they already have a [insert distillery name] on the shelf. Etc.

I recall Chris taking me to the shop in Southern California where he had begun his career. In front of us, pouring some sort of sparkling Rosé for the buyer was a tall and extremely attractive Rep (and I mean a near perfect ten). The buyer though was either not attracted to this individual or was put out more about the products because of the Rep's attractiveness[179]. Either way, this buyer began asking very unhelpful and quite frankly, pointed and technical

---

177. America has a Three-tier import, distribution and retail system. This is supposed to prevent monopolies and price-fixing. It does not.
178. Just one of those casks would be worth more than that now.
179. I believe this is called 'Lookism' the discrimination of someone based upon their looks.

questions. Unable to answer properly, the Rep made the fatal mistake of falling back on reading what was on the label. Having then told the Rep what he thought of them, the buyer waved his hand signalling the sales pitch was over in a most dismissive manner.

I squirmed, not just because I was next, but because the European way, as far as I had seen, dealt with a common courtesy to pretty much everyone in the drinks industry.

Another occasion was the first sales attempt I made in Colorado. The Rep from the Colorado distributor representing ImpEx's brands took me in his beat up Toyota Prius (you're not a sales rep in the US if you haven't at least once owned a Prius) to a large, family owned Wine & Spirits outlet just outside of the main city. I was told before entering that the owner (also the buyer) was a huge fan of Scotch and would be delighted to see us.

It was around 10am and there were a few customers with shopping carts milling about[180]. The owner was in his office which was situated above part of the shop and we were asked to wait downstairs as one of the shop assistants went to get Buck or Chuck or whatever his name was. From the shop floor we could hear everything:

> "Mr Johnson[181] there's a rep downstairs with some Scotch samples for you to try."

> "WHAT?! It's 10 F*****G AM in the F*****G morning? What sort of God damn Sales Rep brings Scotch to taste at 10 in the F*****G morning?"

> "Er, I don't know Mr Johnson. But they're downstairs. Shall I tell them to go?"

> "No, I'll tell them and I'll tell them what to do to themselves if they come here again this early."

I looked at the sales rep next to me who was suddenly very occupied by a stain on his tie. The rest of the day did not get much better. I did have an incredible trip up to the Stanley Hotel just outside of Colorado. This remarkable looking building was where Stephen King[182] wrote "The Shining" and has an equally stunning whisky bar. The two young managers plied me with several of their more incredible whiskies and we chatted for maybe an hour. Although I had only tasted the whiskies (maybe nine or ten) when I stood up to take a tour I

---

180. The shopping cart I approve of. Nothing says 'this weekend is going to be good' like a shopping cart for a store that only sells alcohol.
181. I can't remember his name, and even if I could, probably best not to repeat.
182. I am a huge fan.

swayed and the two young managers laughed at me.

"Don't worry, you're not drunk. The hotel is 7,500 feet above sea level and your system will not be used to it." The hotel is well worth a visit, but you have been warned.

I also made a miscalculation on my first flight to Chicago. I don't know when it started but at some point I suddenly became a bad flyer and to cope with my nerves whilst flying I would drink quite a few gin and tonics. Well more than quite a few. Previously for working visits and pretty much during my family visits I was used to the ten or eleven hour flights to Los Angeles from London. Tucking into my fourth or fifth gin and tonic I had not allowed for the fact that a good flight to Chicago can be there in around eight hours. And, for some reason known only to a man at 40,000ft after having many G&Ts I decided a 'Rusty Nail[183]' would be a really good idea. The flight was unusually calm and I actually tried to get some sleep. But, and this is likely due to the alcohol within me, I am sure that as soon as I closed my eyes the pilot was waking me up with the announcement we were landing. I had a slight issue, very little of the alcohol had worked its way through my system. Somehow I managed to get through US Customs without the ubiquitous hauling into the waiting room to be told that I had once left the US using the wrong passport and without the customs officer realising that either I or he was swaying quite badly.

It was about 6pm in Chicago and I was greeted in Arrivals by Joshua Hatton, the ImpEx Rep for the Chicago area.

"Greetings my friend, we are heading off to Delilah's. You'll love it." He announced.

The Rusty Nail in my brain slowly started to turn. 'Delilah's'? I know that name. Why do I know that name. Think damn it! Oh yes, one of the best whisky bars in the US!! 'Oh shit!', I thought – that is the last thing I need... it was a great bar and Mike Miller was a great host – just don't ask me what he poured me.

---

183. Equal parts Drambuie and whisky (in this case Glenlivet).

CHAPTER 12

Ibs: Irritable Bottler syndrome?

"Single Malt today is a phenomenon in every corner of the world. Like great cuisine the boundaries of taste have been pushed to the limit and in my mind, this has been led by the independent bottlers who in the most part release whiskies in their purest form and fuller flavoured; as single casks without blending different casks to deliver something more untamed. When looking at reviews from respected sources, you will always find that some of the highest rated whiskies are independently bottled. I firmly believe that the Scotch whisky industry would not be as strong and united as it is without the great work of IBs especially over the last 20 years."

SUKHINDER SINGH
Owner Elixir Distillers

It may come as a surprise to learn that there has been little written criticism of the independent bottlers by the distillers themselves. There has been plenty of verbal criticism and much mutterings within marketing departments especially when awards are given out to IBs. The 'named' malts issue is only really a recent complication. Remembering the history of the industry, fillings were sold by their names and there were no stipulations as to when and how that name was used. Let's not forget that Gordon & MacPhail were asked (or had agreements) to represent certain malt distilleries as the owners saw little to gain by bottling it themselves.

Some, like Glenfarclas, have managed to avoid having their distillate openly bottled – mostly by a sort of 'Sword of Damocles' threat of legal action. Interestingly Wm Cadenhead's were challenged by J&G Grant[184] over their open use of 'Glenfarclas-Glenlivet' on labels. Cadenhead's convincingly proved that Glenfarclas used to suffix their name on historical labels (along with several Speyside distillers, wanting 'in' on the fame and perceived quality of 'Glenlivet' and the region). There is no legal mandate for not using Glenfarclas on a label but rarely has anyone felt big enough to challenge the distillery.

Similarly Wm Grant & Sons also took umbrage with Wm Cadenhead in 1987 over their bottling of Glenfiddich and Balvenie Scotch whiskies and using the distillery names on the labels. Brought up in the US District Court for the Central District of California the lawsuit stated:

> "The parties have previously agreed that the Scotch whiskies marketed and sold by defendants which are the subject of this litigation infringed upon plaintiff's registered marks. Plaintiffs contend that defendants should be precluded from making any mention of the fact that its whiskies were originally distilled at the Glenfiddich and Balvenie distilleries. Defendants maintain that they should be able to freely put such information on the labels of its bottles as long as the terms "Glenfiddich" or "Balvenie" are not emphasized in size or colour and as long as the label discloses that the whisky was rebottled by the defendant... the Court made it clear that it felt defendants could make a limited use of the Glenfiddich or Balvenie Distillery names on the labels of its bottles as long as it was not exploitive and there was an appropriate disclaimer.

> "The genesis of the dispute in this matter lies in the fact that plaintiffs have sold original distillate or "new fillings" produced at its distilleries to third parties and whisky brokers since the

---

184. The parent company of Glenfarclas Distillery.

time that its distilleries were built. These third parties generally use the "new fillings" to produce blended Scotch whiskies…

"Until 1984, plaintiffs sold casks of unblended "new fillings" that had been distilled at either the Glenfiddich or Balvenie Distilleries. In 1984, plaintiffs discontinued this practice and began selling casks of blended "new fillings" to third parties. These casks carry new tradenames and are not identified with the Glenfiddich or Balvenie names.[185]"

I recall selecting some quite incredible Glenfiddich and Balvenie single casks for bottling whilst with Wm Cadenhead's, and although none went to the States (because Cadenhead's was not exporting to the US at this time), I can only assume Wm Grant's did not get the outcome they were hoping for.

In 1982 Macallan-Glenlivet Distillers successfully petitioned Gordon & MacPhail to cease using the name Macallan on their labels. The judge, Lord Cameron, was suitably convinced that Speymalt (a subsidiary of Gordon & MacPhail) was 'passing off' their Macallan – that is bottling something with the brand name but not the quality or perceived taste that the customer would expect (despite it being proven to be distillate from the Macallan-Glenlivet Distillery). A year later Highland Distilleries managed to also win an interdiction against Speymalt on the same grounds as Macallan-Glenlivet but this time for bottling Bunnahabhain. The judge, Lord Ross, said:

"[He] was satisfied the distillers had made out a case of infringement of trade mark. If a member of the public was to seek a bottle of single malt described as Bunnahabhain he might receive a bottle of the distillers' or a bottle from Speymalt. [He] was also of the opinion the distillers had made out a case of 'passing off'.[186]"

In December 1990 Gordon & MacPhail (again through their subsidiary Speymalt Whisky Distributors) were this time challenged by Allied Distillers, through their subsidiary JBD over a dispute with the use of the name Laphroaig on their labels. G&M, agreed out of court, to cease using the name Laphroaig on labels and have never bottled a Laphroaig since. In the case of Macallan (which was a unique situation due to some unofficial agreements and arrangements prior to the case) and Laphroaig, Gordon & MacPhail ceased to use their name on any labels, but with Bunnahabhain the practice is continued today. Macallan was reintroduced on the label after the millennium. One can only deduce that

185. Law.justia.com
186. Evening Express January 1983.

Picture courtesy of Photographer Guus Pauka and Marcel van Gils

a further court hearing[187] or out-of-court agreement settled these matters and not in the favour of the distillers.

There was one more attempt by Allied Distillers to try and prevent an IB using the name Laphroaig (see the entry for Murray McDavid in the List of Independent Bottlers at the end of the book). This extraordinary case, which was widely publicised at the time (the Murray McDavid owners never missing an opportunity for some media coverage[188]), is most odd when you consider how many independent bottlings of Laphroaig were available on the market from the likes of Hart Bros, Signatory or Cadenhead's. I guess Allied felt that by picking on a new firm, they might stand a chance (and perhaps send a message). The fact is, as far as I am aware, no independent bottler has been accused of 'passing off' since these court cases.

What makes these cases extraordinary is that in 1994 Diageo took to court a Pavel Maslyukov after he had tried to trademark "Dallas Dhu", "Convalmore" and "Pittyvaich". Pavel reasoned[189] that as these names were from closed distilleries they could no longer be attributed to a brand. One of the key witnesses was Ian Urquhart from Gordon & MacPhail, who informed the court "...that Dallas Dhu means only one thing to the Scotch whisky industry and consumers of fine single malt whiskies: Dallas Dhu whisky from the Dallas Dhu Distillery." Independent bottlers to the rescue..?

In 1983 Philip Morrice wrote in his "Schweppes Guide To Scotch Whisky":

187. Which I can find no evidence of.
188. No such thing as had press...
189. www.ipo.gov.uk/t-challenge-decision-results/o18809.pdf

"Fringe operators: Freed of the burden of financing maturing stocks and maintaining the quality of a particular blend, and, most of all, of advertising it, some smaller companies cause much irritation to the big distillers and blenders by undercutting the heavily promoted main-line brands. These secondary or single-market brands are often put together from whatever source the proprietor can find mature whisky, and the actual process of blending, bottling and transporting is often done on a sub-contracted basis. Quite a different picture from that conjured up by the more traditional companies."

Whether Morrice is referring to just independent bottlers or small blending outfits is unclear but the inference is unmistakable; a lack of care over quality. It is inarguable that some companies have been less concerned with quality than others. But the notion that this is due to a lack of 'tradition' or even of maturing stocks is frankly without merit. For years the bargain basement blend selection was provided by some of the larger blending companies. Conversely some of the very greatest whiskies are bottled by some of the smallest companies. Too often writers and commentators have been caught up in the romance and marketing of the larger blending houses demonstrating with their locale, history and provenance a bona fide 'rite of passage' to unquestionable quality and pedigree. This, when combined with a nostalgic and prosaic romance of the industry, can blindside against the fact that *old* (or *traditional*) does not equal *good* in exactly the same way that *new* does not equal *good* (or untraditional) .

Perhaps the greatest coverage on the subject of independent bottlers was provided by Richard Grindal in his 1992 book "The Spirit of Whisky". Over the course of several pages[190] Grindal, a previous Director of the Scotch Whisky Association gave his take on the independent bottlers:

"This development has not been welcome by everybody and some distillers are particularly unhappy about it. Their argument goes something like this. The name of a distillery – let us use an imaginary one 'Loch Maree', as an example – is in effect a trademark. Not only are the owners of the distillery entitled to benefit from the sale of whisky under that trademark, but it is their responsibility to ensure that the whisky is matured and bottled in a style and to a quality which will enhance its reputation. They cannot have any control over the quality of a 'Loch Maree' single malt whisky put out by an independent

190. Pages 207-209

bottler. If a whisky drinker buys a bottle of 'Loch Maree' which is below standard in any respect, then it is the name of the whisky that will suffer, not that of the bottler.

"The counter to this argument is that the independent bottlers have bought the whisky in good faith and are entitled to bottle and sell it as a single malt whisky from 'Loch Maree', for that is what it is. One has to concede that independent bottlers have made available to consumers a large number of single malts, which they would otherwise not have been available to buy and taste. On recent visits to the Pot Still[191] and to two other well-known whisky shops, Lamberts in Edinburgh and the Soho Wine Market[192] in London, I counted more than twenty-five single malts which are not currently being bottled for sale by the owners of the distilleries.

"This widening of choice to the consumer sounds fine in principle, but people who know their Scotch would, if they were honest, agree that many of these malts, although more than acceptable in a blend, are not worth drinking as single malts. The judgement of whisky blenders who place single malt whiskies in classifications according to quality would be the most reliable guide, and I am sure that they must be surprised to find that some of the whiskies in the lower classifications are being bottled for sale.

"This does not mean that these whiskies are undrinkable, but merely that in the view of the experts they do not have the character, the flavour and the quality to be expected in a good single malt Scotch. There are malt whisky distilleries in Scotland which distil in, shall we say, unconventional ways. I once visited one where they claimed that by adjusting the heads of the stills they were able to produce different whiskies. One would think that if a distillery could produce a malt whisky good enough to be in demand among either blenders or whisky drinkers, it would not need to manipulate its stills to make another.

"The bottling of single malts has become a controversial subject. In essence the argument is not one about consumer choice but about money. Preferring all cowards to remain neutral, the only advice I would offer to a newcomer to malt whisky is that when he has a choice, he should pick the single malt that has been bottled

191. Pot Still Bar on Hope Street, Glasgow. One of the best whisky bars in Scotland.
192. Now known as Milroy's after Jack and Wallace Milroy who started the shop.

by the owners of the distillery. In that way he can know that he will be drinking a malt whisky of the style, age and quality which the distiller believes to be the best for his whisky. Moreover, whiskies bottled by the distiller are more likely to be consistent, as an independent bottler will usually have only limited stocks of mature whisky at his disposal."

Much of what Grindal says is difficult to argue with. As I discuss in more detail in Chapter 14 the relationship of distiller and bottler described by Grindal is unique to the whisky industry. However, reading from a high and mighty seat some thirty years later I am guessing that many distillers would argue quite vehemently with the notion that their malts are simply not good enough to be drunk as 'singles'. I'm not sure the likes of An Cnoc[193], Cragganmore, or Benromach, very much tertiary malts in 1992, would be happy being told their distillate was purely blending fodder.

Like with most things, hindsight makes my criticism sound like hollow point-scoring and, despite the signs, no-one could have predicted the growth in malt whisky sales and prominence from 1992 to today. His argument, as is often the case from blenders and producers, is one of consistency of product. But consistency is not what the modern day drinker is looking for. I am reminded of one of my first days working for Wm Cadenhead's. Poking my nose round Frank McHardy's (then Springbank Distillery manager) door I asked him how he blended batches of Springbank.

"Come on in." Frank said with his genial smile. "I'll show you."

I marched in and stood next to his desk. Expecting Frank to bring out measuring jugs, demineralised water, flavour wheels and any other 'blending' apparatus my little mind could think of, Frank brought out a stock sheet.

"We're about to bottle a batch of Springbank 10 year old." Frank said pointing at a list of casks. "So for this run we'll use casks one through ten. And for the next batch casks 11-20."

I realised I had asked a slightly silly question but it does demonstrate one of the reasons that Springbank is so highly regarded and sought after by malt whisky drinkers. To a certain extent, you never know quite what you are going to get. The batch variation is part of what makes it an exceptional whisky[194].

In 1998 Whisky Magazine was launched through a company called Paragraph Publishing. I have already described my brief time with the company but it is interesting to look at the magazine with regards to how it reacted to the changing face of the industry. No doubt the publishers were wary of

193. Or Knockdhu as it was known.
194. This is no way knocking the incredible skill of blenders who can make each and every batch taste so similar. This batch policy works for Springbank due to their size and following.

highlighting and promoting independent bottlers. At this time, whilst malt whisky was growing at an incredible rate, IBs were a very small part of the industry and Whisky Magazine would have been trying to ensure that the advertisement side, in reality the mid to large distillers, were kept happy with the content. Just three years earlier in 1995 Andrew Dewar-Durie, then Managing Director of Allied Distillers Ltd, had been asked in the Scotch Whisky Review why there were so few independent bottlings of Laphroaig[195].

"Independent bottlings of Laphroaig occur very rarely now. There were clashes where independent bottlers were clearly riding on the back of our marketing effort. This, we hope, is a thing of the past and there is a much better understanding of our roles. Where there are distilleries whose singles we are not selling we are perfectly happy to work hand-in-hand with responsible bottlers who are meeting that niche demand[196]."

It is interesting to note that around five years after Andrew Dewar-Drurie left Allied, the feeling at the company was very different as Rupert Patrick, now CEO of James Eadie explains:

"From an industry point of view they [independent bottlers] bring an excitement, buzz and noise around interesting single malts that the big guys just can't create... When I was selling Laphroaig at Beam, it [awareness of independent bottlers] just didn't feature... we lived side by side very comfortably[197]."

The very first issue of Whisky Magazine carried a letter asking how or why IBs differ. The editor responded:

"The difference between IBs derives from (a) their ability to obtain good casks (which depends on being taken seriously by the producers/brokers, and on good contacts within the industry) and (b) their ability to evaluate the casks that they are offered.

"Some, like Gordon & MacPhail and Cadenhead's (the leaders) hold large stocks, have been in the game for over 100 years and know their business. Others, like the Scotch Malt Whisky Society and Adelphi, have worked hard to win favour and test samples with experienced tasting panels before they buy and bottle... One

195. The interviewer and owner of Loch Fyne Whiskies, Richard Joynson, was incorrect in his question. There were several independent bottlings of Laphroaig available but the UK was not a major lover of smoky whiskies (unlike much of Europe and in particular Scandinavia).
196. It is worth noting that as there were no other whisky periodicals in the UK there is no way this comment will have gone unnoticed by the editor of Whisky Magazine.
197. The Spirits Business 5 March 2021 "The rise of Independent Scotch whisky bottlers".

suspects that others – I'd rather not give names – bottle whatever they can lay their hands on, so long as it has no obvious off-notes.

"So far as storage goes, G&M and Cadenhead's have their own bonds. Others remove the whiskies from the distillery/sellers' bonded warehouse just before bottling. After this the cases lie in duty-paid warehouses.

"One final aspect, so far as I am aware, producers will never try to shift poor casks to independent bottlers. Indeed, United Distillers tells me it makes extra efforts to ensure that malt which is to be bottled from a single cask is especially good. The same may not be true of some of the new wave of 'buy by the cask merchants', where the buyer has no control over the ultimate quality."

Mark Reynier[198] responded in Issue 2:

"I am an independent bottler of the Murray McDavid range of malts... In your letters page, the question concerning independent bottlers was not satisfactorily answered – and gave a very misleading impression... One deduces from the article that the only independents that are any good are those mentioned."

It took the magazine eight issues before an article highlighting an independent bottler appeared – possibly due to the fear of losing large advertisers by focusing on this part of the industry. Its tightrope walk was trying to remain relevant in a changing customer base but also ensuring it had sufficient advertisement to continue. Eventually, with barriers broken, most of the main independent bottlers had good coverage and some became good advertisers.

The advent of mass information online, blogs, vlogs and forums gave no such credence to one side of the trade or the other. It did allow though a constant stream of misinformation from the likes of whisky.com:

"...new young independent bottlers entered the market almost on a monthly basis. Most of them didn't make it from the twilight to the spotlight. Their whisky sources are too dubious, and the quality is far from consistent. Some bottlers have never seen the casks they bottle. They are sometimes called 'armchair bottlers' because they sit at home and have Malt whisky bottled somewhere else. They don't know how the whisky tastes and they don't care. Malt whisky is 'in', and the consumer is thought to fall

---

198. See interview with Gordon Wright.

for any nice story and an exotic Gaelic name."

This, frankly, ridiculous stream of verbal diarrhoea was often repeated by others believing whisky.com was some sort of authority on the subject. There is no empirical evidence that bottling yourself, over having someone bottle for you, has any effect on the whisky at all – you could be called lazy, granted, but it is not an arbiter of care, consideration or quality.

The change of direction by many distillers[199] and resulting growth in sales allowed some within their ranks to pretend they invented the category and at the same time decry IBs as somehow parasitic or detrimental to the industry they helped build. In an interview in 2007 Mike Keiller, then CEO of Morrison Bowmore Distillers stated

> "...it really gets me when the press refer to them [independent bottlers] as innovators. I have even been asked to take a table at a dinner to celebrate them – I think not! For me, they are exploiting a (temporary) oversight of the producers who historically used to reciprocate whisky to balance blends. Over time product got onto the open market and, as we had not tied down how our single malts could be used and sold, these independents have grown and spread."[200]

It is interesting to note that previous Directors and Chairmen of Morrison Bowmore Distillers, Brian & Tim Morrison, went on to found their own independent bottling companies after the sale of Morrison Bowmore Distillers to Suntory in 1994. Keiller also completely ignores the origins of the Morrison whisky story; started in 1951 by Stanley P. Morrison as a whisky brokering company.

Andrew Symington, owner of Signatory Vintage, was asked in 2002 whether what he did [bottling single cask whiskies] upset the marketers:

> "In some cases, justifiably so. I bottle malts at different ages from the brand owner – but that is getting harder to do as they are extending their range to more and more expressions. I've stuck rigidly to that principle but some [IBs] have been mimicking the proprietors, sticking distillery names in big letters on labels with no respect for the trademark owners.

> "It's getting harder for the independents. Glenmorangie has never sold a cask of single malt; they add a tiny measure of Glen

---

199. In response to the change in consumer demands.
200. "Your Shout: Scotch on the rocks" The Drinks Business 10 July 2007.

Moray and call it 'Westport' so 'Glenmorangie' cannot be found in the market. Glenfiddich do the same with 'Wardhead' and more are going to start to do it.' "

The practice of 'tea-spooning'[201], as Andrew is referring to here with the 'Westport', is an interesting case. This alleged process of blending a minute amount of a separate malt with what is in the cask in order to remove the name cropped up on a regular basis. However with the creation of the Spirits Verification Scheme[202] a problem arose. As every single cask is allocated a code for its type (be it single malt, single grain, blended malt etc[203]) and this code is how each bottling warehouse can prove to the authorities that it is labelling the whisky correctly, problems would arise with calling a whisky blended when it was in fact a single malt. In addition to this the physical act of blending, or even tea-spooning would require a completed process form – again, something the authorities could see to prove exactly how much of what had been added (and then follow the product through to bottling to ensure compliance). This came to a head when I received an email from a distilling group:

> "To whom it may concern, we believe that your company is bottling one of our products with the incorrect labelling. We understand you are calling it a single malt when it should be described as blended. Please can you advise how you will remedy this situation."

I gathered my information and replied:

> "Thank you for your email. Please note I have included a copy of the Delivery Order, Shipping Note, EMCS[204], Cask Certificate and a photo of the cask end highlighting the details as originally laid down. As all of these identify the said whisky as a 'single malt' Scotch whisky and not a blended Scotch whisky as you are asking me to call it, I wonder if you could advise how to correctly label the whisky in accordance with all of the Scotch Verification guidelines?"

That appeared to be the end of the matter as I never heard from them again. It does raise a few questions however. Firstly, if the name of the distillery being on a label is a trademark concern then one has to wonder why this issue has not been dealt with. The Scotch Malt Whisky Society (SMWS) decided from

---

201. And I am still waiting to meet someone with a business card that states 'Official Tea-Spooner'
202. SDVS
203. See 'Notes from Author' at the beginning.
204. Excise Movement and Control System – the online form for moving goods under bond.

its formation to put codes on the bottles – starting with 1.1 for the first cask ever bottled[205]. In this way there is no brand infringement and a consumer needs only to either have a good memory or the ability to use a search engine to discover which distillery the contents came from. Assuming this is fine by all parties involved (and with the recent incredible resurgence by the SMWS it certainly appears to be), why has this idea not been more universally adopted? Granted there are bottlers that predate the SMWS (some by decades) but ignoring those, was there not a chance for the industry to lay down some rules or create a charter (allowing independents to at least have the chance to show they understood the concerns)?

The Scotch Whisky Association tried its best to ignore the sector even existed. The organisation, which let us not forget is financed by members (i.e. almost entirely distillers), has pretty much never dared to acknowledge the part that independent bottlers play in the industry. Other than rules and the re-defining of factors affecting bottlers, the SWA has played little to no part in its story. This has maintained the divide between the distillery and the independent.

I asked Ken Grier who was Director of Malts for the Edrington Group (2004 – 2015)[206] how the independent bottlers were viewed:

> "It's very interesting because the independent bottlers played a valuable role in introducing consumers to a range of interesting new styles and distilleries, encouraging drinkers to explore. They were also a key part of the supply and demand ecosystem in terms of stock. As brand owner marketers we were slightly wary of them as we couldn't control the get up or style of our brands as long as they stated the origin of spirit. Many companies tea-spooned and we made sure that we kept a firewall between ourselves and the independent bottlers."

I enquired further as to what Ken meant by a 'firewall':

> "We were always courteous to our independent bottler colleagues but I remember one instance where I declined an invitation to share a platform with one at a consumer facing event as this would have been potentially confusing for the drinkers in attendance to have an official and independent supplier there talking about the same brand."

This is completely understandable, especially given the current climate of demand for, and supply of, branded malt whisky. It does also feel a case of

---

205. Glenfarclas.
206. Also The Macallan Creative Director 2016-2018

'thanks for laying the foundations, we'll take it from here'. However, what is the comeback for IBs? Sell us stock or else! Or else what?

In reality much less has been written than spoken when it comes to criticising the Independent Bottlers. In an industry of cordial relations and constant swapping of skills, staff and products, a pleasant but arms-length approach is often kept and frankly, other than becoming a distiller, what else can the independent company do?

CHAPTER 13

THE END OF CREATIVE WHISKY

"When I started collecting whisky I had not heard of the independent bottlers as was busy understanding the official bottlers. It came as a complete surprise when I discovered that company's like Cadenhead, Samaroli, Intertrade, Sestante and Moon existed. It opened a wild new world which bewildered me at the beginning to say the least, albeit thanks to some friends I was able to start my journey. Amongst these whiskies I had an amazing tasting of several Ardbeg 1967s; all of them were stellar in their own way. Be aware when you enter the world of independent bottlers you will never leave it and you will always be very surprised; be ready to forget everything you know about whisky."

PATRICK DE SCHULTHESS
Malt Maniac

2011 was an incredibly quiet year for the business and Creative Whisky Co was certainly not alone. Several other independent bottlers had begun talking about building distilleries. Arran Distillers had truly broken the stranglehold the larger corporations had over building distilleries when they finalised the Arran Distillery in 1994 – it was the first independently built distillery in Scotland since 1898. The next independent malt distillery would not be built until 2005 when both Daftmill and Kilchoman came online.

Most independent bottlers, other than Gordon & MacPhail (buying Benromach in 1998) and Signatory Vintage (who bought Edradour in 2002) did not begin to show interest until supply of bulk whisky began to look limited around 2011 through 2012. I took a trip to St George's Distillery, established 2006, in Norfolk to take a look at their setup. The then Distillery Manager, David Fitt, was a good friend and showed me around. Their one ton mash set-up was a masterpiece of simplicity and economy and would be much copied over the years.

Enquiries were made to Forsyth's the fabricators of the distillery equipment. A quote of £1.25 million[207] was at least more than £1million than I could muster. Frankly I marvelled at these other bottlers who seemed to have bottomless pits of cash from which to draw on. Many, in conversation, would claim their banks were bending over backwards to help. Mine was still bending the other way to be obstructive.

Supply is a strange thing to explain. I've covered much in the Chapter 'Where do you get your casks?' but a lot has to do with decisions made within the companies holding stocks and that has to do with the situation of the business on a year to year basis (as well as bulk supply manager's decisions). Supply can often come with brands or where stock is overflowing. For instance Signatory Vintage benefited greatly from its relationship with Chivas that allowed a near unique access to their aged stocks (when Chivas was bought by Pernod Ricard, the new owners discovered a huge surplus of whisky).

I was reliant on just a small number of brokers (less than five) that were dealing with large and small blenders looking to offload surplus stock. Often the same makes would do the rounds and I would continually make a list of desired malts to ensure a varied bottling approach. I, and most other independent bottlers, have always tried to ensure a variation in bottled whiskies. Whilst at times a large parcel of a certain malt may come available, no bottler wants to continually bottle whisky from the same distillery for fear of saturating the markets and shelves of their customers and also for fear of wrath (or at least appearing on the radar) of the distiller that owns the brand.

---

207. This was just for the plant. It did not include buildings etc.

It is a sort of game, I guess.

It is no coincidence that between 2013 and 2017 twenty-two new distilleries were opened and only one of those was built by a distilling company[208]. Many of these were independent bottlers seeing the drought as a sign that longevity was only in the form of control over their own supply.

I had never moved in the kinds of crowds that could stump up the £2-3 million required to build a distillery and nor was I tempted to follow the micro-distillery model of the likes of Strathearn or Abhainn Dearg. Distilling was not in my future[209]. I was also reminded of when, around 2003, I asked Stewart Laing why Douglas Laing had not bought a distillery. "We have tried. But every time we got close a parcel of stock would appear that would divert our funds.[210]"

When stock began to be more readily available again I hired Paul McKendrick to aid the business as was at that point working on my own[211]. Paul and I got on very well and I have often joked that on reading through his CV, littered with spelling mistakes, lack of experience, drug dependency and criminal convictions, I noted that his interests were 'Heavy Metal, Whisky & Golf'. "Great, when can you start?"[212]

As supply changed, so did the nature of the business. We were still supplying and bottling casks for Jack Wiebers but were also bottling for Svenska Eldvatten in Sweden, First Cask for the Netherlands, Single Cask Nation for the USA and several other smaller labels. Adapting to what was available we began bottling blended whisky (bought already blended and in casks) and 'unnamed' malts. These began appearing more commonly around 2014 and at first were just a few suppliers wanting to protect their brand name. In almost all cases we knew exactly which distillery they had come from and their anonymity at times added to the appeal – at least in the early days – as drinkers would try and guess the origins of the distillate.

This did lead to one of the more sour episodes for me in the industry. The appeal of independent bottling means that very little knowledge or background in the industry is required to begin. It therefore attracts people with a passing interest who see the ease with which to start and make a profit.

One such person arrived at Creative Whisky and bought a few cases for a couple of his local hotels. Over time he bought more and more and everything was quite pleasant. Small sales turned into the odd cask which

---

208. Dalmunach, built by Chivas Brothers in 2015.
209. Recently I did consider being part of the Dal Riata team opening a new distillery in Campbeltown but withdrew as a Director due to, mostly, a lack of desire to be involved in a distillery.
210. Eventually both Douglas Laing and Hunter Laing would become Distillers. The former with Strathearn and the latter with Ardnahoe.
211. Bottling entire ranges on your own is soul-destroying work.
212. Just to ensure there is no confusion, I am joking, Paul's CV was impeccable and had no discrepancies. He does like Heavy Metal, Whisky and Golf though – that part is true.

was provided with what are termed 'retail ready' labels. Essentially this was enough information to satisfy the Scotch Whisky Association rules and also provide the correct information for any new labels that would no doubt be applied later.

With the advent of the Spirits Verification Scheme (SDVS)[213] all labels can be scrutinised to ensure that from the moment of production through to retail the customer is not being misinformed (or cheated). We had our first SDVS visit and sailed through bar a small hangover from previous packaging that had 'Fine Single Malt Scotch Whisky' – the 'Fine' part now being against the rules. I thought nothing more of the visit until I received an email from the SDVS authorities asking me to show the paperwork behind a cask of Lagavulin 10 year old that I had sold. This was much to my surprise as I had never bottled a Lagavulin 10 year old.

It quickly became apparent that a cask of 'Islay' single malt whisky sold to this new buyer had been relabelled as Lagavulin. What was worse was that he had forged my invoice by scanning it and putting in the new information. The initial fraud being followed up by additional fraud. As with many fraudsters, and no doubt being a newbie on the whisky scene, he had made a silly mistake. Listed in the 'item' section on the invoice he had written 'Lagavulan 10'. Again, thanks to the systems in place, I was able to demonstrate to the authorities that I had done all that was expected of me and was admonished of any wrong-doing. It was another of those lessons learnt and not surprisingly I never saw the snake-oil salesman again.

The buildings we were using for bottling and offices were not fit for purpose and when the neighbouring buildings (complete with additional warehousing, land and log cabin) became available I jumped on them. It took just under a year to complete the purchase[214] but eventually on 15th November 2016 we moved in. To mark the occasion I invited all of my importers, distributors and many other friends for a day of whisky. This was my proudest day having started the business eleven years earlier. Paul took everyone on a tasting tour of the casks before I hosted a tasting with eight of the best casks I had ever bottled[215]. We had a fantastic dinner and afterwards I thanked everyone in the room for their friendship and involvement in getting us to where we were. I was about to finish when my good friend Hasse Peters nudged me and whispered "You are forgetting someone". He nodded to my wife next to me.

213. When this scheme was announced I was very vocal as to the unfairness of it. Each process (Brewing, Distilling, Maturing, Blending, Bottling & Labelling) incurred a fee of £1,600 every two years. This was regardless of size – a plant churning out a huge blend would pay the same fee as my tiny bottling facility.
214. Mainly due to the bank again trying their hardest to put every single obstacle they could find in the way. Eventually we were forced to pay cash which severely limited our cashflow.
215. Strathisla 1969, Clynelish 1982, Glengoyne 1972, Littlemill 1988, Macduff 1973, Ben Nevis 1968, Tomintoul 1966, Laphroaig 1988 and Laphroaig 1996

Very quickly I added "And of course none of this would be possible without my wife." Phew! And again thank you Hasse.

The next day I had a meeting with ImpEx Beverages to discuss stock and future bottlings. It was clear that the US was still not understanding the changing nature of the independent bottling world. Replacement prices for stock were by now climbing at an exorbitant rate. I was able to ignore it for a short while due to the brokering that was going on behind the scenes. Large quantities of good whisky were at regular times being offered and I was able to buy and sell these not only to prop up stock levels but keep up the profit for the business.

Around this time an old friend in the industry had approached me about a business venture. At first I had a vision of hiring him but as the discussions went on it became apparent to both of us that a new company was really the solution. In March 2016 Iain Croucher registered his company and North Star Spirits was born; he and I began a very fruitful and much enjoyable partnership. Creative Whisky took on all of Iain's bottling and warehousing and watched with wonder as this little upstart made a big splash in a short space of time[216].

**Iain Croucher, Alan Hall and the author with
Frank Handgraaf helping himself to a drink**

I had also taken on the bottling of casks for a distillery that had sold several to private owners. This, I had thought, may allow for a route to supply (it didn't) and/or private cask owners looking to sell their cask, or part of, for me to use

216. Iain and I still work together today. The day the laughter dies will be a sad day.

in my range (this never happened either). It did, however, cause an untold amount of stress and I realised just how little some private cask owners knew about bottling whisky. Often we would be asked questions like:

> "I thought it would be in [insert distillery name]'s bottle and packaging?"

> "Why is there Duty on the cask? I am just planning on drinking it and giving it away."

> "I live in America, can you tell me how much it will be to send it to me."

> "I'm planning on selling it to local pubs and shops."[217]

> "I thought the cost of bottling was included."

One of my worst encounters was an elderly man who rang me just after we had bottled his cask. I had emailed him asking for a date for delivery.

> "Ah, Mr Stirk, your email is asking the details of the warehouse we are using. We are wanting this delivered to the house."

> "Ok Mr Smith[218], you'll need to remove the 67 cases from the truck by hand. Have you got someone who can help you with this?"

> "What do you mean remove the cases by hand. I want the whisky delivered to the house."

> "Yes, I'll get it sent to the house but without a fork lift truck you'll need to remove the 67 cases by hand and the truck driver will expect you to have help as will not want to wait around too long in a residential area. I assume where you live has room to accommodate a truck?"

> "I'm not having a truck deliver this. I want the whisky delivered to my house."

> "But there were 398 bottles taken from your Hogshead. I'm sorry but what did you expect to happen?"

> "Listen Mr Stirk, when I buy a bottle from the distillery it arrives in the mail and that is how I want my whisky sent."

217. Which would require an AWRS number – Alcohol Warehousing Registration Scheme brought in to prevent people 'acquiring' alcohol and shifting it to shops and bars.
218. Obviously not his name, although could be as have forgotten.

"Well, I'm sorry to inform you Mr Smith that I am not a distillery and you are not buying one bottle of whisky, you have bought an entire cask and that is being delivered on a pallet."

Here is where he got very angry at me:

"I HAVE A HEART CONDITION AND THERE IS NO WAY I CAN GET THE CASES OFF OF A TRUCK!"

I think I am right in saying this is the only time I ever lost my temper in front of the staff. I shouted back:

"WELL YELLING AT ME ISN'T HELPING YOU IS IT?!"

Once calm was restored he acquiesced. Whilst there was no small print to read, and his contract of purchase was not with me, one would assume a certain level of knowledge before buying a cask of whisky. After that incident, and frankly because there was no profit at all in the exercise, I stopped bottling private casks.

As the prices of casks climbed ever higher I realised that Creative Whisky was not well placed to fit into the new 'premium' nature of the industry. I had spent the last seventeen years selecting and bottling whiskies that were meant to be drunk and enjoyed. Whiskies that came with very little fanfare. In twenty years or so the industry had gone from having very few whiskies over £100 to now having many more than that over £1,000 and there was no end in sight to the increases. I began working on a deluxe range with the few older and rarer casks I had. With my designer Katy Coltart[219], we looked at wooden boxes, engraved bottles, bespoke corks and all of the paraphernalia that came with it. As each item was discussed, the end price to the consumer continued to spiral. I had always sought the advice of distributors and retailers to gauge reception before bottling a new range. The reports back were positive but cagey – it was new territory for the brand.

Around this time I made friends with a collector and buyer that was also working with several international clients that wanted their own whiskies. I discussed with him this new project to get some more feedback. He asked me what the casks were that I was going to use in the series and I sent him the full list. A few days later he replied that one of his clients would be interested in buying the entire list. The amount offered was double the profit I had calculated had I gone through with the entire bespoke boxing, bottling, labelling, distributing and selling. And that is before any marketing, bottles

219. For anyone familiar with the Electric Coo Series, Katy is the designer behind those labels. She has reliably informed me that there are easier animals to draw.

used through tastings and shows and travel expenses. In American speak, it was a 'no brainer'.

This was not the exact moment I knew I was going to sell my business but was certainly part of the catalyst. I was reminded what my boss, Marcin Miller, at Whisky Magazine had said to me once: 'Make sure your hobby does not become work'. In other words 'watch you don't lose your passion'. In truth I had. My role had now become quite detached from the product that had drawn me in. I know the exact moment I wanted out. I was in New York at someone's apartment and we were tasting a large number of bottles from a single distillery. I knew maybe two people from the group of thirty or so. The distillery manager, who had been on tour in the US for a week, had flown in, as the last leg of his tour to be at this tasting and had brought with him from the distillery (and had carried throughout the entire tour) - a special single cask sample, not for retail, to pour for the group. I could tell how jetlagged he was and how much the travel had taken out of him. He valiantly carried on, gave his talk and answered some questions.

Afterwards, and over pizza I didn't want to eat (but nothing else was available), one of the organisers moaned that the distillery manager 'had not much of a personality'. My blood boiled and that was the moment for me - I knew I could not carry on. It wasn't the dismissive nature of the comment, it was more that I was so angry. I realised that for the last two years I had felt like an octopus having its legs pulled in every direction. Demand had never been higher and supply was getting more and more difficult to manage.

I returned to the UK and after talking it over with my wife[220] decided to sell up. My friend who had assisted with the sale of the parcel of older whiskies took a look at my stock and within a few weeks had found a buyer. What pleased me most was that the buyers were not going to continue the business as a going concern and were also not intending to sell on the stock. Whilst there were no stipulations as to what they could and couldn't do (would have been a bit rich coming from someone who had done exactly what they wanted with casks) I was not keen on seeing the brand change or be in any way different to what I had created.

The hardest part for me was the condition of sale that the business was wound up and secrecy was kept over its future. I feel I have always led my business as an open and honest concern and keeping secrets did not sit well. The sign-over day was in August 2018 and due to an already planned trip to see family in the US I was arriving back in the UK just two nights before the Monday signing. A slight discrepancy in the stock records meant pulling an all-nighter beforehand and coupled with jetlag I was in a nervous and extremely

---

220. At first there was sadness after everything we had built up but also realisation that something had to give.

fatigued state of mind on the morning of signing the contracts. I drove into Edinburgh and bought a coffee to perk me up. I then met with my solicitor and had another coffee, followed by another one with the broker of the deal. More than buzzing, I entered into the offices where the documents were to be signed. It was like a scene out of Ally McBeal with lawyers everywhere, and yet more coffee. I had power of attorney for my wife so had to sign everything in duplicate – and there was a lot to sign. At one point my brain froze and I completely forgot how to sign my name. The lawyers hovering nearby began to get fidgety wondering if I had perhaps changed my mind; I'm not sure the remaining signatures were my finest work, but the deed was done.

Done and dusted we all went for lunch and as soon as the first food hit my stomach I began to lose my breath. I made some hurried excuses and left. Driving out of Edinburgh seemed to take a lifetime and everything felt like it was closing in on me. On Morningside Road, always busy even at the best of times, I pulled into a side street and had my first, and so far only, panic attack. My head was swimming and I could barely catch a breath. Thankfully no-one noticed and eventually my breathing returned to some sort of normality. I think the severe fatigue from the jetlag combined with the caffeine that was racing through my system all hit home with the realisation I had signed away the last thirteen years; years that had doubts and fears, stress and heartache but also successes and accomplishments, perseverance and survival. I was proud and sad in equal measures. I did eventually get out of Edinburgh and thankfully have not for one moment regretted my decision.

At this stage only the staff knew[221] and it was time to tell the importers and distributors. Keeping the sale quiet from them was tough, but perhaps toughest was keeping it from Iain Croucher. He came down to the warehouses and looked around:

"Where is everyone? Have you laid off all of the staff?" He asked.

"Yes." I replied. "I've sold Creative Whisky."

Iain was dumbfounded; at first congratulatory until he then realised what it meant for North Star Spirits.

"Shit, guess I'll have to find someone else to bottle for me." Iain said rolling his eyes.

"Yeah, sorry about that Iain[222]."

---

221. All have gone on to better jobs (with better bosses they tell me)
222. It's all good now of course - North Star, with a little help from me, opened their own bottling, blending and maturation warehouse in January 2022.

Whilst this is not the end of my story, it is the end of a company that joins the annals of those buyers, blenders, bottlers and brokers that have come and gone. Creative Whisky will remain only as a footnote, or in an index, or pop up occasionally in collections and auctions. There was never an intention to change the world or the industry. Driven on to survive and find my own path I was privy to some amazing whiskies and met some amazing people. If there is one thing that I will take away from my time bottling whisky and writing this book it is that the people make this industry. The whiskies will change, expressions will come and go, but the relationships and good times will be all that matters in the end.

CHAPTER 14

More good than harm

''I had loved blended and single malt Scotch for many years. In a remarkable moment on Islay in 1983 at Laphroaig, I was introduced to single cask, single malt whisky. What an epiphany! But then I realised it was very hard to come by. My hopes would have been dashed had I not discovered some months later that The Scotch Malt Whisky Society had been formed to independently bottle exactly that. The Society and independent bottlers, over the years, have opened my mind and palate to appreciate the wide world of flavours in Whisky.''

JOHN MCCHEYNE
Master Brand Ambassador SMWS

Checking my calendar I can see that it is time the world hurtled into another recession. Inevitable isn't it? After all, isn't everything cyclical? What's the old saying; 'never throw out anything in your wardrobe that fits, just wait until it's in fashion again'. The 'drink du jour' is whisky. No, wait, let me rephrase that; The drink du jour is 'malt' whisky. A few years ago I seem to recall gin was taking over the world, now gin brands are dropping like flies – and isn't rum the next big thing (how long have I been hearing that)? What's next? Tequila? Maybe Mezcal?

The Artisan Restaurant in Wishaw, Scotland.
It houses the largest whisky bar in the world.

It is not that long ago that large distillers were openly selling new fillings and mature stocks of 'singles' that were not part of their brand portfolio. It is even more recent that some companies were clearing stock to avoid going into the red and/or to remove brands no longer under their 'umbrella'. Meanwhile a group of afficionados, freaks and geeks sought out these weird and wonderful offerings... only for the money men and marketers to get involved. Or rather those identifying something that a quick buck can be gained from.

Malts are indeed the 'new thing', and single casks the latest craze within that sector but the 'independent' discussion is not new, it is just considerably more prominent and far-reaching than it was. The emergence of investment companies promising impossible returns and quoting nonsensical historical one-off sales all shines an unfavourable light on the independents; like Sauron's great eye turning on the plucky little Hobbits. Granted, that's a bit far-fetched but it has to be said when you have had moments in living memory of distillers buying back bottled stock of independent bottlings and claiming it as their own history (okay - to a certain extent) and then public announcements from distillers of sales figures for single casks the likes of which only a few could stump up, it is hardly the Shire folk who are solely to blame.

A definite trend from the smallest to the very largest distilling company has been the premiumisation of their older and rarer casks. Beyond series like the 'Special Editions', or single vintage releases which are readily available you will often see releases that are single cask, market specific and quite openly only available to the uber wealthy[223].

Could any of this premiumisation and specialisation have occurred without independents crawling around in those corners of warehouses[224] that distillers dared not venture when stock was readily available? As we read from Richard Grindal, surely the quality of these second and most definitely of the third tier malts is not good enough to be drinking on its own. Did the IBs help, did they hinder, or is it just now with the mass conglomerations, amalgamations and need to strip out every drop of honey from the hive, that IBs are just a nuisance?

From the history I've outlined, hopefully extensively enough, merchants, blenders, bottlers, buyers and brokers were all part and parcel of, at times, a healthy distilling industry. It has only been since the 1970s that a distillery has been truly self-sufficient (Glenfiddich first but even then was contributing a fair chunk of its malt to Grant's Standfast blended Scotch whisky) – and in a several century old industry that is a blink of an eye. And yet another timely reminder that almost all of the big blends, household names now, started out as independent merchants: "Yes madam, a jar of potted ham, a pound of lard, two tins of suet liver pudding and a bottle of our famous Johnnie Walker blended Scotch whisky? Certainly madam. Sounds like you're having quite the party."

So one point of contention maybe should be put to bed. IBs are not really the new kids on the block. Yes it tends to be the hip and trendy part of the industry. Untethered, boundless and without a department telling it not to, the independent bottling sector has been able to break down barriers and stereotypes that the distillers could only dream of. But new, not really. The change has come because distillers saw the potential of the sector. I am reminded of that

---

223. 'Casks of Distinction' from Diageo are a good example.
224. Mark Watt and I have often joked about building a warehouse with hundreds of corners so that we could keep finding those special 'casks in the corner that we had forgotten about'.

conversation with someone from Diageo whilst sailing around Islay "We are a blending company, we will never bottle single cask, single malt whisky." Oh but they did, and probably faster than that boat was repaired. And why did they? Because every market kept coming back to them asking for it; because that's what the retailers wanted; because that's what the customers wanted.

In all of the countless old whisky books I've read, the author, and I'm not blaming them, indulges us about the skill of the blender. The ability to nose and create a harmonious blend by the careful balancing of flavours and so on. Now, before I start to receive death threats it is a skill and it is not easy - and there are companies, like Compass Box and Woven, that absolutely do not fit into what I'm about to say; I know I am not alone when I confess that were I to count up my bottles currently open, other than the dozen or so blends pre 1980s and Compass Box, there are about four or five blends on my shelf (Johnnie Walker Black, Chivas Regal 18 and a few single cask blends from IBs – I'm counting those). Malts; single cask or otherwise, number over 200.

My point is those writers from the 1930s to 1990s that have chopped down forest's worth of print in order to proclaim the merit and talent of blenders were a couple bullet points from a complete presentation. Let me put it this way, their blanket appreciation of blends was like coming across a fantastic theatre; Striking, beautifully made, artisanal craftsmanship; architecturally and aesthetically magnificent. They would stop and eulogise over the majesty of this building. But just possibly, a more fulfilling experience would be go to inside that theatre and meet and make friends with all of the characters therein.

Again, before I get struck off any lists (or added to any) I am not suggesting for a moment that blended whisky is defunct. Far from it – in fact, give me the stocks and time and I would be a blender, not a single cask bottler[225]. I guess the point I am really making is that it is no longer sufficient for drinkers to hear a blender discuss how each component is part of a symphony and together they make an incredible, and harmonious noise; as there are enough among us who pay to hear the solos and/or will pay the same attention to a soloist as we would an entire orchestra.

Blends must not however be forgotten, and I for one would like to see more companies in the ilk of Compass Box creating magnificent whiskies from stock we otherwise would really never have the opportunity to taste. Even today, a period in the Scotch whisky industry never seen before, where the selection of malt whiskies on shelves is maybe ten times the amount of blended expressions available, blended whisky still accounts for around 88% of all Scotch whisky bottled and consumed[226]. And, to counter my previous analogy about the theatre, one can look at malt whiskies as individual colours on a painter's palette. Each

225. If course I would do both. We all know that...
226. Maybe even higher for 'consumed' as there seems to be less of these collected than malt whiskies.

bright and vivid in their own right, but when expertly mixed and applied; hey presto, a Monet or a Turner.

But this leads me on to the crux of this chapter. If all of these malts are now available, from the companies that distil them, what is the function and future of independent bottlers? Why do we need them anymore? When I, and many of you reading this, began their journey into Scotch whisky there were plenty of single malt whiskies available but there were plenty unavailable. Currently there are only a small group of malt producing distilleries in Scotland that do not have an official bottling[227]. Are IBs now just a parasitic group, riding the coattails of the marketing of other firms (as per Keiller's comments in Chapter 12)?

There is a marketing overlap - it is impossible to avoid. But I would argue that this overlap is akin to sales of all whisky being impacted should a hero be seen to drink any brand of Scotch in a movie. Or more pertinent perhaps, the sales of all cognac rose off the back of Busta Rhymes' song "Pass The Courvoisier". And let us not forget that had IBs not been bottling named malts when it was the neglected sector, those distilleries re-born (like Bruichladdich and Ardbeg) would not have had the catapulted start they have enjoyed. Much of the heavy lifting and groundwork had been done.

It would be wrong to ignore the pleas and exasperations that distillers have, mostly in private, revealed to me (and others). Whisky bottled outside of the control of the company that owns the brand is a challenge. We have all likely had a bad expression of a whisky from an independent bottler[228] and should you be fairly new to that particular distillery it is possible that the 'bad bottle' could put you off buying more from that distillery – even from the brand owner. That has certainly been the case and there are and have been bottlers that are not the most selective when it comes to what they put in the bottle. Gordon Wright was amazed to find, when he joined Wm Cadenhead's, that no-one was tasting the whiskies prior to bottling. The idea was that the customer can decide on their quality – many of these 'dumpy' bottles are now quite legendary but this is a very flawed business model and Gordon took it upon himself to begin a practice of selective cask choice.

Unlike, therefore, a blending house that can disguise or 'lose' bad casks into the mix, single malt and, especially, single cask bottlers have the potential to negatively highlight a distillery. The converse of this must also be true however. As malts began to be bottled from almost every distillery, some of the offerings from the distillery owners were not, at least for the malt whisky drinker, showing the distillery in its best light. It is not my intention to pick out any brands, but it was clear that the malts were being given just a token effort. Anyone wanting a good example of what that distillery had to offer needed therefore to turn to the

227. Dalmunach, Balmenach & Roseisle.
228. No single bottler gets it right 100% of the time. Creative Whisky was definitely guilty of this.

independent bottler. (You can't call this free advertising though as the original spirit was sold at a profit.)

Independents have also been at the forefront of myth-busting and aiding the industry to un-pick some of the tropes that were ingrained in previous decades. One good example is Macallan. This brand spent decades convincing the customer that whisky had to be of a certain colour and that 'good' whisky should only be matured in ex-Sherry casks. They weren't alone but were certainly at the forefront of the 'Sherry cask' movement. So much so that even the SWA started to believe that there were only a few 'traditional' cask types for the maturation of Scotch whisky[229]. It was therefore a great surprise, not least to a friend of mine that worked in Macallan's warehouses, when the Fine Oak Series was launched in 2004.

This is not a criticism, in fact many malt drinkers were crying out for a non-Sherried Macallan – it is an excellent spirit after all. But without independent bottlers highlighting the fact that Macallan was available in something other than first and second fill ex-Sherry vessels, and remarkable to boot, would this release have ever occurred? And down this lane we can point to a myriad of examples. Finishing, odd ages, batch variation, higher strengths, funky labels, cask or filling details – all pioneered, or at least championed by independent bottlers.

Perhaps then you could argue that when the golden period of independent bottling was over it was time for the sector to move on. Perhaps IBs have overstayed their welcome? Certainly that is the feeling of some of the distillers. You only have to look at the view of most IBs that purchased or built a distillery to see how actively they have prevented other IBs from getting stock of their distilleries (do as I say, not as I do). Some of the newer distillers, the likes of Ardnamurchan, Glasgow and St George's have openly worked with IBs, recognising perhaps, that the IBs can gain access or coverage in certain ways the distillers have not.

I am reminded of Amrut; a single malt whisky made in India. Through a slow process of continually breaking down preconceptions, stereotypes and prejudices this 'world whisky' (a term that is generally given to anything not from one of the major whisk(e)y producing countries[230]) began to get some coverage. This took a much helpful leap when, due to a close association with Robin Tucek of Blackadder Intl, a cask was chosen, bottled by Blackadder Intl and duly submitted to the highly read, if short-lived, Malt Maniac[231] Awards. It won the coveted 'Best Peated Whisky' award (yes, you read that right, an Indian

229. Around 2001 the SWA tried, unsuccessfully, to suggest that ex-wine casks were not traditional. It can be argued that ex-wine casks are the most traditional. And, whilst I'm giving the SWA a hard time, let's not forget that they once tried to insist that previous contents of the cask had no effect on the flavour of the maturing spirit.
230. Scotland, Ireland, Canada, USA & Japan
231. The Malt Maniacs were a group of whisky enthusiasts spanning the globe. Each highly respected for their knowledge of the industry and their depth of knowledge of tasting whisky.

whisky was considered better than all of the other peated Scottish entries).

I am not suggesting that Amrut would have not got to where it is today without this recognition but perhaps Robin's assessment of the stocks available, combined with the reputation his brand had, helped Amrut gain some much welcome recognition and helped break down some of those stereotypes.

Similarly we can look at some of the practices that IBs were either the first or certainly the most vocal to highlight - either *for* (cask finishing or higher strength bottlings) or *against* (colouring and chill-filtering) - that distillers openly adopted when launching new or re-designed malts. But is the argument here really just a system of point scoring? Afterall the arrangement and situation is, I believe, unique. Where else, in any industry, can a third party buy the product of a single factory and use its name openly, and without agreement, from the factory that made it. Add to this the fact that the product has spent years maturing (often in a third party warehouse and third party wood) and could have changed hands multiple times (and possibly cask) before becoming the final product. It is a special case, and to the outsider, a quite baffling *modus operandi*.

Perhaps, here lies the nub of the issue; it is a unique industry and a one of a kind co-existence. It has always tried to be different and played upon its 'specialness'. Its formative years were transformed by incredible people taking an equally remarkable product and presenting it to the masses in a special way. The industry enjoys, repeatedly, retelling how it was born out of a cottage industry and then transformed by remarkable adaptation, skill, belief and marketing of those names that still adorn many of the blends we drink today. Scotch whisky has continually moved and adapted to changing times and tastes and IBs have, at least for the last thirty-forty years, been at the forefront of this movement.

Being smaller, generally speaking, IBs have been able to greater reflect the preferences and personality of their bottlings. From the early days of James MacArthur, Pip Hills (with SMWS), Robin Tucek (Blackadder) and Andrew Symington (Signatory) you could get a glimpse into what they enjoyed drinking (possibly supply was such that they could pick and choose in a much more selective manner). But even when supply was not from the 'golden era' the personalities of the bottlers very much shines through the selections, packaging and company message in a way that distillers are not able to. If you look at the wild and whacky labels from the Thompson Bros, Decadent Drinks and Elixir Distillers you can see a freedom of expression and identity that is hard to match.

Which neatly brings me onto the delicate subject of imitation being the highest form of flattery. It would be hard for any company releasing a series of malts to have not been influenced by the methods, labelling and marketing of the IBs. I've already discussed the practices that were highlighted and either championed or shunned (depending upon whether they were good or bad for the whisky). The first, and some may argue best, large scale malts release was the Manager's Drams[232]. Released initially in 1987 each bottling was hand-picked by the existing distillery manager and the labels were as basic as they come. This is the closest any company has got to what the IBs were doing (hence why the bottles now fetch extremely good money at auction).

But this series, like the Flora & Fauna series (which has no official title so Michael Jackson nicknamed them thus), was never intended for mainstream release. As, like most things that are good, word got out and demand forced their release into the wild. Clearly the biggest nod towards the IB 'style' was the release of the 'Rare Malts Selection' by United Distillers (later Diageo). This range would not have looked out of place had it been launched by Cadenhead's or Gordon & MacPhail and would in turn be an inspiration for brands like The Ultimate and Exclusive Malts.

Other ranges like Chivas Brothers 'Cask Strength Edition' are very much a nod to the simple and data loaded bottlings as per Signatory. Available only at their distilleries, these bottlings are labelled with notes such as 'Bottled straight from the cask' and 'non chill-filtered' and include all of the information that malt whisky enthusiasts want (and distillers had been reluctant to include). Ardbeg's attempts to make their brand feel personalised, fun and friendly is much more aligned with how IBs had been approaching the industry. It is interesting to note how different the marketing and positioning of Glenmorangie is to Ardbeg despite being the same company.

It is also worth considering the incredible variety of artist collaborations on labels and other partnerships to raise the profile of malts (and blends). Was all, or at least, some of this ground broken by small independent bottlers that wanted to have fun with the category?

The level of adaptability and individualism has allowed the IB sector to remain fun, fresh and engaging for the consumer. Scotch whisky, as we saw during the 1980s, was stuck in a bit of rut. Too many executives could not see past case sales of the blended brands they owned. Tinkering with labels and messages was almost *verboten* and the idea that this push for 'singles' and greater transparency was nothing more than a fad was heresy. IBs, as Serge pointed out in his foreword, often cared little for any brand heritage, instead offering the customer something they otherwise could not obtain. And from this grew the whisky geeks; but these geeks were not a fad and turned out to be among the greatest selection of unofficial ambassadors this, or any, industry could ever wish to have.

---

232. Released by United Distillers – now Diageo.

CHAPTER 15

SIGNATORY VINTAGE

"I'm extremely glad I discovered independent bottlers very early on in my whisky discovery. On several occasions I've found the official bottlings from distilleries to be dull or not really to my taste, only to find independent bottlings were excellent. Sometimes a whisky distillery decides to paint only in certain colours, but then independent bottlers are the ones that show you the rest of the spectrum from those same distilleries. To me they're an invaluable part of the industry, not just the well-known names but also very small boutique bottlers or independent shop bottlings, which are often cherry-picking casks that offer something special."

RUBEN LUYTEN
WhiskyNotes.be

Interview with Andrew Symington.

The wind is blowing the rain at near right-angles as I drive my car along the small, pot-hole ridden track towards Edradour Distillery. A Flying Spur Bentley (there is some money in these parts) nearly runs me wide; two large cars are almost too much for this wee road and I begin to wonder how little joy the bus drivers must have greeted this journey with their load of tourists heading towards 'Scotland's Smallest Distillery'[233]. With the equally stunning and considerably more accessible Blair Athol Distillery situated in the heart of Pitlochry, just two miles away, it is odd to think that it was Edradour that the bus loads would seek out to let their passengers buy a £2.50 miniature.

"I got to the point where I hated the buses coming in." Andrew Symington, owner of Signatory Vintage and Edradour Distilleries, would later reveal to me. "It was made worse by the shop having the entrance and exit in the same area – there was no escape. Once you were spotted you were caught, no matter how busy you were."

Andrew kindly invited me up to his distillery as these interviews are far better in person than over a Zoom call. When he first sees me he laughs as it has been well over a decade since we had last seen each other.

"You used to have a full head of hair." He points out. I nodded; there's no reply to be made however as Andrew is still sporting a full frock. To get out of the rain we head into the warehouse where the bottling hall and cased goods, much ready for dispatch, are situated. The warehouse is quiet but activity is ongoing despite the signs and barriers everywhere outside to prevent access and parking (clearly this is a problem at times). As Covid forced the distillery to close its shop Andrew and the team decided that enough was enough and the sense of relief is palpable.

"We have no intention of re-opening the shop or distillery tours." Andrew informs me "There simply isn't enough stock to warrant a shop and we don't have the time or inclination to re-start the Visitors Centre again for a while. If, or when we do, it will be in a different format."

I first met Andrew whilst working for Whisky Magazine. We both mention a few names, now some twenty years on, a couple are no longer with us.

"I remember you then." Andrew says laughing. "At the first Whisky Live in London. You spent an age at my stand asking lots of questions. I remember Damian Riley-Smith [owner of Whisky magazine] coming up to me after you left and said 'He spent a lot of time at your stand, what was he up to?' I just said you were keen to learn."

233. It used to be.

Picture courtesy of Photographer Guus Pauka and Marcel van Gils

I was keen. Signatory and what Andrew *did*, along with his no-nonsense approach to the industry really struck me. At a time when the industry was desperately trying to cling on to some part of its 'tartan and tweed' history Andrew's direct approach was not only a breath of fresh air, but also in line with what the new breed of malt whisky drinker wanted. I am fascinated by his story; his mixing with people like Brian Morrison (Morrison Bowmore Distillers), Peter Russell (owner of Ian MacLeod Distillers) and Brian Ivory (of Edrington), the 'old boys network' as Andrew calls it, who would get together for lunches and discuss the industry.

"They would bring these amazing whiskies with them for each other to try and naturally it piqued my interest. Eventually it was arranged that some would be bottled for the hotel and the Prestonfield Whisky brand was born."

These first few casks were bought from and organised by Morrison Bowmore but very quickly it became apparent that this bit of 'fun' was becoming a real business.

"When I started the Prestonfield Whisky bottlings the hotel were initially behind the project. But when I started buying packaging and boxes and so on and bills were getting up to £100,000, they began to realise that this was quite alien to their business of being a hotel and decided it was not really for them. They had no issue with me continuing the Prestonfield range and using the name. All remaining stock was sold off and then I bought my own casks and started Signatory – I've still got the Prestonfield Whisky name; the history attached to that is our history."

Signatory is the second largest independent bottler in the Scotch whisky industry and has held that position for some time. When you consider that Andrew was just 23 years old when he started bottling whiskies for Prestonfield and 25 when he began Signatory it is one of the myriad of success stories that gets added to the Scotch whisky archives. It is also worth remembering that in 1988, as Andrew was creating Signatory, the Six Classic Malts were launched by Diageo. Malts were still a very 'new' thing.

Through contacts made at Prestonfield, Signatory began its bottling program using a small office in the back of an existing bond owned by William Muir & Co Ltd (of Leith). Casks on occasion could be stored there and Andrew would bottle entire casks in miniatures using a two head filler and hand capping machine.

"I still have these old machines. Who knows, maybe we can have a museum for all of this stuff one day."

A few years in this small office and Andrew began applying to Customs & Excise for his own bonded warehouse.

"We were being knocked back by Customs & Excise, several times in fact, but by chance I was in Spain when the Trade Secretary John Gummer (now

Lord Deben) was in attendance. In front of a large entourage he said to me something along the lines of:

"Oh, Scotch whisky, you boys are doing well at the moment."

To which I replied: "Well, actually I'm having trouble with Customs & Excise granting me a bond. John told me to give his Secretary my business card and within two weeks we had full permission – automatically all the problems magically disappeared. The quantity levels, the thresholds that you had to jump through to get permission, suddenly vanished. John Gummer was annoyed that Customs was holding back business.[234]"

This allowed Signatory to move to a new site on Newhaven Road just outside of Leith. The company built up excellent partnerships in Germany and France, countries that are still big markets. Andrew's son, Andrew Jr joins us for part of the tour; at 18 years of age he is learning the business and shows an eagerness belying his age.

"It was tough." Andrew says nodding towards his son. "For much of his youth I wasn't around. Building up Signatory and buying Edradour took years of hard work and I was absent through just being busy. Often I would be working on the holidays, even Christmas day sometimes."

Andrew Jr nods but in a knowing agreement. His father's efforts are steeped in everything around us.

"Edradour was not your first choice for a distillery?" I asked.

"No." Andrew says, picking up an errant bottle lying on a cask. "The first distillery we tried to buy was the old Caledonian grain distillery near the station at Haymarket. Most of the site had been sold for housing bar the main structure and tower, but it was too late to utilise the building as most of the land was about to be sold, the deal really being done. We then considered Ardbeg, but that was a journey that was never going to happen. We had a great trip to scout the distillery with Iain Henderson (manager of Laphroaig at the time). He took me to the site and basically said 'the best thing you could do is bulldoze the entire thing and start again'. The process to tender was by auction with sealed bids – a Dutch guy called Hans Fontaine was running it and I said 'give me a clue on price Hans'. I had built up quite a rapport with him as he was intrigued how a little guy like me was going to get anywhere near buying Ardbeg. Hans suggested the bid would need to be over £5 million so we bid £5.2 [Glenmorangie bought Ardbeg in 1997 for £7 million]. I didn't know how we were going to do it, or where the additional money for renovations would have come from. Glenmorangie had the money to come in and completely renovate so probably for the best I lost the bid."

This led Signatory to approach Chivas about buying a distillery. Although the purchase came with incredible access to stock, something that would propel Signatory's inventory, the distillery came with its own issues[235].

"When we bought Edradour in 2002, twenty years ago, we had problems with some of the stock being soapy. This was due to the previous distilling team often using domestic soap in the distillation process[236]. Chivas were very good about swapping some of the stock but even so it took years of careful cask management until our own distillate had eradicated the problem."

As we head around the warehouse I marvel at the odd boxes stored at the top of the pallet racking. Three butts surrounded by empty bottles is the beginnings of possibly the greatest, limited run blends ever. Andrew pulls out a half empty bottle – 'Linlithgow[237] 1970' – a quick sip reveals juicy fruits and sweet oak – whisky from a bygone time.

"These are all of the leftovers from the casks down the years. There's four pallets of the stuff and we are blending by age."

I last visited Edradour when Chivas owned it and marvel at the transformation by Andrew in the last twenty years. One of the first things Andrew did was hire Iain Henderson and ask him to make a peated version. This spirit, which first came off the stills in 2003 was called Ballechin and has been a huge success for the company. Edradour Two, an exact replica, was built in 2018 and is directly opposite the original distillery. Unlike the original distillery the plant is well laid out and can be viewed at nearly every angle.

"Everything possible has been replicated to the last detail; really we have just increased the capacity."

I study the decorated mash tun.

"Made to exactly the same specification as the original mash tun, even to the paint – the only difference is that this one is stainless steel and not cast iron. The stills, which are hand riveted, are exactly the same. In fact we had to get the cooper, who had just retired, to come back in to do the riveting as he was the only one who could do it."

True to Andrew's word, there is even a Morton Refrigerator cooling the worts. As the oldest distillate is only four years old we shall have to wait and see if the industry has another 'Caperdonich or Linkwood[238].

"When I started it was possible to buy casks from almost every distillery." Andrew states. We are sat in his now disused visitor centre; on three walls are the history and memorabilia from Edradour's near two hundred years

---

235. Not least, 10 days after receiving the keys floods caused over £300,000 worth of damage.
236. It is common practice to use a special detergent to help prevent the Wash from boiling over the still. If not monitored however, this will still occur causing soapiness to enter into the spirit. Domestic soap is not commonly used or recommended...
237. Otherwise known as St Magdalene
238. Examples of when the industry built identical distilleries adjacent to existing distilleries only to find the spirit markedly different. Caperdonich Distillery was originally called Glen Grant No 2.

of history[239]. "This was still the time when the great blending houses within companies had their own management teams. Now, however the market has radically changed. If you are unable to offer aged whisky for trading then there is really nothing much available. Signatory is set up for many years to come and who knows how the market will change in the future, but I doubt we will ever see it return to how it used to be.

"We are maturing over 35,000 casks and have plans to build another distillery, again matching the equipment here exactly, which we hope will be in the Freyburg area of Germany."

It is impossible to prevent the colour of my cheeks from turning a little green. Andrew and I have already discussed the sale of Creative Whisky and he completely understands my reasons of diminishing stock. It is such a strange and unique industry but like all industries if your stock is going out faster than it can come in the light at the end of the tunnel gets dimmer with each shipment.

"Yes, I understand. As I said - you can't trade if you don't have good stocks to trade with. We are cutting back supply to those bottlers that use our stock (and our name on the label). We just found this was competing with our own products. China has been a big boost to our sales and we could supply them more so there is no need for us to supply casks with our name to others."

As there's not much for me to add here. Andrew changes the subject.

"Ah." He says pointing to a row of butts. "These are those 1991 Edradour butts that are soapy.[240]"

I mention how markedly different Edradour is now to when I first started drinking it[241].

"I always knew it would be a challenge to turn it around, but it was a good challenge."

And really that's what separates Andrew from the rest; a challenge to him is always worth overcoming. There were countless others that could have realised the potential of single cask, single malt whisky but Andrew was a pioneer and frankly peerless. His drive and commitment have kept him growing, sometimes at a frightening pace but sometimes just with rebuilding a brand. I do not think it an overstatement to suggest that all who came afterwards owe a debt of gratitude to the ground broken by Andrew. Signatory was the first, the best and the largest of the new wave of independent bottlers.

---

239. Established in 1825
240. Andrew informs me that there is a process of filtration that will remove this from the whisky but will more or less strip it of all colour too.
241. It is now a highly sought after, multi-award winning whisky.

CHAPTER 16

The Future

"In the 1990s - when I became aware of whisky - it appeared to me that much of the excitement came from independent bottlers; they were enthusiastically releasing non chill-filtered, uncoloured, natural strength, single cask whiskies - the real deal it seemed to me - while at the time some distillers tended to focus on a standard range of predictable age statements at 40%."

MARCIN MILLER
Spirits Entrepreneur

When I suggested to several of the independent bottlers featured in this book that my original title was 'Independent Scotch – The Fall & Rise of the Independent Bottlers' many of them suggested the subtitle should be 'The Fall, Rise & Fall of the Independent Bottlers' such was their feeling regarding the future for the sector. One only has to read the personal accounts in the list at the end of this book to know that there is an overly pessimistic view towards the continuation of independent bottling. And who am I to argue having sold out due to the constraints and costs of re-supply?

But, as Serge observes in his Foreword, haven't we heard all of this before? Weren't the distillers proclaiming the end of 'singles' as early as the 1970s and again in the 1980s. Weren't some of the early bottlers proclaiming the end of the golden era as early as the 1990s? Well, yes and no and maybe. This industry is so cyclical that who can tell what the future holds? When Andrew Usher created his first brand of O.V.G[242] in the mid 19th Century did he or the industry even acknowledge that he was an 'independent bottler'? Distilleries were mostly independent at that time and none survived by selling a single brand.

Rather than try and pretend I, and others, can foretell the future, I shall instead discuss what the future could mean without independent bottlers. And in so doing add a little more to what I wrote in Chapter 14.

In November 2022 I attended two festivals; one in the north-east of England and the other in Rotterdam, in the Netherlands. The first was wholly devoted to independent Scotch whisky companies and the latter was about 80% independents the rest being 'official' bottlings. 'So what' you might say - some festivals are almost exclusively official bottlings (as is Travel Retail these days).

It is still the case that many of the more interesting stands at a whisky festival are those from the independent bottlers. Speaking to you, the converted and educated whisky drinker, we know all too well what some of the larger and more established distillers are pouring. I am reminded of attending a Whisky Live in Glasgow a number of years ago where the Laphroaig[243] stand had the 10 year old and Quarter Cask open for pouring. On the stand behind the representative was a bottle of the newly re-released 15 year old. Upon asking to try that I was informed that it was just for show. I explained that I already owned both the 10 year old and the Quarter Cask - protestations that fell on deaf ears. Thankfully Hunter Laing had an exceptional 14 year old Laphroaig bottling on their stand – independent bottlers to the rescue again.

Would the industry really miss this tiny, drop in the ocean? Wouldn't it just carry on regardless without it?

Simply put, yes of course it would continue. Just as the industry carried on when most single malts were available only from independent bottlers. Just

242. Old Vatted Glenlivet.
243. One of my top ten whiskies – I'm drinking it as I type this.

as it has whilst selling bulk Scotch to the Japanese (and other markets) for admixing to create their own market blends. Just as it did when it openly sold fillings to brokers, investors and the general public. The difference now is the interest; the public demand, desire and attention. Never, in its possible 400 year history, has Scotch whisky (and all whisky) had such a level of attention, scrutiny and desire for transparency.

When the first crofters lifted that clear, hot and rather alcoholic glass of Uisge Beatha[244] to their friends to try, not one of them ever asked what their fermentation times were or whether a longer worm-tub made a difference. That level of inane[245] scrutiny and 'geekiness' from the public would not really come about until the 1990s (and became intense much later – and really only by some Belgians and many Germans[246]). Part of the great beauty, mystery and risk of this incredible product is that no-one, and I really mean absolutely no-one, knows what a whisky will really be like until it has been distilled a few seasons and matured in a few different types of cask for a number of years.

And this is really, deep down, what makes this drink so special – no-one knows what will happen, years from the moment that clear spirit hits the inside of the wooden cask. The modern whisky drinker, unlike all that we saw the industry resist during the 1980s and 1990s, wants variation, novelty, nuance and insight. *Vive la différence* Serge would likely say. At the forefront of this movement is the independent whisky company.

The recent and remarkable craze of independent distilleries, the likes of which the industry hasn't seen for over one hundred years, is the new difference. Arran, whose trailblazing and quite colourful story has its own book[247], showed the whisky industry it could be done[248] - and even Harold Currie, the man behind the distillery, believed it would predominantly survive supplying spirit to blenders. On Arran's heels comes a long and quite prestigious line of independent distilleries; Daftmill, Kilchoman, Wolfburn, Ballindalloch, Kingsbarns, Ardnamurchan, Annandale and many, many more. Some distilleries have been bought from the large conglomerates and returned to private ownership; Edradour and Benromach we have already mentioned but also Bladnoch, Glenallachie and Tormore.

This new independent sector of the industry are easily the most exciting and ground-breaking pioneers. Challenging old myths, tropes and misgivings, these new companies have succeeded where larger distillers would not have thought possible. Some like Daftmill and Ballindalloch, no doubt without

244. 'Clearic', 'new-make', 'makes-you-go-blind', 'hairs on the chest', 'hairs off the head' etc
245. Of course this is not silly, it is very, very, very serious.
246. I'm joking. Some Belgians, and all Germans.
247. Written and published by Neil Wilson.
248. The eagle-eyed will note I have ignored Speyside Distillery. It has only really been a distiller of merit in the last ten years or so.

the financial restraints of others, have sat back and waited until they felt their whisky was just right. Others have, in my opinion, done themselves no favours by trying to sell spirit (often with whacky names or naïve ambitions that it makes a good mixer), but most have shown an incredible depth of flavour and style with whisky once deemed too young.

Helping this is a customer base that is educated, understanding of the financial constraints involved with running independent companies also accepting of modern day practices with regards to a single distillery offering several different expressions. These new independent distilleries are all bottling at 46% or above. None colour their whisky. None rely on a single type of cask. None rely on a single age statement. Most offer cask strength versions. Most offer single cask expressions; market specific bottlings; packaging and labelling that tells the customer what they want to know. The reps of these new independent distilleries are often on the younger side; full of passion, knowledge and eager to engage.

It's as if they watched what a generation of independent bottlers were doing and thought 'hey, that seems to really appeal to the customer'. Perhaps the independent bottler was preparing the way – laying the foundations if you will – for these new independent distilleries to have a footing for future success.

I believe I can even take this a step further. Not only have we seen the resurgence of small independent distilleries, we are also witnessing a change in the large conglomerates attitude to malt whisky drinkers. Remember if you will my story about the Diageo marketing person that informed me they were a blending company? Well not only is that not true anymore (it wasn't really true then either), Diageo is now committed to the revival of two of the most iconic distilleries that independent bottlers undoubtedly shone a light on (and kept alive). Without independent bottlers getting their hands on Port Ellen[249] whisky its name would have slipped away as quietly as Glenlochy did. Brora, often ridiculed by blenders for making such an inconsistent malt (so inconsistent they rebuilt the entire distillery), is now reborn, not because Johnnie Walker Red or J&B Rare need it for their recipes, but because the malt whisky drinker, now a big force in the buying public, adored it.

Ardbeg, revived in 1998, did so because IBs were bottling some iconic releases. Bruichladdich would have been forgotten, other than Illeach's (Bruichladdich was a firm favourite of the Islander's), had it not been for the odd IB bottling. Rosebank, at the time of writing, nearly completed by Ian MacLeod Distillers, revived not because Ian MacLeod are missing Lowland whisky in their blends, but because it became an iconic IB bottling. And

---

249. And here we have to thank the Monopolies & Mergers Commission who, inadvertently, forced the break-up of part of Diageo and with the break-up a huge parcel of Port Ellen found its way into the hands of Independent Bottlers. Sadly not into my hands.

beyond this we see a willingness, not evident as little as maybe five or ten years ago, to pander to the malt drinker. Single cask bottlings, market exclusives, enormous variations in cask types, finishes, strengths, ages and a transparency in packaging and process that is frankly completely refreshing.

Would any of this have happened without the likes of Adelphi, Wm Cadenhead's, Douglas Laing and perhaps most significantly Signatory? And let's not pretend that it has all been plain-sailing for these companies. The fervour and rapid sales of single cask bottlings that we see today is a very modern phenomenon. I could fill an entire book with stories on just how tough it was to sell whisky ten, twenty and (albeit not my stories) thirty years ago. In researching this book I have marvelled at the continual astonishment by retailers, journalists and commentators over the prices that were being bandied about for new bottlings. When I worked for Cadenhead's the shops used to have a separate blackboard *just* for the closed distilleries; St Magdalene, Littlemill, Port Ellen, Dallas Dhu, Banff, Coleburn, Glen Albyn etc. An entire blackboard – and they were a hard sell!

I recall the satisfaction in convincing a couple of English tourists that rather than each buy a bottle of some run-of-the-mill 10 year old (that they could likely find in Oddbins in England) they should pool their money, with a few quid more and get a 1967 Glenfarclas-Glenlivet that I had recently selected. It was about £70. Reluctantly, and only after having sampled it, they agreed. I recall that in 2000 Adelphi were selling a 1977 Highland Park for £50 – I bought one off of Jamie Walker (for a bit less) as it was not flying out the door. Even when I ran Creative Whisky Co I remember being at a whisky festival in London with a recently bottled four year old peated Bunnahabhain[250]. I don't think I sold a bottle during the festival and continually had to explain why my £35 bottling was more expensive than the Bunnahabhain 12 year old standard bottling at around £25 per bottle. IBs had to persevere, educate and stick to their convictions[251]. But, arguably, this perseverance has paid dividends to the industry.

So to speculate on the future, we have to encapsulate the past. This incredible industry that for too many years ignored the potential of its own produce is now reaping the benefits of a period of overproduction that allowed independent bottlers to flourish. Does that mean independent bottlers will continue; almost certainly, but I am just as certain that they will have to adapt to market conditions. Some simply won't survive – that's the natural order of things. Some of the new breed of independent distilleries will not survive; again history of the market has proved this to be the case.

Which leads me on to the question I have least wanted to tackle with the

---

250. This was and remained the youngest whisky I ever bottled.
251. I'm going to acknowledge here that they also had to sell what they had. One way or the other.

writing of this book. It has been easy to tell my little story, even easier to ask others to write theirs, and it has been enjoyable and revealing researching the modern history that has led the industry to where it is. But how does the industry carry on? Prices of mature stocks have never been higher. Overall demand from companies within and without the industry has never been greater. The question must now return: "Why would a distilling enterprise sell its produce to independent companies?" And frankly, this is the 'what is the future of the independent bottling industry' question in a nutshell.

Realising the enormous quantities now being produced and lack of evidence that future growth will match this stock piling – coupled with the fact that the world is entering into recession (and the cost of living will be squeezed for millions of families), distillers are, for the most part, not starved of cash or investment and currently do not need to change their course. There are few signs indicating closures, layoffs or a sudden need for cashflow. I feel a little like a famous UK weather forecaster called Michael Fish who, days before one of the largest storms to hit the islands, proclaimed 'there is no storm'. Could the scenario that faced the industry in the 1970s, 1980s and 1990s return whereby distillers are forced to unload large quantities of stock? Let's not forget that the industry still relies on the mass sale of bulk blends to prop up the deluxe, and more profitable sector of the industry.

The most recent figures[252] indicate that consumption is around 84% of production and the industry is sitting on enough stock to last ten or eleven years. This is around 5 billion litres of alcohol (not forgetting that maturing stocks hit the 1 billion litres of alcohol mark in 1963/64 – consumption as a percentage of production then was around 45%). Throughout the post war period the industry has maintained a stock to consumption ratio of around 7-10% (dipping as low as 6% in 1986 and around 10% now which is the highest).

Will these conditions return the IB sector into a near free hand in offering single malts to the market? I sincerely doubt it. We no longer have the brokers providing this link and I believe even if we are on the verge of another 'Whisky Loch' the distillers will fight tooth and nail to prevent masses of their stock suddenly being dumped into the open market. Can there then be a future for the distiller and independent company to work hand in hand. Has Compass Box provided the industry with the business model? Will brands like Vintage Malt Whisky Company's 'Finlaggan', Douglas Laing's 'Big Peat' and North Star's 'Vega' range be the link? Quite possibly. We are maybe a decade away from really seeing what will happen, such is the speed of change in this industry, but IBs, being the flexible and mercurial beasts they are will be planning for this. To really allow their survival though, those that hold

252. *Scotch Whisky Industry Review* 2020

the power over supply will need to be open to a greater dialogue. As Angus MacRaild from Decadent Drinks puts it:

> "Independent bottlers should exist and they serve a clearly defined market and by and large do a good job. The image of them as 'parasitic' and opportunistic is, in my experience, false. The majority of them exist to serve, and in response to, genuine whisky geekery and enthusiasm. They aren't charlatans out to make a quick buck off the back of some vast distilling company's hard work; those that do attempt that approach tend to disappear as soon as they realise what hard work it really is."

Whatever happens I am confident that the 'independent' sector and spirit to this industry will always exist. It was around at the beginning, it made the first brands, opened the first markets and it was this spirit of adventure and of breaking down barriers to markets that brought Scotch, be it blended or single malt[253], to the world.

---

253. And all of the other variations.

INDEPENDENT BOTTLERS

Compiled by Thijs Klaverstijn & David Stirk

This list is by no means exhaustive. There are numerous companies that offer single cask bottlings and many more that have bottled under their own label. To list all of these would require a continually updatable database and as Whiskybase.com has just such an incomparable system in place, printing the entire list of brands would be simply pure theft from their site. These are many of the notable independent bottlers either in their own words or written and researched by David or Thijs.

Acorn

Founder Seishi Tsuta began his drinks career working for Oddbins in London during the late 1970s and early 1980s. After a decade-long stint with a Tokyo wine and whisky specialist, Tsuta branched out on his own in 1996 and started his independent label, Acorn. Based in Sakado City, Saitama, he focuses on single cask whiskies. Early bottlings under Tsuta's Acorn Natural Malt label included Lagavulin 1984, Port Ellen 1982 and Glenlivet 1972. Today Acorn exports to Australia, Taiwan and Europe (among others). Tsuta also opened the Whisky Plus store in Tokyo in 2014.

A D Rattray

www.adrattray.com

Originally called A Dewar Rattray, this was a revival of a firm that goes back to the mid-19th Century. The history of the Morrisons is a long and varied one intertwined with brokering, bottling and distilling Scotch whisky. Stanley and Brian Morrison inherited the firm Morrison Bowmore Distillers Ltd from their father Stanley P Morrison in 1971. Stanley P Morrison had been an incredibly successful broker of Scotch whisky in the '60s, and had bought Bowmore Distillery (1963), The Scottish Trading Co (1967) and Glen Garioch (1970). In 1984 the Morrison brothers added James Sword & Co (a blending firm) and Auchentoshan Distillery to their portfolio.

In 1989 the Japanese firm Suntory bought a 35% stake in Morrison Bowmore Distillers Ltd. A Dewar Rattray, a blending company that had originally been established in 1868, was bought from a family member in 1993. A year later Suntory completed their takeover of Morrison Bowmore Distillers (though they then merged with the American company Beam in 2014 to create Beam-Suntory).

The firm of A D Rattray (as it is now called) remained with Stanley 'Tim' Morrison and began operating as an independent bottler with the launch of Stronachie Single Malt. Two years later the first of their single cask bottlings were launched. In 2011 they opened the A D Rattray experience, a shop in Kirkoswald, Ayrshire and six years later they returned to distilling with the impressive Clydeside Distillery in Glasgow.

Ardnamurchan Distillery

Adelphi Distillery Co Ltd

www.adelphidistillery.com

With a name like J. Walker it is maybe difficult to not have an association with Scotch whisky. But Jamie Walker, the creator of Adelphi Distillery Co is not from the Johnnie Walker stable of whisky, but rather the A. Walker & Co that took ownership of the Adelphi Distillery in Glasgow in the 1870s. Archibald Walker's great grandson, Jamie Walker, started the independent bottling firm of Adelphi to explore further single cask bottlings.

Presentation was purposely simplified with infuriatingly small text. The idea was to let the whisky do the talking – no packaging and filigree to get in the way. Jamie always looked for the fun in what he did and brought a sense of humour to the independent bottling world.

Alex Bruce: "I began my career working in fine wine in Scotland, initially for Justerini and Brooks and then running a franchise for Friarwood. In addition to the vast stock portfolio of parent company, Diageo, when I was at J&B, I always looked forward to visits to our office by Jamie Walker, the then owner of Adelphi. He would invariably be accompanied by a large box of single cask samples which offered a whole new dimension in flavour and rarity. He was therefore a go to supplier when we opened a retail shop for Friarwood in 2003.

"However, as it happened, when I contacted him to ask for a stock list, he replied that he had just sold Adelphi to two West Coast businessmen, Keith Falconer and Donald Houston. Subsequent calls and meetings with the new owners ended up in me accepting their offer to take on the running of the business. Adelphi was undoubtedly a niche IB in those days. I remember taking on about four or five casks and an assortment of bottled whiskies, but it was exciting times. We had an almost inexhaustible supply of real gems from the 1970s-1990s and despite many just not being suitable for single cask bottling, I quickly built up our stock with the help of mentor Charles MacLean.

"By 2007 it was becoming obvious that demand for IB whiskies was in full flow, and I began to witness some early supply constraints. We began the plans for our own distillery, and Ardnamurchan Distillery was born.

"Over the years we have grown the Adelphi business from niche IB to distiller and our export from three countries to thirty-five, all of which was beyond our early expectations or plans but, like many others in our industry, we have had to adapt. Personally, even though the heady days of multiple casks of Springbank, Ardbeg and sherried Macallan at prices that we (and our clients) could enjoy are very much over, I truly believe that the new era of Single Malt focussed distiller is every bit as exciting, and provides for a consistency of quality and variety of flavour going forward that we could never have imagined back in 2004.

"I feel incredibly lucky to have been given the opportunity to grow a business in the industry that I had always wanted to be part of. I also don't believe that anyone could have predicted quite how the industry would change in the first two decades of this century - huge global growth in awareness and demand for Single Malt whisky coupled with the inevitable tightening of supply, and the unprecedented growth of new distilleries.

"In terms of Adelphi as an IB, the challenges have simply been around continued supply of bulk stock that we are proud to put in a bottle. We have managed to grow the company to a decent level and maintain that and, now with our own maturing stocks of Ardnamurchan, have a much welcomed new stability, but will certainly never be complacent. As the company has grown we have had the inevitable challenges of keeping the infrastructure up to speed, building our own warehouse for bottling and logistics in 2010 and keeping pace with a suitably dynamic team that can cope.

"Ardnamurchan is much the same, just on a different scale. Not just the design and build of a greenfield distillery in a very remote part of the country but, now eight and a bit years on, with seven warehouses almost full, a growing operational team, a fully-functioning visitor centre and shop and an ever-changing supply chain keeping us on our toes.

"One of the aspects that I am really proud of is the creation of a new and sustainable circular economy in such a remote place. The distillery has provided added value in several important areas on the peninsula: long term employment that is already allowing young families to remain and build a future there, locally produced and utilised animal feed, new levels of tourism and an extended season, and the opportunity to trial and drive environmentally sound production methods. All of the above and, subjectively, a tasty whisky too.

"I can recall Jamie's late 1970's Ardbeg bottlings being sensational, as were his heavily sherried Glen Grants and the odd butt of Springbank thrown in for good measure. In my time, inheriting the majority of the 2003 bottling of 'The Whisky That Cannot be Named 1953' got us off to a decent start, and it has been followed by a very decent 1976 Macallan, two butts of 1965 Lochside Single Blend, more Springbanks and very recently a beautiful 36yr old Mortlach[254].

"I have also really enjoyed progressing our fusion whisky series, blending Scotch with international distilleries and, in particular the first Glover malt whisky which contained some very special old Scotch whisky married with the legendary Hanyu from Japan."

Artful Dodger
www.artfuldodgerwhisky.com

Sebastian Woolf: "Woolf Drinks Ltd was established in 2012 to provide rare wines, champagne and spirits to merchants around the world. I entered the bottling business in around 2014 as a customer asked for me to seek out a cask of Glenglassaugh. I found one through my contacts and it turned out to be a 40 year old fully matured in an ex-Sherry cask. Given the trusting nature of our business I agreed to buy on their behalf and committed funds. As it transpired the customer chose not to buy the cask. I was left with little to no cashflow and a cask of Glenglassaugh I didn't know what to do with. Running parallel to this I was becoming more frustrated with the wine industry. I found that while the Chateau can produce excellent wines, they had no idea how to appeal to a new generation of drinkers and as such at each en-primeur in Bordeaux that I attended (along with tastings in London), I noticed the age of the consumers were all knocking on heaven's door.

"The appeal of Scotch was that I could take a product which has been expertly created and imagine a brand that would entice new drinkers to the category. The traditional view of Scotch by most consumers was that of tartan, bagpipes and cigars. New drinkers wanted to be excited by something different. Back to the cask of Glenglassaugh - I chose to work with a design company

---

254. I am nodding my head vigorously. This is an amazing dram.

Artful Dodger whiskies bottled for their Cut Your Wolf Loose Bar

called Stranger and Stranger for this and called it 'The Hunter'. We released the bottles at RRP of £750 at the premium end of the market and realised that consumers loved the design and packaging and of course the liquid.

"I then worked on another brand idea, Artful Dodger Whisky. Bottled in 50cl bottles allowing more of different whisky styles to be purchased by customers for more reasonable prices. I had access to whisky stocks through contacts made and realized early on that in order to keep the bottlings going any profits made on anything the business did should go straight back into cask whisky stocks. I did not want to be a bottler who worked on a 'single cask to bottle' model nor one who committed cash to buying five to ten casks and then hoping the brand would sell when in bottle. I had to make sure the stock was right and that we had the diversity to work with. Any stocks we didn't want we could place with other independent bottlers making sure the liquid ended up in glass. I am very meticulous in the way I wanted the bottles to look. Corks from Portugal, Glass from Spain and labels made in Italy. BREXIT screwed up everything overnight. Buying all these elements beforehand was tough to plan but now it's a logistical and costly nightmare.

"I would not look to enter the market now given the cost of liquid and limitations on warehousing and bottling. When starting out eight years ago on the journey most of the smaller warehouses were able to accommodate new brands for bottling. You could plan releases effectively and not worry about any mishaps causing delays as they could be easily remedied. Now with the cost of liquid being so high that bottling the product makes it impossible, the cost of dry goods (glass, corks, boxes, labels etc) going up daily and storage/ bottling halls at a premium, it makes no sense. I see a new indie bottling company appear each week. I have no issue with this as long as the RRP of their bottles is competitive in the market. Most of the time they are not and in fact might just have an adverse effect on the indie market as a whole giving customers a negative view on the cost/price of a bottle from an indie bottler.

"Above all IBs are here to help promote Scotch whisky. I wanted to showcase what could be done in a sexier way. I wanted to open up the category to new consumers and play a small part in the change which was long overdue. Unfortunately, I think the success of smaller independent bottlers could well lead to their downfall. I don't see it as a coincidence that I was able to buy stocks from distilleries like Clynelish, Laphroaig and Glenrothes but to name a few, and now apparently due to 'global demand' the stocks are allocated to in-house projects. I think it's more that the IB has done such a good job of promoting the distilleries that larger corporations now think they can do it in-house without our help. I think they are wrong and in the next three to six years we will see a switch back as the corporations will have too much whisky stock and will need it to go somewhere."

Alistair Walker Whisky

www.alistairwalker.com

A work placement at Burn Stewart Distillers in 1997, where his dad was Managing Director, got Alistair into the whisky industry.

"I only joined the whisky industry to get some work experience on my CV but I never left."

Six years later Burn Stewart was sold and both Walkers left as dad, Billy, acquired and set up The Benriach Distillery Co in 2004 and Alistair again worked under him. Twelve years later and yet another sale saw Alistair at a crossroads. Billy would go on to buy and establish Glenallachie Distillery but Alistair decided it was time to strike out on his own.

"I wanted to stay in the whisky business, but this time entirely under my own steam. Buying or building a distillery are both cost-prohibitive so independent bottling seemed like the obvious fit.

"I established the Alistair Walker Whisky Co in 2018 and spent the next twelve months securing suitable stock. In June 2019 I launched the first batch which was an ambitious nine casks – the first of which was a 26 year old Glen Keith – this is still one of my favourite drams from everything I have released."

Now nearing his one hundredth cask, Alistair's 'Infrequent Flyers' series have quickly become an established and respected brand in a sea of new companies.

"I have a fairly simple business model being a one-man band; if the whisky doesn't impress me, I don't bottle it. I have no targets to meet so have the luxury of time to allow casks and re-racks to mature to their full potential."

Berry Bros & Rudd
www.bbr.com

A name perhaps more synonymous with fine wines and champagnes, Berry Bros & Rudd's contribution to the whisky world should not be overlooked. Established sometime in the 1690s near the palace of St. James in one of London's most exclusive parts, the wine merchant had a dalliance with bottling pure malts, blends and the odd 'single' before launching the 'lighter' styled Cutty Sark blend. The label was notable for its simple yet appealing label featuring the famous old clipper 'Cutty Sark' which had just retired and also for the use of 'Scots' whisky rather than 'Scotch'. The artist, James McBey, like many Scots, preferring the correct adjective to the more common one.

Picture courtesy of Photographer Guus Pauka and Marcel van Gils

Robertson's, a large blending firm in Glasgow, bottled the blend for Berry's and post prohibition in the US saw substantial growth. By the mid 50s however, the success of Cutty Sark was causing Robertson & Baxter Co (the company by now had reverted to its original name) supply problems. Over half of R&Bs output was going to Cutty Sark, so much that R&B were having supply issues to their other, and sometimes, older customers. In 1956 an agreement was reached and R&B became the sole suppliers of the blend.

Since then the association has benefited both parties. In 1961 Cutty Sark was the first blend to break the one million case barrier to the US and in 1962 the brand was released in the UK. The partnership ended in 2010 when Edrington bought from Berry's their shares in Cutty Sark and then Glenrothes in 2017.

Much of the more recent Independent Bottlings came about when Doug McIvor joined Berry's in 2000 and the development of the company as an independent bottler grew from there.

Interview with Doug McIvor: The first time I met Doug he was general manager of the whisky shop Milroy's. As a young whisky drinker, No 3 Greek Street, better known as Milroy's of Soho[255], was a must visit when in London. I had already read Wallace Milroy's "Malt Whisky Almanac" – the very first book

255. And to those older than me, Soho Wine Market.

that catalogued available malt whisky – and had heard from everyone and anyone that this shop was a mecca for people like me. Doug sold me a bottle of Ledaig – I find it remarkable that I can still recall what I bought (though cannot remember what it tasted like). This was around the late 1990s and Doug was already a renowned whisky expert from his time working with John "Jack" and Wallace Milroy.

"The job at Milroy's was just by chance. I had been working in the wine industry, retail and wholesale, and as was moving back into London noticed an ad for a wine and spirits merchant with a W1[256] address. It took several months for Jack to stop asking who the new guy was. The shop when I joined was about 50:50 wine and whisky but it was quickly becoming *the* place for anyone wanting a good bottle of whisky."

Jack Milroy was forced into selling Milroy's in 1993 but stayed on as General Manager until eventually leaving and Doug took his position. The new owner, John Scott, was preparing the business to simply move it on and Doug sensing his days could be numbered looked for another job. This led Doug and the logistics & export manager, Bridget Arthur, to join a soon to be opened store that Wallace Milroy had been a consultant advisor.

The new store was situated on the corner of Jermyn Street and St James's Street in Mayfair, London. Up there with the most expensive and exclusive addresses in the world, this shop was a converted bank complete with vaults and three floors. Working for Whisky Magazine at the time I was invited to the opening along with Michael Jackson who was to cut the ribbon so to speak. I had met Doug before the opening and had been privy to the ongoing work; the scope of which was staggering with bespoke shelving and cranes brought in to remove parts of the interior. There was not going to be a swankier whisky shop anywhere in the world. The opening night was a huge success and anyone in the whisky industry that could make it was there. Michael Jackson said a few words to officially open the store and at one point motioned over to the three owners who were standing together in a corner. As soon as the room had got their first look at the three owners of the shop, all felt that something was a bit fishy with this enterprise.

A few months later I called in to see Doug and his new place of work. The shop was stunning but remarkably poorly stocked. Despite the pretence of being *the* whisky shop bar none, it consisted mostly of the more common whiskies and prices that one would expect from any run-of-the-mill whisky shop – not one situated in Mayfair. No special editions, hard-to-find rarities locked in cabinets; I recall nothing over £100. Doug shrugged his shoulders and was fairly non-plussed with the new venture. I guessed correctly he

256. Central London.

would not stay long. Doug jumped ship before the shop closed in 2002 and the company of Vintage Hallmark went bust less than a year later owing £77 million to mainly American investors. The owners; Richard Gunter and Robin Grove were both prosecuted for fraud[257] and the third party, the accountant David Lamb, took his own life before the court hearings in 2003. The shop is now owned by the Italian gun maker Beretta.

"I was quite lucky that I could move just down the road to Berry Bros & Rudd when I realised things were not what I thought they would be at Vintage Hallmark." Doug remarked.

We are sat in his first offices, steeped in hundreds of years of history – the original blend for Cutty Sark was made in a room next door. A few years after Doug joined the office became the shop for the spirits portfolio before a new, and frankly fit-for-purpose shop was opened around the corner on Pall Mall.

"I had built up a good network of contacts and friends within the industry so was able to slowly build up the spirits side of Berry's portfolio. When I joined the business felt that this was just to serve their wine customers with things they would want. The company had a long history of independent bottling but this had been just the odd cask really that would be brought down to the cellars and hand bottled."

Doug slowly built up the number of export partners and over the years the branding has changed from its quite basic origins to the classy and deluxe presentation it now has.

"It is really the people that have kept me active in this industry." Doug admits. "It is unique that you can spend a weekend working with direct competitors and you are all friends at the same time. I still have many friends from my earliest days with Milroys."

Doug and I are now round the corner from his old office at a small pub called Chequers Tavern. Over a pint of London Pride we talk about mutual friends and a few who are no longer with us. The passing of Wallace Milroy in 2016 is brought up and we cannot ignore the all too recent tragic loss of Dominic Roskrow.

"The last time I saw Dominic I was sharing a pint with him here." Doug recalls. "He was one of my closest pals in the industry."

There's nothing I can add so we both stare off into the adjoining buildings.

"You see that window?" Doug asks breaking the silence and pointing to a large window two stories up in the building opposite. "That's where Jimi Hendrix played his first gig in London." Now how do I top a fact like that? I don't even try, I just get us another beer.

---

257. It was discovered that by use of a UK registered limited company and a boiler room style investment scheme the company obtained over £30 million as investment into spirits and wines. Gunter was sentenced to four and a half years. Grove was later acquitted.

Blackadder Intl

www.blackadder.com

This independent bottler is named after the fugitive 17th century Presbyterian preacher John Blackadder, who evaded authorities for seven years before being imprisoned on the Bass Rock. Blackadder International was founded in 1995 by Robin Tucek and John Lamond, who had previously worked together on *The Malt Whisky File* (published in 1987). Lamond left the business in 2001, and Blackadder is now run by Robin and his daughter Hannah and son Michael.

Robin properly caught the whisky bug during a visit to Glen Grant distillery. He tasted a sample straight from the cask, an experience that instilled his personal philosophy on whisky. Robin became convinced cask influence was something unique which could never be replicated by big bulk, mass market releases. Therefore, cask is king for Blackadder. Almost to an extreme.

The Raw Cask series is the best example of Blackadder's dedication to cask strength, single cask whisky. The idea for it came about when Robin needed to find a way to amplify the natural element of his releases. It bothered him that many whiskies proudly displayed they were non-chill filtered. 'They might not have been chill filtered but are still heavily filtered.' And so, he saves cask sediment that is filtered out and divides it evenly amongst all bottles. This is Blackadder's way of assuring each of their whiskies is completely natural and 'raw'.

Blackadder has other ranges such as Peat Reek, Smoking Islay, Red Snake, A Drop of the Irish and Black Snake. The latter is produced from a vatting of casks finished in a single butt. It starts its life in first-fill ex-bourbon casks. They then put three of them into new Oloroso or Pedro Ximénez sherry butts and leave them for around a year for further maturation before bottling two thirds of the cask. They are a kind of mini solera.

Robin has a strong partnership with Japanese importer Gaia Flow. Together they worked on establishing Shizuoka, a young distillery that made headlines for using some of closed distillery Karuizawa's equipment, including one of the stills. Asked about his official involvement in Shizuoka, Robin's trademark humour shone through in his answer.

'I was the first person from overseas to stand under an umbrella, as it was raining, on the site of the distillery. I was also there for the ceremonial blessing of the site and at the official opening ceremony. So, as you can see, there is a very close connection between our two companies.'

The Bottlers

The Bottlers are a no-frills independent label produced by Raeburn Fine Wines in Edinburgh. Their traditional straight Cognac-style bottles (imported from France) are adorned with a simplistic yet effective label that contains all necessary information. One exception is the label designed for a Bunnahabhain 1978 by Scottish abstract painter Callum Innes. Their first outturn in 1993 included single malts from closed distillery Glenugie and Highland Park. The Malt Maniacs, with whisky blogger extraordinaire Serge Valentin leading the way, were especially instrumental in driving the popularity and fame of The Bottlers' releases.

That Boutique-y Whisky Company
www.thatboutiqueywhiskycompany.com

Toby Cutler: "It all began at Maltstock 2012... a car full of Master of Malt folks and assorted hangers-on descended upon Nijmegen, Netherlands. Ben Ellefsen had filled his car with his buddies and some whisky. Hours later they were pouring drams from bottles adorned with illustrated labels and, lo, That Boutique-y Whisky Company was born!

"The initial idea wasn't fun, it was (yawn) addressing a business need. We had no way to put out 'single malts' from named distilleries. As odd and indeed unfeasible as this sounds – it's true. We had the Master of Malt Single Cask Range, we had our Secret Bottlings Series for those secret drams where we weren't allowed to reveal the sources, but if we wanted to release a single malt in its most common sense (a blend of casks from one distillery), we had no vehicle. TBWC started out with a singularity of vision, something that didn't need to be safe, it could afford to be dangerous (sorry about that first set of labels, everyone!). It wasn't our core business so we could afford to push the envelope. It didn't need to succeed, but rather could sink or swim on its own merits.

"The label ideas began more like a superhero-y thing but as we sat and did briefs, we realised there wasn't even the need for that next-level, graphic novel attention to detail. There was always something fun or interesting that jumped into view. In fact, that made the distilleries that didn't have an exciting back story even more fun creatively, inspiring daft ideas. A dinosaur fighting a shark? Here's looking at you, Aultmore!

"So in a way, Boutique-y was made by and for a very particular type of whisky nerd. The brand zoomed out from chemical processes, technical jibber jabber,

Picture courtesy of Whisky Auctioneer

historical dates, but somehow made use of all these elements of "the meat" of any given whisky distillery thanks to the great skill of illustrator Emily Chappell.

"The realisation of the labels is a huge part of it and they always have been. Polarising for traditionalists, not modernist or fashionable, there's arguably nothing appealing about it to 99.624%[258] whisky consumers; it's for people who are more about the enjoyment and the fun than the image or the boast or the luxury lifestyle. Don't get us started on the bottle size. Ridiculous!

"What's at the *heart* of a great bottle though? It's the liquid, stupid![259] After all what we do is very simple - we sell people pleasure, the liquid is paramount. 'Traditionally' laying down stock from new make and supplementing that with interesting parcels that arise from time to time has been the sensible way to go for an IB (with good planning and some spare cash to lay down), but not for these crazy fools. Being a part of a quickly growing, tear-up-the-rule-book-at-every-opportunity company has meant that securing and nurturing liquid has not always been as easy as it could have been. However, we've muddled through with some thick skin, a very generous set of suppliers and a little bit of luck. Whisky really is a great industry to work in. When everyone you deal with is interested in one of the greatest products of humankind's interaction with nature, nice things tend to happen more often than not.

"But the prices! My first bulk whisky purchase back in the heady days of 2014 was a handful of 10 year old first-fill Arran casks from a private seller. I felt like a terrible buyer, offering what I felt to be an over-the-odds price of £15 per litre of alcohol to get the deal over the line ('I've got another interested

258. Toby assures me that 0% research has been done on this figure.
259. With apologies to Mr Carville.

party...'). Soon after that, £150 per litre of alcohol for 25 year old first-fill Oloroso matured Macallan? I must be INSANE. At the time of writing in 2022 I'd think it was my Birthday twice over if I saw the same spirit at ten times that price! Time changes perspectives though, entering the market as an IB now would be a very difficult thing to do. Liquid prices, logistics, Brexit, dry good costs (assuming you have a friendly glass supplier with stock!), storage and bottling hall availability are all much harder to come by, or far more expensive, in 2022.

"With a broad range of palates in the business it was inevitable we were going to be a truly global independent bottler. Our first non-Scotch bottling was from the wonderful FEW distillery in Chicago in 2014, quickly followed by Overeem from Australia, Rock Town from Arkansas, Paul John from India and Millstone from the Netherlands.

"This idea solidified in 2020 with the concept of quarterly themes. A theme could be anything from 'Ryes of the World' to a focus on one particular country, style, cask type or region. This pushed the envelope design-wise while drawing on a wider whisky palette than ever. We've now bottled whisky from England all the way back to... England and nearly everywhere in between. Logistically and legally, let's say it's a challenge, but a lot of fun and my goodness, there's *incredible* whisky being made by a lot of very hard-working and creative people out there. Tasmanian rye made in a tumble dryer anyone?

"As I write, the post-Brexit trade deal with India is being negotiated. If that includes a large reduction in import duty for Scotch whisky, there won't be a lot to go round for us IBs without a very large increase in distilling capacity and time. Perhaps whisk(e)y from around the world is what a large part of the future looks like for IBs? There'd be no complaints in TBWC towers if that were the case.

"And what of the people? Conceived in the unique mind of Ben Ellefsen and executed by a very large cast of characters over the years. There really are too many to call out here but it would be remiss of me not to mention our very own Boutique-y Dave Worthington, a legend in his own breakfast time. Whisky porridge, anyone? Emily Chappell, artist extraordinaire and keeper of the stylistic flame. Felix Dear has been instrumental in building relationships with dozens of new distilleries around the globe.

"Reflecting about writing this piece I realise I am lucky to be in a unique position. I've been a trade buyer of, consumer of, bulk buyer for, logistics co-ordinator for, blender of (once!), cask selector for, label brief creator for, occasional marketer of and salesman for, That Boutique-y Whisky Company's whiskies. It's been quite the ride so far for this cartoon-y little whisky brand from Tunbridge Wells that recently celebrated its 10th Anniversary. It's still the most fun we have on a day to day basis and we always look forward to the next flavour, the next label, the next story."

Càrn Mòr

www.carnmorwhisky.co.uk

One of Scotland's foremost whisky families is behind independent bottler Càrn Mòr. The Morrisons started out as grocers during the 18th century, but have since filled the role of blenders, bottlers, whisky brokers and distillers. Much of their modern legacy lies in the family's former ownership of Bowmore, Glen Garioch and Auchentoshan.

Càrn Mòr is part of Morrison Scotch Whisky Distillers, which was originally incorporated as John Murray & Co on the Isle of Mull in 1982. It was set up by the Bartholomew family, who started out as producers of Columba Cream, a Scotch whisky liqueur. They renamed their business to The Scottish Liqueur Centre when it moved to Perth in 1996. Perth has been of historical importance to the whisky industry; blenders such as Arthur Bell, John Dewar and Matthew Gloag all called it home. And in Perth is where The Scottish Liqueur Centre caught the attention of the Morrison family almost a decade later.

In 2005 father and son Brian and Jamie Morrison bought in. They did so in partnership with Kenny Mackay. Together they brought a wealth of whisky experience and knowledge. Kenny Mackay previously worked with blender Peter Thomson (Perth) Ltd. Brian Morrison's father was Stanley P. Morrison, renowned former owner of Bowmore, Glen Garioch and Auchentoshan until they were sold to Suntory in 1994.

When Brian, Jamie and Kenny acquired The Scottish Liqueur Centre, they wanted to revive some of Perth's Scotch whisky heritage. The trio's first step was to increase independent bottling of Scotch whisky. The Scottish Liqueur Centre had sporadically been releasing single cask whisky even before the Morrison's and Mackay's became involved. The Beinn a'Cheo range was kept alive initially but replaced over time by brands that still form the heart of modern-day Morrison Scotch Whisky Distillers' independent bottling arm.

Single malts started to appear as part of Càrn Mòr's Celebration of The Cask range in 2008. Not surprisingly some very good Bowmore and Glen Garioch were (and are still being) bottled under this label. In 2012 the Strictly Limited range was added. More affordable, but quality daily drinking whiskies. Nowadays there's also a high-end range called The Family Reserve.

The second step was purchasing the mothballed Old Perth brand from Whyte & Mackay. It was relaunched as a blended malt in 2013. This was a milestone for Kenny Mackay especially, as Old Perth was once owned by his former employer, Peter Thomson (Perth) Ltd. Old Perth has since grown into a well-respected brand with a strong core range and the occasional vintage release. To reflect the company's move into the whisky sphere, and certainly also to highlight its family heritage, the name was changed to Morrison & Mackay in 2014.

But the third (and maybe most bold) step was the construction of Aberargie Distillery. Its first cask was filled on November 1ˢᵗ, 2017. And it signaled the return of the Morrison family to distilling. It also put in motion one final name change. Morrison & Mackay became Morrison Scotch Whisky Distillers in 2020, a year after sole ownership transferred to Brian and Jamie Morrison.

Claxton's

www.claxtonsspirits.com

Adrian Hoose: "Whisky, for me, is much more than a drink and being able to work with it is a passion realised. We formed Claxton's in 2011 but didn't really begin running it as a business until 2015 when we released our first range of single cask whiskies. The first few years certainly had some challenges; in many ways we were very new and the independent bottling world was full of established names. Bit by bit and market by market, we developed a loyal following by concentrating on diversity and quality single cask bottlings. By 2018, we realised we needed our own warehouse, eventually settling on an old farm steading on the beautiful Dalswinton estate in Dumfries and Galloway.

"From the moment we rolled our first cask off the lorry things stepped up a gear and we now have two main ranges; the Warehouse Series and the Exploration Series. Each are single cask ranges bottled either at cask strength,

for the Warehouse Series, and 50% for the Exploration Series. The Warehouse Series tries to evoke the roaring 20s with its Art Deco feel and offers a more traditional and uncompromising approach to bottling single casks, whilst the Exploration Series is a much more modern presentation offering the customer a slightly different take and the chance to step outside their comfort zone.

"In addition to this, we are now developing a core range, including the already released Grain Barn 30 year old (a single grain Scotch whisky that brings the story back to the Dalswinton warehouses where grain used to be stored) plus a selection of quality focused single malts and blends.

"Since establishing the warehouse in 2019, we have worked with companies like Coachbuilt to create bespoke blends at our own facilities and now export to a dozen markets having released hundreds of expressions. Not bad from having just the single cask we started with.

"What started from the pleasure of drinking single malts and discovering independent bottlings from the likes of Cadenhead's, Signatory and Douglas Laing, we now run our own bonded warehouse and get to open and taste many maturing casks each week. We are proudly independent and every member of the team is truly passionate about what we do."

Chapter 7

www.chapter7whisky.com

Chapter 7 is an independent brand started by Selim Evin, whose passion for whisky was instilled by his Scottish grandfather. They went on a tour of Scotland when Evin was 16. "We'd roll up to distilleries, knock on the door – this was long before every distillery had its own visitor centre – and I'd be captivated by the language and lore of the spirit."

Many years later, when Evin was looking for a change in his life, it was obvious the business he wanted to move into. The brand initially started out in Switzerland in 2014, but as the business grew, Evin found partners to help him move Chapter 7 to Perth, Scotland. The brand's name was inspired by literature, and the label design by cask end prints. The typography on their labels comes from UK street signs.

Finally, the name Chapter 7 is inspired by Shakespeare's Seven Ages of Man monologue, which explains the seven parts a man plays over his life. A helpless infant, a whining schoolboy, an emotional lover, a devoted soldier, a wise judge, a clueless pensioner, and a corpse. "I love whiskies aged in bourbon barrels and more spirit forward whiskies, meaning not strongly influenced by the wood but rather whiskies that are balanced, layered and sophisticated thanks to age and magic rather than finishing and colour."

Daily Dram

www.thenectar.be

A brand from importer The Nectar, Daily Dram is the most prolific independent bottler of Belgium. Casks are selected by founder Jan Broekmans and marketing director Mario Groteklaes. Founded in 2006, The Nectar quickly established themselves as one of the foremost independent bottlers on the European mainland. The early colourful labels (courtesy of Serge Valentin) and curious anagrams for distillery names (Adieu Lina, Womb Ore, Huh! Bin Banana) are memorable. Their current labels are a bit more civilised; but probably more stylish too.

The Dava Way

www.dunphaildistillery.com

The Dava Way uncovers, curates and bottles spirits that exemplify and celebrate flavour, balance and uniqueness. Casks are selected to typify distillery characters, showcase individual production techniques and demonstrate a broad spectrum of maturation styles.

The bottler launched in October 2022 and is led by Dunphail Distillery's Director of Whisky Creation Matt McKay. This highly traditionally-focussed distillery will be commencing production in early 2023 - becoming one of only two distilleries in Scotland to floor malt 100% of its barley on-site.

Decadent Drinks

www.decadent-drinks.com

Angus MacRaild: "I started properly getting into whisky as a teenager by reading a lot of books about it. I was interested before that as it was something distinctly Scottish and my Dad liked Islay malts like Laphroaig and Caol Ila so it was always something on my periphery growing up. My earliest memories of indy bottlers was kind of a muddle of seeing names like Signatory and Gordon & MacPhail on the shelves of Loch Fyne Whiskies in Inverary, while also looking online and reading about more exotic names such as Samaroli.

"I twigged very early on that Indy bottlers were important and different. It seemed quite obvious to me that what they offered was more exciting and more interesting and detailed from a drinking experience perspective. The higher ABVs, the single casks or smaller batches - these were all revelatory and stood very clearly apart from what most OBs were doing at the time. I remember distinctly discovering the SMWS for the first time and then reading up about them and being blown away.

"I think if official bottlings provided a lot of the basic landmass of my whisky education in terms of basic distillery styles and general profile variations. Then IBs added colour and detail and nuance and generally filled in the landscape with all manner of intrigue and subtle variation. You cannot really understand the variety and depth of variation in Scotch Whisky without IBs and what they bring to the culture. It was certainly IBs which were the most alluring and fascinating to me in terms of both newer releases and the world of old style or historic bottlings, which I got very quickly and deeply into through working and meeting people at Ardbeg distillery while at university in 2005 and 2006.

"I never anticipated I would be a bottler myself. My memory of what other bottlers had said was that it was just so hard and frustrating to find good casks, and this was being said pretty much since I first started in whisky. For me it came about by chance really, I was asked by my business partner, Iain McClune, if I had any ideas for bottling and would like to collaborate. By luck I had been thinking at that point for a while that it would fun to find a cask to bottle for my Whisky Sponge blog. So I just suggested we use Sponge as the brand and from there it evolved quite naturally and pretty quickly. About six months later we felt there was traction in it and we decided to formally start a company, which became Decadent Drinks. I think we were lucky to have good industry contacts and relationships. Certainly my relationship with Signatory was, and continues to be, invaluable. Andrew was very supportive which helped a lot. Also I was determined not to just do whisky but to be diverse and embrace many other spirits and types of drink (hence Decadent *Drinks*).

"I feel that the overwhelming reception to what we have done so far has been positive. It is an extremely challenging environment in which to do Indy bottling, stock access, pricing and competition are all intensely difficult, so we face problems every day. But the feedback to our philosophy, our products and our way of doing things is generally positive I find, which is highly motivating. We try to embrace having fun, not taking whisky or life too seriously, and of course we do our best to bottle interesting and high quality products.

"The future for IBs is deeply uncertain. I think the mainstream industry has never appreciated Indy bottlers and what they have done for whisky and whisky culture. Many brands have accepted their massive value hikes without acknowledging that this was hugely underpinned by the work of Indy bottlers in an era when single malt enthusiasm was still hyper-niche. They are rapidly pulling up the drawbridges of access and controlling pricing as well as busily

Angus MacRaild

getting rid of distillery names - all of which is essentially tantamount to a boot on the throat of Indy bottling as an industry and culture. For those that do survive, I believe the future lies in diversification of product away from just whisky (we already see this quite widely) and also in working with the many smaller, newer and independent distilleries, not just in Scotland but around the world, who understand and recognise the value of Indy bottlers in spreading the word on specific whiskies. But that latter aspect will take time and a lot of work.

"I have been very fortunate in my career to taste a lot of the great and iconic Indy bottlings. Whiskies such as Laphroaig 1967 and Bowmore Bouquet 1966 Samaroli will linger beautifully in my memory for the rest of my life. But I would also point out more humble bottlings that were important to me personally, such as an old 1998 Cadenhead Longrow which really switched me onto that distillate. I first, properly, discovered Bowmore thanks to an old Murray McDavid 1988 single cask. I also lost count of the number of astonishing old Longmorns, Springbanks, Lochsides and Laphroaigs that I fell in love with thanks to indy bottlers over the years. For some distilleries, such as Port Ellen and many of the other old lost names (Glenlochy and Glenugie in particular) there are really *only* Indy bottlers to thank for our experience of those makes.

"From my own bottlings, I am of course a big fan of our very first bottling, that gorgeous 1981 Glen Moray. That was a privately owned cask that we were really fortunate to get. But the ones I'm most proud of are things like the Equilibrium I, the Jura 27yo Edition 46, the Ardnamurchan triptych: bottlings where I was able to be a bit more creative and play a more active role by mixing together different casks and vintages. Essentially creating interesting and hopefully good quality bottlings that wouldn't have otherwise existed. That's what I really enjoy most about Indy bottling, is the creativity of it. Indy bottling is essentially a response to, and an expression of, geekery. It's whisky culture's equivalent of Comic Con in bottled form. That was true for the ancient and long lost Berry Brothers and G&M bottlings from the 19th century, and it's true to today in a much more diverse and global way. Which is amazing, and something we should do our best to preserve and support. Whisky would be an astonishingly impoverished culture without Indy bottlers."

Douglas Laing & Co.
www.douglaslaing.com

Whisky is a family affair for Douglas Laing & Co., an independent bottler from Glasgow founded in 1948 and currently led by the second and third generations. The company boasts an impressive range of Scotch single cask brands, blended malts and blended whisky, including the Remarkable Regional Malts, Old Particular, McGibbon's and The King of Scots – the blend that started it all.

Having served in the RAF during World War II, founder Fred Laing Snr (full name Fred Douglas Laing) encountered the American owners of The King of Scots brand, then established in New York. This blend, reportedly with a higher malt content than usual, was first created in 1886. Laing Snr initially was asked to accommodate bottling and shipping of The King of Scots from the Glasgow docks, but soon acquired the brand along with a handful of casks, which was enough to last him a year.

It was to be the start of Douglas Laing & Co., but replenishing stocks for his newly obtained blend was difficult in post-war Scotland. Through determination and sheer relentlessness Laing Snr was able to set up small filling programmes with distilleries, most of them without any written contracts. Remarkably, many of these handshake deals are still in place, even after some of the distilleries were taken over by bigger companies.

The King of Scots, and Douglas Laing & Co. by proxy, really found its footing during the 1970s, when travel retailer Duty Free Shoppers (DFS) asked the independent bottler to launch an assortment of blended Scotch whiskies for affluent Asian globetrotters. It was also during this decade the company attracted probably its most infamous customer, Ugandan dictator Idi Amin, who had proclaimed himself 'King of Scotland'. Intrigued, Laing Snr wrote to

Image courtesy of thewhiskyvault.com

him, suggesting Amin should drink The King of Scots if he were truly King of Scotland. Not long after Douglas Laing & Co. received an order for 200 cases.

This order was part of what became known as the 'whisky run', an almost nightly visit of Uganda Airlines to Stansted Airport in England, where planes were loaded with Scotch whisky and other luxury items. Amin, who relied on the army to keep him in power, supplied these products to his officers and troops to win over their loyalty. An African proverb summed up Amin's rationale: "A dog with a bone in its mouth can't bite."

Sons Stewart Laing and Fred Laing Jnr joined the company in 1967 and 1972, respectively. Both worked at other whisky companies before stepping into the family business, such as Whyte & Mackay, White Horse Distillers and Bruichladdich. McGibbon's, a brand of blended Scotch whisky sold in golf-shaped decanters, was one of their first major successes when it was launched in 1976. The blend was intentionally named after their mother's maiden name, so that any mistakes the then relatively inexperienced Stewart and Fred Jnr made wouldn't besmirch the good name of Douglas Laing & Co.

While gaffes may have been made, McGibbon's became immensely popular in the Pacific. The whisky industry was going through rough times in the

1980s, when many now iconic distilleries were closed. But Douglas Laing & Co. prospered, in large part thanks to their deal with DFS and the sales of McGibbon's. It won the company the Queen's Award for Export in 1990, an achievement Fred Laing Snr was no longer around for to witness; he passed away six years earlier.

During the ensuing years Douglas Laing & Co. slowly shifted focus to bottling single cask single malt whisky. It wasn't necessarily a smooth transition, as Fred Laing once remarked. "It was a nightmare for us to make the transition from bottling 1,000 cases of King of Scots to start bottling 321 or 289 bottles, and selling split-pallet loads," he said in an interview with The Spirits Business in 2021. But eventually ranges like Old Malt Cask and Provenance brought them great success. However, a friendly bearded fellow joining the company in 2009 arguably made even more waves. They were somewhat ahead of the curve with the launch of Big Peat, a blended Islay malt with a distinct label adorning a drawing of a big Islay fisherman. Many of the company's importers were sceptical and the whisky was often ignored at trade shows. Initially cases were even sent out for free. But in the decade-plus since Big Peat has grown into one of the independent bottler's biggest earners.

By far the most seminal moment in the independent bottler's modern history (and maybe ever) came in 2013, when brothers Stewart and Fred decided to go their separate ways. They had different views on the way forward and decided an amicable de-merger was the best solution. Fred Laing Jnr retained the rights to the Douglas Laing name, and Stewart formed a new company called Hunter Laing & Co. (Hunter is his middle name.) Whisky stocks and brands were split between the brothers. Some hard decisions were made, but in the end the brothers more or less took turns in choosing what assets they wanted to keep, with Fred setting his sights on Big Peat.

In the same year succession was put into place, as daughter Cara Laing and her husband Chris Leggat joined the company. Together with his daughter and son-in-law, Fred Laing Jnr created a whole range of Remarkable Regional Malts alongside Big Peat, including accessible, fun blended malts for each of Scotch whisky's official regions. Douglas Laing & Co. also embarked on what might be their most ambitious project to date: building their own distillery and new headquarters on the banks of the river Clyde in Glasgow. Clutha Distillery's opening was initially supposed to coincide with the company's 70th anniversary in 2018, but building is now expected to be completed in 2024 (at the earliest).

Facing delays on their 'Campus Project', which is how they've come to refer to their future head office and distillery, Douglas Laing & Co. acquired the small Strathearn Distillery in 2019. Cara Laing referred to it as an historic landmark for her family. For the first time in over seven decades of business they could add distiller to their credentials.

Duncan Taylor Scotch Whisky Ltd

www.duncantaylor.com

The original firm of Duncan Taylor & Co was established in May 1938 as a cask brokering and trading company in Glasgow. This firm was acquired by American importer Abe Rosenberg, who made his fortune importing Scotch (including J&B) post World War II. He used the firms links to store casks of Scotch whisky he bought for future blending projects. It is estimated that Rosenberg built a portfolio of some 4,500 casks before being put up for sale seven years after Rosenberg's death in 2001.

Euan Shand, previously part of the Bennachie Whisky Co, acquired the stock in 2002 along with company name and therefore returned it to Scottish ownership:

"The average age of casks at the point of the takeover was 33 years old. It included an incredible A-Z of the best and most interesting whiskies available on the market. This included old casks of Macallan, Bowmore, Glenlivet, Laphroaig etc.

"Negotiations for the company took nearly a year – the family were tough negotiators. Part of the deal, prior to acquiring the company, allowed me to check every cask in situ – which meant travelling to numerous warehouses and distilleries throughout Scotland.

"The industry in 2001-2 was still going through the post dotcom doldrum of all industries and of course 9/11 happened in the midst of my negotiations with the Rosenberg family. It was a very up and down year.

"My modus operandi was and still is to hold a large quantity of the best spirits in cask, basically a carbon copy of Rosenberg's plan and that is what I have done. We hold a large collection of casks now in the 30 – 60 year old range as well as casks for the younger expressions."

During his time creating products with Bennachie, Shand had been interested in the vatting and blending part of the industry which would see a return with several new brands for Duncan Taylor. DTC gained a reputation for bottling exceptional single cask malt and grain whiskies. Whilst Duncan Taylor were not the first to bottle single grain, single cask bottlings they were at the forefront and gained more recognition for doing this than any other bottler.

With the purchase of Duncan Taylor came the rights to the name Black Bull Blended Scotch Whisky and the new owners reinvigorated the brand bottling several expression including an extraordinary 40 year old expression.

Elixir Distillers

www.elixirdistillers.com

Elixir Distillers was born out of the bottling arm of The Whisky Exchange, founded by Sukhinder and Rajbir Singh in 1999. Originally an extension of Sukhinder's passion for single casks, the first bottling under an Elixir Distillers own label was a Single Malts of Scotland Tomatin 30 Year Old in 2002. It would remain a small brand until 2013, with between 10 and 20 casks bottled a year and sold mainly through The Whisky Exchange and a few, likeminded, importers around Europe and in Japan.

In 2008, Sukhinder launched the Elements of Islay brand, with a focus on creating small batches of Islay whisky, celebrating the key characters of Islay with a focus on flavour rather than age or vintage. In 2009 he launched his second Islay range, Port Askaig, a non-distillery declared Islay Single Malt, named for the village on the north coast. In 2010, he also entered the world of Rum with Black Tot.

The key strength for the business was always that it was entirely done for the love and enjoyment of finding whisky rather than to simply make a profit. Supported by the successful retail and wholesale business, Elixir Distillers was able to buy larger parcels of casks and manage their evolution over longer periods of time. The business changed from one of discovery to that of custodians.

Today, the philosophy is even more focused on flavour, with blending a key component to liquid creation. There are many similarities between the business history of Elixir Distillers to that of John Walker & Son, Chivas Regal, etc, with the business first being a shop, moving from whisky bottling and blending and now into distillery ownership and operation. Though Elixir Distillers maintains its single cask lines and the people selecting and creating liquid have been the same for over a decade, the focus has very much moved to a longer-term view in all regards, as they look to control more facets of liquid creation.

In 2021, Sukhinder and Rajbir Singh sold The Whisky Exchange along with its sister business Speciality Drinks, to allow them time to focus on Elixir Distillers as an independent bottler, blender, and distiller. In 2022 they announced the purchase of Tormore Distillery in Speyside. Work on their distillery on Islay, Portintruan, is due for completion in 2024.

Hart Brothers Whisky

www.hartbrothers.co.uk

In 1964 brothers Iain & Donald Hart started the company of Hart Brothers as Wine & Spirit Wholesalers and Scotch Whisky Blenders. The family history had been steeped in the licensed trade back to the 19th century around the Paisley area.

Alistair Hart joined in 1975 and the company began bottling single cask whiskies. The company was sold to Campbell Meyer & Co Ltd in 2007 and Alistair Hart continues to select the casks today. *For further information see Meadowside Blending.*

Hunter Laing & Co.

www.hunterlaing.com

While only established in 2013, the story of Hunter Laing & Co. began well over half a century ago and includes esteemed brands such as Old Malt Cask and Old & Rare. The only reason they are a relatively new Scotch whisky bottler and blender is because they (sort of) spun-off from Douglas Laing & Co. Or de-merged, as founder Stewart Laing has referred to it.

Stewart has a long and storied career in the whisky industry, first getting his feet wet as an 18-year-old at Bruichladdich Distillery, followed by a stint

Donald Hart

at Stevenson Taylor & Co, a wine and spirits company. But it was a foregone conclusion he would join the family business founded by his father, which he did in 1967. Stewart and his brother Fred Laing Jr would enjoy great successes at Douglas Laing & Co. First as deputies and later as the head honchos. [More details in the section on Douglas Laing & Co.]

Hunter Laing & Co. was created after the brothers had differing visions on the way forward and decided to split. Fred Laing Jnr retained the rights to the name Douglas Laing & Co, while Stewart Laing formed his new company with a fair share of Douglas Laing's assets. He was joined by his sons Andrew and Scott, who in turn merged their existing company Edition Spirits into Hunter Laing.

Just three years after the seminal break between the brothers, Hunter Laing & Co. announced an exciting new chapter. And when the first new make spirit flowed out of the stills of Ardnahoe Distillery in October 2018, the young independent bottler officially joined the ranks of distilling companies. Located on the northeast shores of Islay with a stunning view of the Paps of Jura, Ardnahoe has the capacity to produce one million litres per annum. While the spirit in the distillery's warehouses is now legally whisky, there are no plans for an inaugural single malt yet.

Ian Macleod
www.ianmacleod.com

Ian Macleod Distillers have quietly slowed down their independent bottling arm in recent years, focusing more on their single malt brands; Glengoyne, Tamdhu and the newly revived Rosebank. The company originally started out as a broker when Leonard Russell Sr made his first foray into the whisky industry in 1936. But Ian Macleod's history takes us back a few years earlier even.

When Ian Macleod & Co was acquired by the Russell family in 1963, it had been incorporated since 1933. With it also came the acquisition of Isle of Skye, a blended Scotch whisky that's still an important part of Ian Macleod's business and legacy. Other blended (malt) brands include Sheep Dip, Pig's Nose and Hedges & Butler.

Independent bottlings of single malt whisky may have never been the core business for Ian Macleod. But they've provided whisky enthusiasts with a steady stream of releases regardless. In the late 1990s and early 2000s they started releasing single malt (and often single cask) whiskies under their labels Chieftain's and Dun Bheagan. And then there's Smokehead, from an undisclosed Islay distillery, which was first launched in 2006. It remains one of Ian Macleod's most popular single malt brands to this day.

Intertrade / High Spirits

Ferdinando 'Nadi' Fiori is part of Italy's impressive legacy of independent bottlers of Scotch whisky – as much as Silvano Samaroli, Ernesto Mainardi and Pepi Mongiardino are. Many of his bottlings are highly sought after, whether released under the High Spirits, Intertrade or Turatello labels.

Fiori opened the Taverna degli Artisti in 1970 with his brother. This restaurant and bar was located in Rimini, a popular seaside town in northeastern Italy. With the growing enthusiasm of his patrons for not just whisky in general but single malt specifically, Fiori traveled to Scotland and London regularly. There he would select whiskies that were not available in Italy. This went on for quite a few years during the 1970s, until a friend suggested Fiori should go to Elgin. There he met with Mr. George Urquhart of Gordon & MacPhail. As Fiori would later describe it, this 'was the real beginning of my whisky adventure.'

The two struck up a friendship, and Urquhart took Fiori under his wing, further introducing him to the world of whisky and sharing many inside stories. Initially Fiori imported batches of just 15 to 20 cases of whisky at a time. Until he met someone working for bottler and retailer Robert Watson of Aberdeen. With that chance encounter Fiori officially moved into the independent bottling game in 1981. He purchased casks of The Glenlivet, Glenfiddich and Glen Grant. All of these were labeled 'For Nadi Fiori'.

Just three years later Fiori established Intertrade in partnership with the Turatello Brothers, Italian beer distributors and traders. Fiori remained responsible for bottling single malts from the vast stocks of Gordon & MacPhail, while Turatello arranged distribution. Some of the first official Intertrade bottlings have become nothing short of iconic, such as a Laphroaig 1966 and Highland Park 1955, both bottled in 1985.

Like his Italian contemporaries, Fiori understood the importance of label design. 'At the time most normal whisky releases had a very dull presentation', he shares in an interview with Whisky Auctioneer. 'The independent Italian bottlers first of all showed good style and fantasy, see Moon Import followed by Silvano Samaroli. I thought that it had to be done so and I did it my way trying inspiration from very old books/labels and using the skills of an artist that was a good friend of mine.'

Taverna degli Artisti closed in 1999 and Fiori started a second independent bottler, High Spirits. With this company he bottled a series for one of Italy's most renowned collectors, Valentino Zagatti, to celebrate his 50th year of buying whisky.

Jack Wiebers Whisky World

Jack Wiebers Whisky World was one of the first independent bottlers established in Germany. They made a name for themselves through coveted series of single casks such as Old Train Line, Gentle Noses, Classic of Islay and Great Ocean Liners. The origin of this bottlers name is a curious one. Jack Wiebers doesn't formally exist, but instead is a nickname of founder Lars-Göran Wiebers, given to him because of his fondness for Jack & Coke.

After initially starting out as an importer and distributor of whisky in 1996, Wiebers graduated to independent bottling three years into his whisky adventure. In 1999 he launched the Castle Collection, which included whiskies from lesser-known distilleries such as Balmenach and Tomatin. This was by design, as Wiebers wanted to turn the spotlight away from the big distilleries that already received so much attention.

The company's headquarters is in Kreuzberg, one of Berlin's edgiest districts; it's full of punks, anti-fascists, musicians and artists. Many of the labels are designed by Wiebers himself, but he enlists help from creatives such as painter Alfred Prenzlow, with whom a close friendship developed over the years. His brother, Sven Wiebers, is also a well-known artist. His work is featured on a series of independent bottlings, Wiebers Brothers.

James Eadie

www.jameseadie.co.uk

They say that most family businesses don't survive more than three generations. That was certainly the case with the original James Eadie business. Whilst it might not have been 'shirtsleeves to shirtsleeves' the once-famous company created by the founder in this instance had all but disappeared when his great-great grandson decided to revive the business and show what the fifth generation could do.

The original founder, James Eadie, was born in Blackford, near Gleneagles in Scotland, in 1828. At the age of 14 he came to England to work in his uncle's tea business before establishing his brewing and bottling business in 1854. By the end of the 19th century Mr. Eadie was the owner of a well-reputed brand with more than 200 pubs across the country. In the words of Alfred Barnard, who met Mr. Eadie in the 1880s, he was 'a self-made man, justly proud of his success, and one who, by indomitable perseverance and industry, has achieved commercial prosperity, far exceeding his most sanguine expectation.'

Mr. Eadie's most famous logo was his Trade Mark 'X'. Registered on 16 May, 1877, it is one of the oldest trademarks in the world. The whisky made under this logo was produced until the 1940s, with the majority of the few existing bottles kept as treasured family heirlooms. 'Bequeathed to him by his father,' Alfred Barnard wrote approvingly of Mr. Eadie's 'ancient Scotch mixture', and having opened one of the last remaining bottles in the process of reviving the Trade Mark 'X' blend, we can attest to this whisky's remarkable quality.

After thirty years working for Macleod's, Diageo and Beam Suntory, Rupert Patrick took the decision to revive the whisky business of his ancestor, bringing the brand back to life in 2016. James Eadie Ltd had been dormant for over fifty years, and had not produced whisky for nearly seventy. Rupert was surrounded by the drinks trade as he grew up. His father was one of the first-ever Masters of Wine, and two Eadie uncles, Alastair and Jeremy, made their careers in whisky and beer, following the family tradition. Leon Kuebler and Hugh Barron, both of whom started their whisky careers in retail form the nucleus of the James Eadie team, alongside Rupert.

The initial goal of the revived James Eadie Ltd was to re-establish Trade Mark X as a high-quality premium blend. The chance discovery of Mr. Eadie's 19th century ledgers enabled us to pinpoint precisely which distilleries he was buying from, as well as the age profiles and wood types. Only whisky from the same distilleries used by Mr. Eadie in the Victorian era are included in today's Trade Mark 'X', and the modern incarnation has gone on to win multiple gold medals as a result.

Leon Kuebler: "We are guided by the rich heritage of the James Eadie brand in everything we do.

"Our Cask Finish range gives whiskies an additional maturation in the types of casks held in Mr. Eadie's Victorian warehouses – Sherry, Madeira, Marsala, Malaga and Brandy – with particular care taken to pair the spirit with complimentary flavours from the wood. Whiskies rarely seen in a century, such as 2021's bottling of Cameronbridge 22 year old finished in a Marsala Hogshead – inspired by Mr. Eadie's regular Christmas Day purchases of Cameronbridge in Marsala casks.

"Our Small Batch whiskies, which combine two to four casks from one single malt to focus on distillery character, feature unique designs for the labels, each one inspired by the name of one of Mr. Eadie's pubs.

"And this year we published a book, 'The Distilleries of Great Britain & Ireland', featuring a long-forgotten series of 124 distillery profiles written between 1922 and 1929 which, with more than 640 contemporary photographs restored by the British Library's digitisation team, brought one of the earliest records of the industry back to life."

James MacArthur

Founded in 1982, James MacArthur aimed to select whiskies from Scottish distilleries that were lesser known or closed. This independent bottler's best-known range were the Old Masters series. Bottled at cask strength, the back label of each bottling included a short history of the distillery. While the company was officially dissolved in 2022, their last single casks were released three years earlier. Three from Tomatin and another three from Balmenach.

Kingsbury

While incorporated in Aberdeen, Kingsbury almost exclusively release their single malts for the Japanese market. The company was founded in 1989 by owner Katsuhiko Tanaka, who selects the casks with assistance from Springbank distillery's Gordon Wright. (He is officially one of the directors of Kingsbury since 2017.) Many of its early casks were sourced from either Cadenhead's or Douglas Laing, although later casks come from a wider variety of origins. During Kingsbury's three-plus decades of existence they've always remained highly selective about who they source their casks from. Of the hundreds of casks that have been bottled, several have become cult classics, including some 1960s and 1970s Islay single malts.

Kintra Spirits
www.kintra.nl

Erik Molenaar: "During the summer of 2009 my young family and I were on a three week trip through Scotland. The second week was spent on Islay and while the little kids took their afternoon nap I would race across the Island for a quick visit at a distillery.

"It was during those days that I decided that I wanted to do more with whisky then just drink it. I was a frequent visitor of tastings and whisky festivals but I wanted to do more. So while sipping from a Laphroaig 18 year old that I had purchased at the distillery I decided to become an independent bottler.

"Back home I was caught up in everyday life again and it took another eight or nine months to finally present the first bottles. The very first whiskies bottled under the "Kintra Single Cask Collection" were a 13 year old Glenallachie refill Sherry cask and a nice peaty Ledaig from Tobermory distillery. Back then it was fairly easy to get my hands on good quality whisky at decent prices. We bottled one after the other, old Glen Grant 42 year old, Clynelish 16 year old, Dalmore 9 year old, Caol Ila 25 year old - the list went on and on. Even Port Ellen was presented under the Kintra label....it was only six bottles that were a leftover from a bottling job for another customer, but still...!!

"Specialty retailers started working with the brand and we managed some export and things went very well for the first couple of years. It was still however a 'don't quit your day job' affair.

"In 2015 I decided to make it a full-time affair and bottled more whisky; and more importantly, started my own distillery – the Wagging Finger Distillery was born. The whisky business in general was booming to such an extent that pricing of aged casks was starting to go through the roof. Subsequently I started to bottle fewer casks or took to buying younger casks that today are still maturing. To make up for that we started to import more brands and became a wholesaler in Scotch and Irish Whisk(e)y, French Cognac and Armagnac. Rum also makes up an increasing part of our portfolio. We still bottle a couple casks per year as and when we find them. Our standards are high so we reject over 90% of casks offered. Our customers expect a very good whisky when it is bottled under the Kintra label… so I'd much rather not bottle anything for a while until I run into a cask that ticks all the boxes. As David has said in this book, a small independent bottler is only really as good as their last bottling."

Lady of the Glen
www.ladyoftheglen.com

Gregor Hannah: "My dad served in the Black Watch regiment and during a particularly cold night in Inverness he was offered the chance to escape that to join the army pipe band. Through that opportunity he travelled the world doing tours of America, Japan and Europe. Upon leaving the army he played at weddings, Burns Suppers and family events and as is the custom for these events he was given a bottle of Whisky so over the years he accumulated a Whisky collection which he never paid a penny for! As a kid I found his reverence for Whisky inspiring and I loved the branding of the different bottles despite having no real knowledge of it.

"During a very unhappy spell working in an office I decided I wanted to start my own business in the Whisky industry and since I lived in Scotland I had a proximity to a market leading product with its premium nature. I felt it was suited to a small business model because it didn't require huge economies of scale and investment to provide a relatively comfortable lifestyle. However, even small businesses require investment and I had zero savings so I applied

to the bank for a loan to help with my commute to work – I used this money to purchase two casks and create the brand Lady of the Glen, which was named after the Green Lady ghost of Stirling Castle.

"It has been 10 years since the business started and what was a part time business that could go either way for many years now has a more settled status operating from our own bottling hall with a really good and committed team. We won the Independent Bottler of the year for Scotland and globally in 2022 and this was a huge achievement considering our limited portfolio, small capital budget and relatively short time in the industry. I am still the sole director and we are an independent business which was always my ambition.

"Going forward there are a lot of concerns weighing on the business; the rising energy costs will drive up the cost of spirit which we buy from suppliers; the weak pound makes acquiring casks from Europe less cost effective in conjunction with higher transport costs across the board. In the UK I have deep concerns about how the IB market will continue due to duty rises, the cost of living crisis and the impending recession impacting disposable income. Also the deposit return scheme is going to add a further cost and bureaucracy burden to the Scotland market alone. It is certainly not a positive view I have, and the cask investment side of the industry has driven the cost of casks up while also creating a more divisive and cynical consumer base."

Little Brown Dog

www.littlebrowndogspirits.com

Little Brown Dog are distillers and bottlers based on a farm in rural Aberdeenshire with a growing reputation for bottling excellent whiskies and spirits in a sometimes less than conventional style. Established as a business in 2018 but really began in 2012 as a way to label whisky samples shared with friends and as a series of whisky experiments with the results shared online. The compnay is named after Andrew's dog who was his constant companion on distillery visits and went everywhere with him. The logo is Banksy the dog in profile, and the copper colour references the colour of stills as well as the dipping dog used to sample casks.

Because of their origins sharing drams and experiences, Little Brown Dog is built around sharing information and drinking whisky with friends. They inherently believe whisky is a social spirit, with its cultural place in society and history being the accompaniment to all the important things that happen in your life, births, marriages, deaths. The guys at LBD are immensely proud to be part of the tradition of independent bottling in Scotland but their bottles are presented and advertised in less than traditional ways. They never take

themselves too seriously and try to promote their products as something to be enjoyed by everyone, not an investment or an ornament, it's something to be experienced. Product launches are usually accompanied by in-house photos and videos that range from amusing to bizarre, who else would recreate the Italian Job as the Moray job but using swans rather than Mini Coopers? The early projects, whisky experiments shared online like #projectFRANKENCASK and #projectPEAT grew up on Twitter and as such social media has always played an integral part in the way that LBD share their story.

As committed spirits geeks, Little Brown Dog are keen to showcase different spirit categories, having bottled world whiskies, brandies, rums and calvados. If it comes in a cask and interests the team then they will bottle it. The focus however is on Scotch Whisky. For a single cask to be bottled it must be high quality as whatever ends up in a bottle represents their palate as bottlers, but the criteria for bottling also extends to showcasing individual casks with character. There must be a reason to single out that particular cask for its style or flavour and give it the attention it deserves.

Lombard

The Lombard-Chibnall family can trace its roots back well over 300 years. Records from 1762 show they owned wine merchants, a cooperage business and a local pub. But Lombard Scotch Whisky was founded by Margaret Lombard-Chibnall in the mid-1960s. The company started out as a bulk supplier of whisky, but later moved into blending and bottlings its own brands, like Driftwood, Anchor Bay and Smoking Ember. Lombard bottled single casks from the late 1990s until 2017, although in certain years there were no new releases from them at all. Probably their best-known series is Jewels of Scotland, which includes some highly-rated bottlings from Springbank, Brora, Tomatin and Lochside. The company was dissolved in 2019.

MacKillop's Choice

The story of Mackillop's Choice is that of its namesake, Lorne Mackillop. During university he worked for André Simon Wines in London's posh Belgravia neighbourhood. From there he worked his way up the wine ladder, becoming the world's youngest Master of Wine in 1984 along the way. Mackillop is also heir to the chief of the Mackillop Clan, which was almost wiped out in the aftermath of the Battle of Culloden.

The switch to the spirits industry was made during a deep recession when many small wine firms went under. Mackillop joined Angus Dundee Distillers (owners of Tomintoul and Glencadam Distilleries) as their master blender in 1993. In the late 1990s he started Mackillop's Choice. At the launch event in New York, Lorne presented a line-up of single cask whiskies, mainly from Speyside and all over 28 years old. New releases have slowed down lately – the last outturn dates from 2020.

Meadowside Blending
www.meadowsideblending.com

Donald Hart: "I started in the whisky industry in 1964 working with my brother, Iain, who was a young whisky broker trading as Iain G Hart Ltd, from a small office above my father's dental surgery. My Aunt (Kate Hart) was the first female licensee in the area of Paisley. From my brother and his work I learnt all about stock, invoicing, delivery orders and how deals between stock owners and blenders worked. Iain had done his training under Russell Paterson, father of the well-known blender Richard Paterson, and the company W R Paterson Ltd in Stockwell Lane, Glasgow.

"We were dealing with the main brokers of the time which were Stanley P Morrison, the Hillmans, Lundie, Peter J Russell and a few others. The brokers were mainly based in Scotland but there were also quite a few agents in London.

I would help out buying and selling but the margins on these casks would be just pennies – sometimes just six pence on a hogshead, however the volumes were much larger and it was a lucrative business.

"Most of our work was helping the blender's to balance and manage their holdings and we would get phone calls from different companies looking for certain makes and ages. Eventually we looked to expand and bought the residue of J B Rintoul based in Edinburgh. This consisted an old Bedford truck including a driver/salesman and a handful of customers in the Glasgow area. At the time we were selling a lot of South African wine and the driver would head down to the Greenock area delivering at the end of the week. We were also using the firm of W R Paterson to do our duty paid bottlings.

"The business developed from there and we eventually got our own premises in Fourth Street, formally called The Glenvey Blending company. This had a duty paid bottling line and we bottled our own casks as well as casks for others – this included bottling vatted cask samples which was permissible at the time. These were the days when cask samples could be removed without issue and many companies would just vat these large samples together into a cask and we would bottle it for them. It wasn't long before HMRC put a stop to this practice (much to the dismay of blenders). I learnt how to use all of the bottling machinery some of which was from a company called Purdy. In 1975 Alistair, my other brother, joined us from Whyte & Mackay where he had been Director of Blending (working with Richard Paterson).

"We had acquired the Barrhead Bond which was a big move for us – we had our own uniformed Excise officer inspecting everything we did. Sadly there was no real money in the blending we were offering (this being the time when cheap blended whisky was everywhere) so we would try and encourage companies to use our site for storage, even offering free transport (could you imaging doing that today). Eventually we decided it wasn't profitable enough and Burn Stewart took over in 1985. This meant we were no longer employers, or premise owners so we headed back into brokering.

"There began a real interest in named single malts (we had watched the likes of Gordon & MacPhail and Peter Russell gain market share with their single malts) and Alistair used his experience to source casks that we began to bottle under the name of Hart Bros. We had some fantastic whiskies around this time, the likes of 60s Laphroaig and Macallan – some of these were bottled for Oddbins and now fetch thousands of pounds. We were selling them for around £20 a bottle at the time. Cask prices were fairly consistent and there was no premium paid for any names or makes.

"In the early 1990s, during the recession, there was a big push to promote Scottish produce around the world and my brother and I would head off to faraway places like the US, Japan, Cuba, Brazil and all around Europe to attend

Meadowside Blending latest release:
Vital Spark

Andrew Hart

trade shows presenting our Hart Bros whiskies.

"When Hart Bros was eventually sold in 2007 I took some time out. It was strange as my entire professional life had always been working with a brother and under the family name. Hart Bros had been sold to Campbell Meyer & Company; Alistair continues to work for them bottling whisky under the Hart Bros name and I am pleased to see the brand doing very well. Eventually though in 2009, and now working with my son Andrew, the Meadowside Blending Co was born (as we were based out of Meadowside Quay) and we registered the brand The Maltman for our single cask, single malt releases – I am also a Maltman through the Trades House of Glasgow, so it seemed a fitting name.

"With the hard work of Andrew we developed the business and were surprised and a little taken aback at how welcoming the business was to this new enterprise. It seems all of the work I had put in over the decades, with retained friendships, opened doors for the business with no lost heritage. We increased our markets to the point where we now comfortably sell what we bottle and have introduced several new brands to the fold including The Grainman for our single grain whiskies, The Granary for our blended grain whiskies, Excalibur (for older blended whiskies) and The Vital Spark (for an un-named, heavily peated, single malt), all of which are gaining traction with our customers.

"My life has been spent in this incredible industry and Andrew and I are both proudly Keepers of the Quaich and the company is a member of the Scotch Whisky Association. I started when malt whisky was just an add-on, something that was considered a passing fad, and now malt whisky is everywhere and from every company. The Hart family has gone through many phases, from brokering, to blending, warehousing and bottling, and now with my son Andrew, we do our best to offer exciting releases and working with a selection of excellent importers and retailers. It is a fantastic industry and after working in it for 58 years I am delighted to still be a part of it."

Malts of Scotland

www.malts-of-scotland.com

German independent bottler Malts of Scotland has consistently churned out single malt releases since the company was founded in 2005. Mostly Scotch whisky, but also Irish, Indian, and American whisky. Led by Thomas Ewers, Malts of Scotland has a whisky lounge, cask warehouse and shop in their hometown of Paderborn. The company's Standard Range is usually anything but, while bottlings from their Warehouse Diamond and Amazing Casks series are among the best they have to offer. Ewers has also partnered with a nearby distillery to create his own whisky, The Westfalian.

Moon Import

Having built a legendary reputation during the 1980s specifically, Moon Import is one of Italy's most exceptional independent bottlers. Founder Pepi Mongiardino was truly a pioneer, but it was a fortuitous meeting with another Italian whisky legend that nudged him in the right direction.

Working for Pernod and with brands such as Ballantine's and Miltonduff, it was during this period in the 1970s that Mongiardino really started to appreciate single malt whisky. His employer's marketing budget was sizeable. So, he visited high-end restaurants and came across brands like The Macallan and Glenlivet. When that business took a downturn and he was asked to work in France or Germany, Mongiardino pivoted.

Enjoying dinner at Cantarelli, his friend's restaurant near Parma, they struck up a conversation about how Mongiardino should move forward. It wasn't long before their talk turned to Mongiardino's love for whisky. That's when his friend introduced him to Silvano Samaroli, who just happened to be dining in the other room. Advice was given. A friendship was made. It gave Mongiardino the courage to strike out on his own. Moon Import was born in 1980.

They say you make your own luck, and that's certainly what Mongiardino did. He used a reference book to check which whiskies weren't yet imported to Italy. He came across Bruichladdich - a foreign name for him at that time. He cold called the distillery, and fate would have it that the call was answered by an Italian. The next day Mongiardino flew out to Scotland, and he soon signed a contract. For the next five years he would be importer of Bruichladdich. He would later also sign deals with Tamnavulin and Tullibardine.

Just a few years into his new-found adventure as an entrepreneur, Mongiardino bottled his first whisky. The Half Moon series took its name from the semi-circular typography on the labels. The range included single malts from Glenlivet, Macallan, Glen Moray, Glen Grant and Tamnavulin. This was during an era when casks weren't bought from a spreadsheet supplied by brokers. Instead Mongiardino visited warehouses around Scotland, sometimes sampling 40 to 50 casks at a time. Later he also started to buy from private cask owners.

Moon Import's most iconic series are likely The Birds, The Animals, The Costumes and The Sea. And not just because the whisky is revered. Inspiration for the labels was drawn from the 18th century German encyclopaedia, Brockhaus Enzyklopädie. From a design perspective, they've been massively influential. A line can be drawn from those releases to labels of independent bottlers today, such as Archives, The Whisky Agency and Sansibar.

Almost two decades after Moon Import was founded, Mongiardino and his longtime friend Samaroli collaborated on a series of bottlings, Dreams. Included were single malts from Bowmore, Caol Ila, Dailuaine, Glenrothes, Linkwood, Mortlach and Longrow.

Murray McDavid

www.murray-mcdavid.com

Named after two family members, Murray McDavid was set up by Mark Reynier, Simon Coughlin and Gordon Wright in order to establish a brand for selling through specialist retail stores and exporting. The company set out to establish itself as slightly different to other bottlers offering predominantly vatted releases at 46% (without colouring or chil-filtering). Garish colours and witty descriptions added to the appeal and the company found great success through established channels and importers such as Hanseatische (HAWE) in Germany. The first use of 'Clachan a Choin' (Gaelic, allegedly, for 'The dog's bollocks'[260]) appeared on these bottles and would later adorn Bruichladdich bottlings.

Murray McDavid were one of the few IBs to get into direct trouble with a producer. Having bottled a nine year old Laphroaig in 1997 they received a letter from Allied Domecq's solicitors with a cease and desist order and were accused of 'passing off' and 'breaching copyright'. Eventually, and no doubt scared by a legal bill the owners could not afford and did not want, they gave in and, in keeping with the ethos of the company, bottled a Laphroaig in the very next batch called 'Leapfrog'[261]. A year later a judge in the Court of Session, Edinburgh dismissed Allied Distillers claims. It is interesting to note that Allied described Murray McDavid's bottling as "...inconsistent quality and pungent taste of the product was likely to damage irreparably the reputation of the Laphroaig sold from the Islay Distillery." The judge, perhaps understanding what a bottle of Laphroaig tasted like better than Allied, responded with "I do not consider it likely that to allow Murray McDavid to continue to bottle the modest quantities of whisky from the Laphroaig Distillery bearing labels indicating that was the source of the whisky would be irretrievably detrimental to the pursuers' reputation and goodwill." As is the way with these things, this bottling became infamous and the management at Allied Domecq were left looking rather silly.

Murray McDavid was used as the vehicle to offer and buy Bruichladdich Distillery in 2004 and from it the Mission series was launched, casks being selected by Jim McEwan. When Remy Martin acquired Bruichladdich in 2012 Murray McDavid was not part of their plan and was sold to ACEO Ltd in 2013 who have run the business since. Still specialising in outlandish colours the company have recently released their Cask Craft Selection.

---

260. For those not acquainted with this phrase, it is slang for the very best of something. When you think about it, it is a terrible phrase.
261. Something to do with an American customer mispronouncing 'Laphroaig'.

Gordon Wright: "I joined Springbank first as a director at the behest of my uncle, Hedley Wright, who had inherited it after the early death of his father. It had been a family company since 1928 and my uncle, having no children, naturally wanted the company to continue in the family. I immediately decided to get more involved than just a director and as this appeared to please my uncle I moved down to Campbeltown in 1990 and began work.

"I had been hoping for a period of hands-on experience, learn the distilling process and get a feel for the company and brand etc, but as I arrived, the export manager walked into the office, said something like 'that's me then' and was never seen at the company again. Before I joined, Springbank had experienced a difficult period during the '80s and prior to '89 when normal distilling began, had only really made any spirit during '85 & '87 (and this was to satisfy the needs of just one customer). From '89 onwards the distillery began filling with the idea of promoting its own brand.

"Even then Springbank was generally regarded as one of the top-tier malts but until the surge in demand for malt whisky in the '90s much of what kept the company, and small bottling warehouse, going was the growth in Cadenhead's. When I joined a small amount of Cadenhead's were being exported but most was being sold in the UK and through the Edinburgh shop on the Royal Mile which opened around '86. The inventory was incredibly impressive and I recall meeting Andrew Symington, owner of Signatory Vintage, who would come down to try and buy old Springbanks. He had been sold some when he managed the Prestonfield House Hotel. My uncle wanted to keep him at a distance realising that perhaps selling everything we had was not the wisest move, but, and I think he regretted this later, was quite positive about Signatory using the same 'S' as their logo as Springbank's. Perhaps he thought it would do the brand good.

"The largest independent off-license chain at the time was Oddbins and Cadenhead's did great business, maybe as much as half of our turnover, with them. Nick Blacknell (now Global Marketing Director for Chivas) was the Buying Controller and used to come up and visit once a year. He and his small team would taste cask after cask to plan bottlings for the year. Most of these bottlings would sell around the £30 mark and now can fetch five or six thousand. Oddbins also asked for a 12 year old, ex-Sherry Springbank and we made the 100 Proof bottling for them. We didn't have any 12yo stock but we did have older whiskies – thus it was a huge success and ended up being exported as part of the core range. I believe after I left the business with Oddbins was abruptly halted and all Cadenhead bottlings remained branded solely for Cadenhead's.

"Most of the Cadenhead stock was being purchased from Broker's and Distillers through a company my uncle owned, which acted as a sort of holding company. I had the very good fortune to meet and work with a company called Okura that also acted as a holding company for some of the Japanese blending

SPRINGBANK CASKS

Those of you with a bit more dosh to squander on drink may be interested in a full cask of Springbank. There are six cask options starting with a 330 bottle bourbon cask costing £850 (excluding duty and vat—payable on removal) including 10 years maturation. Further details on request.

CAVEAT EMPTOR

With a top-of-the-range new sherry butt (660 bottles) from Springbank costing £1,850 (the reasonable going rate) we wonder why there are 'Wine and Spirit Investment Advisors' offering whisky casks of unknown provenance for £3,000+. Be warned, there are some very dubious offers being touted.

Taken from Scotch Whisky Review
Autumn 1995

companies. They were able to sell some quite amazing stock as and when it was not required (or when cash was more convenient). This allowed me to buy some old Talisker and Lagavulin amongst others.

"Through a sale made in the shop in Edinburgh, Cadenhead's broke into Japan and eventually, and often with help of Springbank, into several other overseas markets including the US. Although the two brands were never sold collectively it often helped sales of one to have the other. This got us into Germany and Italy and slowly into other emerging markets. In 1995 the London shop opened just off Covent Garden and before I left there was talk of the first international store in Germany.

"In 1991 I met Mark Reynier and Simon Coughlin who ran La Reserve, a high-end wine and spirits outfit in London that had five stores. Cadenhead's and Springbank were selling bottlings to them exclusively and also began selling casks to the general public through the stores and via bottle purchases (by adding an advertisement within the packaging). This was a huge success (at the time one cask sale would allow Springbank to make two more).

"When it became apparent that my uncle was thinking about taking the company in a different direction, in other words, without me, I began thinking of a venture to safeguard my future. Along with Mark and Simon we set up the company Murray McDavid in 1995 and began bottling and selling through the

La Reserve stores and also existing customers. The bottlings were brash and bold and we had a lot of fun with the marketing and names ('Leapfrog' being a particular favourite). We were less interested in cask strength whiskies but were very keen that we tried everything we bottled (you might be surprised how little of this went on in other companies at the time). The brokers liked to play poker and would always ask 'what are you looking for?' and never tell you what they had. Sometimes they would supply samples and sometimes you would have to buy blind. I remember at the time that we were selling a Bowmore 1989 for just £28 a bottle and had the audacity to charge £125 for a 1965 Springbank.

"As a team and through the company of Murray McDavid we bought Bruichladdich Distillery. Originally we had put a bid in for Ardbeg but Glenmorangie outbid us (only by £2 million). Bruichladdich was likely a better fit for us at the time however as Glenmorangie had to invest more millions (which we didn't have) to get it going again.

"In 2004, although still a shareholder in Bruichladdich, I started Alchemist Beveridge Co and began introducing more Cognac and Armagnac to my customers. Since 2013 I have been exclusively acting as a commissioned broker and have ceased bottling Alchemist. Sales are to existing bottlers and other brokers and I have no plans to recommence bottling."

North Star Spirits

www.northstarspirits.com

Iain Croucher: "My attendance at school was vapid, which stood me in great stead for next to zero qualifications. This gave me the perfect springboard to attend not one university. I did all of this with gusto. My appetite for fun and devoid of any skills, led me into the most colourful world of tending bars where I began my whisky peregrination.

"My journey with spirits got underway in Glasgow, in a French Brassier called Malmaison in the mid 1990s. A very polite and generous Japanese chap bought a Rémy Martin XO and said, *'one for yourself'*. I took that 25ml of 40% cognac with gratitude (and haste), ran around the bar away from the observant custodian and my boss Ken McCulloch. Sitting on top of five crates of 1991 Pavillon Rouge du Chateau Margaux and 4 cases of Schweppes tonic as a foot stool I sank that dram like I was celebrating the end of a week-long hunger strike. I'm sure it was that moment I understood that spirit in whatever form could taste 'gallus'. This led me to develop my pallet with all things liquid, including wine and single malt scotch whisky

"To skip a couple of hazy decades, I sold a pub that my folks and I owned to start work for the Morrison family and their Dewar Rattray bottling company.

I was now in an arena where I could taste and spend time analysing great whisky and the industry as a whole. It was a great experience in many ways, as I got to peer behind the curtain of the magical world of single casks and how they are presented by a company that had no part in the production of the liquid.

"Towards the end of 2015, I was in a position of having some access to some remarkable scotch whisky and given an opportunity by this supplier to go out on my own. As I had nothing to do with the production of this liquid and knew I had fantastic friends and importers around the globe. It was up to me to fill in the blanks the best I could. This is when the name North Star came into my world. It fit perfectly, true north, a navigational tool, an accurate timepiece millions of miles away but also perennial and relevant.

"Supply and a name are hardly a business model, so I reached out to a few friends in the industry (such a remarkable industry, help is never far away) and one of them, indeed the writer of this book, asked me to come down

Iain Croucher

and see his operation. I had known David for a few years from festivals and events so travelled down the M74 to visit his operation in Thornhill. And that was really the birth of North Star Spirits Ltd; whilst being able to show off my ill-spent youth on his pool table.

"A few months later the very first North Star bottling, a phenomenal Arran 20-year-old, rolled off the bottling line and I began to make sales through contacts in Germany, Australia, Netherlands, Sweden, Italy, Canada and throughout the UK. Since then, I have been able to continue my passion to unearth rare and wonderful parcels or single casks of whisky that highlight the quirkiness and uniqueness of all whisky.

"Early on I was able to begin a range of uber-premium blended malt whiskies that I named 'Vega' – continuing our constellation theme. I was very keen to show that the blended sector is every bit as exciting, and rewarding, as the single malts sector – this led me to also bottle several blended Scotch whiskies. These incredible blends put North Star Spirits on the map, and I am very excited of the potential of this category in the future.

"Whisky, and in particular independent bottlers, acts like a time machine. Nosing a whisky can take you back to a moment, place, or time. I was privileged to be able to buy some casks of Springbank whisky and I can vividly recall the first time I nosed these whiskies straight from the cask – it was like I was back in the wee toon; memories just come flooding back.

"North Star Spirits, from the moment we came up with the name, strove to stand out. Our packaging and philosophy has never been to stay at the back of the bar or shelf. We bottle whisky to be eye-catching and most importantly, to be drunk, enjoyed and shared. Consciously we strove to make the company look and feel forward thinking and I believe this is one of the many reasons that we won 'Independent Bottler of the year' from the Scottish Whisky Awards in 2020 & 2021 – something I am particularly proud of.

"As a company we are now expanding our operation with new premises and look forward to working with many new companies and suppliers. We will continue to seek out those interesting and rare parcels that keep up excited about what we do and the customer intrigued and wanting more."

Samaroli

www.samaroli.com

The name Samaroli sends a chill up the spine of whisky enthusiasts, collectors and investors alike. Certain bottlings of Silvano Samaroli, such as the Bowmore 1966 Samaroli Bouquet or the sherry cask matured Laphroaig 1967, are regularly mentioned as some of the best whiskies to have been bottled. Ever.

Picture courtesy of Whisky Auctioneer

Like many of his contemporaries, Samaroli initially got his feet wet as an importer of Scotch whiskies. He set up Samaroli Import in 1968 and became the official Italian distributor of blends like Chequers and Abbot's Choice. He also imported an exclusive cask strength Linkwood for famed collector Edoardo Giaccone in 1969, followed by several of his own limited and special releases. But the true transition from importer to independent bottler came a decade into his love affair with whisky.

Samaroli bottled his first outturn in 1979. Almost by accident. He imported a series of Cadenhead's so-called "dumpy" bottles; single malts from Springbank and Macallan (among others). But since Mario Rossi were the official importer of Cadenhead's, Silvano was required to re-label them. A task he happily took upon himself, including the design of the labels – a series of water colours.

This was quickly followed by Samaroli's first true independent releases in 1981, the cumbersomely named The Never Bottled Top Quality Whisky Series. They're probably better-known by its more concise and more easily remembered moniker, the "Flowers" series. It showcased whiskies from uncommon distilleries, such as Millburn, Teaninich, Coleburn and North Port. These were possibly the first-ever commercial bottlings of these single malts.

The 1980s were Samaroli's most prolific period. He began to promote cask strength whiskies, a rarity up until that point. Especially outside of Italy. By the end of the decade almost all his whiskies were released at cask strength. He was a pioneer and visionary in that sense, and many others as well. For one, he was a champion of bottle ageing also – on the label of a Clynelish 1983 it says "Refined inside the bottle since September 2002."

One of the important but sometimes overlooked chapters of the company's history is Samaroli's relationship with Anacleto Bleve, whose Rome shop *Casa Bleve* was an important client. The two bonded by common interests and a similar passion for whisky. They became friends and mutually beneficial business partners. With no heir to leave the company to, Samaroli turned to the Bleve family in the early 2000s. Anacleve's son Antonio underwent an apprenticeship and took over the day-to-day running of the business in 2008. However, Silvano Samaroli remained involved until his passing in 2017 at the age of 77.

Today, Samaroli is still an important part of the independent bottling landscape. The company regularly release single malts and blended malts, combining multiple casks from various vintages. The colourful, artistic labels are elegant and evoke a sense of flair. They have also branched out into rum.

Sansibar
www.sansibar-whisky.com

Sansibar's origins are unlike most: this German independent bottler was originally intended to source rum and whisky for the eponymous restaurant. Located on the remote island of Sylt, the first Sansibar restaurant was just a humble beach kiosk. But over time the restaurant has become a cult fine-dining destination. And what started out as a modest bottling operation has now become an internationally respected independent bottler. In 2016, Sansibar collaborated with Italian bottlers Lions and Whisky Antique for one of their most ambitious projects to date; Antique Lions of Spirits was an homage to the iconic labels of Moon Import.

Scotch Malt Whisky Society (SMWS)

www.smws.com

Known for their whimsical tasting notes and bottling names, the Scotch Malt Whisky Society has played an important role in promoting cask strength single cask whiskies. Their members now number north of 35,000. And their bottling codes have collectors drooling. The SMWS may have been founded during an era when the Scotch whisky world economies were in decline, but they have been thriving ever since.

Apparently, in the 1970s you could just go up to certain distilleries, load up a cask in your boot, and drive away like it was the most normal thing in the world. When Pip Hills, founder of the SMWS, heard of this while visiting a friend in Aberdeenshire, the first seed was planted for what would become the world's largest whisky club. Excited, he headed home to Edinburgh, convinced a few friends to chime in, and set his sights on a cask from a family-owned distillery in Speyside.

John Grant, owner of Glenfarclas, allowed Hills to purchase one 10 year old quarter cask. Word about it quickly got out. As the contents of the original cask diminished, two other casks were purchased. Surprised that single cask whisky wasn't marketed to consumers, Hills eventually began pondering his own syndicate – or society, if you will. The Scotch Malt Whisky Society was officially established in May 1983. Some of the other founding members were writer W Gordon Smith, actor Russell Hunter and architect Ben Tindall[262].

From the outset it was decided not to mention the distillery on the label. Not because it was thought to be a clever marketing strategy. It was seen as a *sine qua non* – a necessity. Hills was warned that distillery names were trademarked, which could result in unwanted legal troubles down the road. Also, the Grant family of Glenfarclas was (and is) notoriously against independent bottlers mentioning their distillery name on labels. But Hills wanted to bottle a single cask Glenfarclas as the Society's first release. And so, they had to come up with a plan.

The unusual system of coding bottles was invented to protect brand names. The very first number on an SMWS label represents the distillery where the whisky was made. Glenfarclas is 1. Glenlivet is 2. Bowmore is 3. And so on. (Entire cheat sheets are shared online). The second number stands for the release of that particular distillery. For example, the code given to the Society's first-ever independent bottling is 1.1 – their first release from Glenfarclas. Eight years old from an ex-sherry cask.

262. And Doug McIvor's father.

Image courtesy of thewhiskyvault.com

The numerical labels have since become an unintentional trademark with enormous appeal to collectors. Over the years the system has expanded to different spirit categories. Letters were introduced to classify bourbon (B), Cognac (C), rye whiskey (RW) and Armagnac (A). The SMWS presented its 150th unique distillery in May 2022, cask 150.1 from a distillery in the south-west of Ireland. Almost 40 years since that first cask of Glenfarclas.

Membership soared in the 1980s and early 1990s, but founder Pip Hills resigned in 1995 and left the Society entirely a few years after. In retirement he became a successful author and now once again regularly speaks at SMWS events. He received the Dr Jim Swan Award at the Scottish Whisky Awards in 2022, a lifetime achievement award in recognition of his trailblazing efforts.

Without Hills the SMWS continued to flourish. It was acquired in 2004 by Glenmorangie, who expanded the society to include more than 26,000 members worldwide, with branches in 19 countries. For its 25th anniversary in 2008, the Society redesigned its bottles for the first time (but not the last). The new bottles were shaped somewhat differently. And the labels included an extended tasting note. Around 350 single casks were bottled annually by the time the SMWS was sold to Artisanal Spirits Company in 2015. Among the investors were a couple of the original founding members.

The Society started to invest heavily in global expansion. Local brand ambassadors were appointed. And deals were made to partner with over one hundred bars in more than twenty countries, including the UK, United States, Thailand, Japan, Sweden, Germany and the Netherlands. Most importantly, a large emphasis was put on e-commerce. All SMWS sales were funnelled through a newly launched web shop. Initially the Society's output was offered to non-members as well (at a hefty surplus), but this was stopped after feedback from paying members.

The SMWS has four members' clubs around the UK. The very first and oldest one has been the Society's base since 1983. Dubbed The Vaults and located in Leith, Edinburgh, it is the spiritual home of the SMWS. A second members' club at Greville Street in London was acquired in 1996. The money for it was raised via a private share scheme for its members. The third location is 28 Queen Street in Edinburgh, which was opened in 2004 and also houses the Kaleidoscope Bar, which is open to non-members. The newest members' room opened at 48 Bath Street in Glasgow in March 2020.

The latest milestone for the Society came on 4 June 2021. On that date the Artisanal Spirits Company made its debut on the stock market. The company is now listed on the Alternative Investment Market of the London Stock Exchange. Funds of the public offering were used to further invest in whisky stock, casks and venues.

Scott's Selection

Named after Robert Scott, former distillery manager of Bladnoch and Speyside Distillery, Scott's Selection started bottling cask strength whiskies in 1997. Robert was reputed to be one of the finest noses in the business, so he was tasked with selecting casks. One of the shareholders of Scott's Selection was Ricky Christie, son of industry legend George Christie, who had founded Speyside and North of Scotland distilleries. The last ever Scott's Selection bottlings were released in 2012.

Shinanoya

The well-known Japanese food and liquor shop/distributor Shinanoya has been around since 1930. Their shops are scattered across the country and usually include a great selection of spirits. But it wasn't until 2007 that they started releasing their own independent bottlings. Because of their longstanding relationships within the whisky industry, Shinanoya has been able to release a steady stream of high-end whiskies. Some of their series include Kinju-Zue, The Chess, The Sixth Sense and Instrumental Solo. Shinanoya has also done numerous joint bottlings with other independent bottlers and brands.

Silver Seal/Sestante

www.silversealwhisky.com

Silver Seal and Sestante might not be the same, but they are very closely related. Both are seminal independent bottlers. Both are part of Italian whisky heritage. And both were founded by Ernesto Mainardi. "Mr Mainardi has one of the best noses in the world – he's an artist," says Massimo Righi, the current owner of Silver Seal and an influential whisky figure in his own right.

Ernesto Mainardi's first encounter with Scotch whisky was as a bartender, but his formative whisky years were spent working for Co. Import. They imported Gordon & MacPhail to Italy and when the business' owner died, Mainardi took over the distribution rights. As you do when you're Italian, he travelled by scooter from Parma to Inverness and Elgin. It took him four days. Once arrived he befriended George Urquhart from Gordon & MacPhail. It naturally gave him access to a number of exclusive bottlings. Mainardi also imported whisky bottled by George Strachan, such as Rosebank, Glen Grant and Tamdhu.

The name Sestante is derived from Il Sestante, a bar Mainardi opened in Parma in 1977. It translates to sextant, a navigation instrument primarily used for the purposes of celestial navigation. Mainardi thought it the perfect name for a company that invites people to explore the world of whisky. And the Italians took to exploring whisky like no other nation before.

Righi says, "Italian people are collectors. They enjoy fashion and art. They like to eat and drink well. Every area has their own food traditions and recipes. My area is very famous for tortellini. It's completely different from how it's made five kilometres away. It might be a little thing, maybe some more mortadella, less cheese, different kinds of cheese.

"The same principle applies to how Italians drink whisky. We're not content to drink the same whisky over and over. We always look for different whiskies."

Mainardi's first independent bottlings were released in 1985; two Bowmore's, a 14 year old from 1971 and a 20 year old from 1965. In an interview for Emmanuel Dron's seminal book Collecting Scotch Whisky, Mainardi claims that his Bowmore 1965 was the best Bowmore Ian Morrison ever tried.

Sestante was known for releasing two versions of its single cask whiskies, one at 40% abv and the other at cask strength. Mainardi also released a fair number of whiskies bottled in crystal decanters, selling around 3,500 of them. This was a tradition he picked up during his days at Co. Import, who made several Macallan-Glenlivet decanters with Gordon & MacPhail. Mainardi continued this tradition at Sestante in partnership with Edinburgh Crystal.

The 1990s were a relatively quiet period for Sestante, and the company was dissolved in 1999, only for Mainardi to start over a year later. He began Silver Seal in partnership with Douglas Laing, seemingly picking up where he left off. Some of Silver Seals "First Bottlings" are Macallan 1976, Lochside 1979, Port Ellen 1969, Linlithgow 1974 and Ardbeg 1972.

Mainardi first discussed selling Silver Seal to Righi in 2007, and a deal was struck not long after. Righi, who already owned the acclaimed retailer Whisky Antique, acquired the Silver Seal brand and its stocks. "I have more of a fiscal mind. Everything must be in order. Mainardi is like Maradona. Amazing footballer, not a great accountant."

Righi carried the Silver Seal brand into the 2010s and beyond. He does not think of other independent bottlers as competitors and regards Silver Seal as his work of passion. Cask selection is usually his sole responsibility. "I try cask samples during different times of day, but the most important time for me is after dinner in the evening. The technical people, or whisky geeks, think it's the best to drink in the morning. But in the end, when you drink whisky it's often after dinner, during your free time. Whisky is now more technical than emotional, and I believe whisky should be more emotional than technical."

Single Cask Nation

www.singlecasknation.com

Founded by two Jewish chaps and a Jewish adjacent Scotsman (which sounds like the opening to a joke you can't tell in 2023), Joshua Hatton, Seth Klaskin and Jason Johnstone-Yellin formed Single Cask Nation as the independent bottling wing of the Jewish Whisky Company in 2011. When Seth left the company in 2018 to pursue other ventures, the company began trading as J&J Spirits Ltd.

Having built their industry reputations with separate well-known and well-respected whisky blogs (Jewmalt and Guid Scotch Drink – guess which one ran which blog!), Joshua and Jason had spent several years championing the cause of independent bottlers posting hundreds of reviews of oftentimes cask strength, single cask releases across their two platforms. At Joshua's prompting, it seemed a natural next step to wade into the world of independents for themselves.

Heralded from its inception as "an American-based independent bottler doing business in the Scottish tradition" Joshua and Jason travelled the length and breadth of the United States pouring cask strength, single cask bottlings for whisky lovers who, at that time, didn't even know single casks were a thing, let alone the names of the distilleries from whence the casks had come.

"When we first started," says Jason, "we'd be in a room of self-professed whisky lovers and we'd ask them if they'd heard of Arran, Kilchoman, or

Benriach, which were our first three bottlings, and not a single hand would go up."

Gradually, though, a loyal following began to coalesce around the nascent company and "the Nation" (the name given to the fans of the company) began to take shape. While early Single Cask Nation offerings were exclusively available through the company's online portal in 2017 the independent bottler added a separate line of retail offerings across the United States.

"People ask us," says Joshua, "what's the difference between the bottles on your website and the bottles on my local retailer's shelves. Well, we like to think of the online portal as a Special Projects Division, the place we can offer, for example, an American rye finished in an ex-Kilchoman cask or a first fill bourbon cask Dailuaine accidentally finished in a first fill sherry cask! Online releases that might be a little unusual but that will instantly resonate with the Nation who tend to enjoy the interesting offerings that tell a different kind of story."

Jason picks up the thread at this point, "The retail line needs to speak to a consumer who maybe hasn't heard of us before and simply wants to know that what's offered in the bottle is top notch liquid. We can't rely on the retailer to move that bottle for us. It must speak for itself and get itself sold."

The company continues to build on its hard-earned successes and to date there's a podcast called One Nation Under Whisky, a whisky tour company; Whisky Geek Tours, and a currently mothballed series of whisky festivals; Whisky Jewbilee. In 2019, when J&J brought on Global Sales Manager, Jess Lomas, the retail line expanded to include the UK, Canada, Germany, Sweden, Israel, and Japan. In 2021, they hired a Sales Manager for the Americas, Elijah Ammon, to continue growing the brand. The four are currently hard at work on a line of regional single malts bottled at 47.4% that focuses more on flavour than provenance and hope to release those to the public in the not too distant future.

Svenska Eldvatten

www.eldvatten.se

Svenska Eldvatten is an independent bottler that began mainly releasing Scotch whiskies but have also bottled several single cask rums, Swedish whiskies and even a single cask Tequila. The company was established in 2010, with the first release in 2011 (a single cask Bowmore 2000, 10 years old).

The history of the company started much earlier for the two founders and owners, Tommy Andersen and Peter Sjögren. Both were already fans of Scotch whisky; the interest growing from numerous trips to Scotland, visiting distilleries and fairs, buying and trying whiskies, arranging tastings, starting a whisky club and ultimately buying casks. Eventually they gave up their daytime jobs and started full time with the company.

The company is based in Göteborg on the rugged Swedish West coast. "Svenska" simply means "Swedish" and "Eldvatten" means "Firewater" – this is to clearly reflect that the owners are Swedes and that it not only whisky they bottle.

The company releases roughly twelve bottlings every year with over 80% of them being Scotch whiskies. Svenska Eldvatten doesn't buy casks with young whisky for maturing, making all their casks ready to be bottled straight away. Every cask is handpicked, tasted and chosen in the warehouses and both Tommy and Peter need to give each cask a thumbs up before giving it a green light for release.

Thompson Bros Distillers
www.thompsonbrosdistillers.com

What started as part-time work in the family hotel (Dornoch Castle Hotel) led brothers Phil and Simon Thompson into a crash course initiation into the world of whisky, bottling and distilling. By 2008 both brothers were full time in the hotel business and began expanding the whisky bar. At this time much of what they were buying was from Gordon & MacPhail but they began attending auctions in the central belt, and more provincial ones, picking up weird and wonderful bottles of whisky as they went.

This led them to being part of the group that would 'gather', collectively buying and bringing incredible whiskies to drink together (one of the first ones being an 1899 Glenlivet that was bottled for a company in Bristol and shipped to Australia). As Phil remembers:

"These Gatherings were giving us a real insight into this world of old whisky and old bottlings. We were learning from the likes of Serge Valentin, Olivier Humbrecht, Marcel van Gils, Emmanuel Dron – people with vast knowledge of bottlings. This got us to raise the level in the hotel bar again although it was also just when prices started to go crazy."

A visit to Strathearn Distillery convinced the brothers that a distillery could be built at a fraction of the cost and in a way that would allow them to 'tinker'. Sites at Loch Ness and the Black Isle were considered but buying the land was out so the distillery began on part of the Dornoch Castle Hotel grounds. Distilling commenced in 2017 and at first it was felt a gin could bring in sufficient funds.

"We quickly realised we had vastly underestimated the amount of money we would need to get the distillery off the ground. I was asked to do a pop-up whisky and gin bar in in Osaka, Japan. We realised that the gin was never going to be enough to keep us going but I happened to go to the hotel bar that night

Picture courtesy of Marcel van Gils

and met a local called Kimura-san who had previously been at our hotel in Dornoch. Kimura-san had just begun importing and was very excited about what we were doing and said he would take the gin and the distillery bottlings once they were available. But then asked if we could get any whisky.

"I said 'I don't really know', so I spoke to Iain Croucher at A D Rattray and he supplied us with a cask and it snowballed from there. We were able to buy things we liked and we were able to buy things like Caroni rum and this grew into more and more markets. We kept to our philosophy of good whisky at good prices. This really seemed to resonate with a group of consumers and stuff started selling out – so we introduced a ballot system but maintained the UK stockists whilst still exporting."

The Ultimate (Van Wees)

www.ultimatewhisky.com

The Ultimate is the boldly-named independent whisky label of Dutch importer and distributor Van Wees. They've bottled well over 1,000 casks since the first series of releases in 1994, which included Ardbeg, Port Ellen and Macallan from the 1970s. *Pater familias* Han van Wees is often credited with teaching the Dutch how to drink whisky.

Van Wees was founded by Hubertus van Wees in 1921, originally selling tobacco. His sons Han and Ben joined him on January 1st, 1954. But the two brothers had been helping in their father's store since long before. As the tobacco business was trending down, Han van Wees decided to become a licensed spirits retailer not long after joining his father's company.

There was one issue: only a limited number of licenses were available in the city of Amersfoort. Exhibiting his entrepreneurial spirit, Han came up with a clever ruse. The regulations allowed him to start selling liquor unlicensed if he sold more than 10 litres per transaction. So that's what he did. And he never looked back.

The origin story of Van Wees' foray into whisky is part of Dutch whisky lore. In the 1960s the MS Hornland was damaged on her way to the Port of Rotterdam and sank in the Nieuwe Waterweg ("New Waterway"), which connects to the North Sea. On board the MS Hornland were many sea containers filled with whisky and champagne. They were all acquired by Han; at a nice discount of course.

It appeared this whisky (mostly blends) was of much better quality than what was usually made available for the Dutch market. Having spoiled his new whisky hungry clientele, they started asking for single malts. Han convinced Gordon & MacPhail and Cadenhead's to bottle exclusives for the Netherlands, including young Ardbeg and Laphroaig.

But the company's longest and most important relationship is with Signatory Vintage. Andrew Symington is a friend of the family and most (if not all) whisky bottled as The Ultimate is sourced from the warehouses of Signatory Vintage.

Han's son Maurice has been working in the business since 1987. He's currently the managing director of Van Wees. And the fourth generation has entered the company as well, Julie and Joël — Maurice's children and Han's grandchildren.

Vallinch & Mallet Whisky

www.vallinchandmallet.com

Davide Romano: "Before starting Vallinch & Mallet I was a portfolio manager of a hedge fund and I was looking into alternative investments for the fund, I was already a member of the SMWS so I knew a bit about single casks. I was then put in contact with Fabio Ermoli through a mutual friend in Italy and we started selecting some casks. Fabio comes from the wine world - previously he had a wine shop in Milan but then decided to work solely as an importer of whisky.

"When it was time to start the new company that would buy and sell casks for the fund I realised that I wasn't really interested in the pure speculation since I had chosen those casks by tasting them. I proposed the fund manager to bottle them creating a new independent bottling company, still profitable but different. After he refused, I immediately resigned and started V&M with my own savings, it was 4th September 2015.

"We had no export markets and 1,100 bottles to sell, I started knocking here and there and some people responded positively after tasting the samples, country after country came on board and we are now distributed in 20 countries worldwide.

"The philosophy has always been bottling only what we like. Fabio and I need to agree on a specific sample before it's bottled, regardless the name, age, or the difference in experience we had and have. I wanted also to show my "double" identity, Italian but in a way a bit more British than before after years living there, so the design, aesthetics and packaging needed to show that without impacting the prices too much. I designed everything (logo, labels and so on) myself, never used a graphic designer, this way the packaging cost was greatly reduced. I managed to have a product that was the way I wanted at the same price level of the majority of similar bottlings. The packaging, made in Italy by small family businesses, no mass production of course given our volumes.

"We reinvested 100% of the profits in casks since year one. I put aside enough savings to allow the company to grow for a while. I have been able to build a good portfolio of casks that will be our future now that the prices are spiking. Basically we can decide what to buy and bottle and what to take from the existing stock, lowering the average cost. We have also started re-racking casks since 2016 so we now have some sort of maturation program with good Bodega Sherry casks.

"We were lucky enough to start in a period when it was still possible to bottle older whiskies at a fairly decent price. We did a Port Ellen 32 year old, Bowmore 25 year old, two Springbanks (21 year old and the latest a 24 year old), I think we are the last young bottler that was actually able to do a Port Ellen.

"Nowadays we have expanded to rums as well with the same philosophy and taste above all. Ageing, distillery name and so on are of course important but I don't care if I have an Enmore that I know will sell, if it's mediocre I'm more than happy to leave it to someone else. I also want to have diversity across the whole range of whiskies and rums, by age, price, type of maturation. Our bottlings should be for drinking so I'm sometimes happier to do a young whisky that is very good and correctly priced than an important name that will only end up in collections. Money is money, but if I wanted to make a lot of it I would have kept my previous job for sure.

"The reason I wanted to be an IB was to be able to sell what I liked, without having to push a particular product just because I was making it. This way the only thing that matters is my way of choosing products, no marketing speak required, if a product is good it will sell; you can fool the public once or twice but after that you are done.

"The future of IB for me is into becoming bottlers of "good spirits" going beyond the boundaries we've had for years: whisky drinkers, rum drinkers, Armagnac drinkers and so on. What I'm trying to do with The Spirit of Art collection is exactly to stop dividing the public into sectors and just saying 'look, this is really good for me, try it, enjoy it, it doesn't matter what product it is, just enjoy it!'. Life is too short to not be open minded..."

The Vintage Malt Whisky Co Ltd
www.vintagemaltwhisky.com

Andrew Crook: "My father Brian started in the Scotch Whisky trade in 1978 initially as Export Sales Manager for Eadie Cairns and Company, then owners of Auchentoshan distillery. He worked with them for five years and then joined Stanley P. Morrison Ltd, owners of Bowmore. Shortly after joining Morrisons, they bought Auchentoshan so within a few months of leaving he was getting his old job back! During his nine years at Morrison Bowmore, he was made Sales Director, overseeing the brands repackaging and introduction to the Duty Free market. Then under the ownership of the Morrison family, Bowmore did not have the budget to take the brand truly onto the world stage. This changed following the Suntory takeover in the early 1990s, with the new owners having big ambitions for the brand. The company then set up two divisions, one for Bowmore and another for all the other brands but Brian was left to work with Auchentoshan and felt he would be more or less starting again. He felt his energies would be better served starting from scratch with his own company so he made the decision to strike out on his own at the age of 50. VMW was formed in April 1992.

"In his time working with Bowmore, Brian had built up good connections with importers around the world and was confident that if he started his own company, there would be enough friends in these markets to help support him with distribution arrangements. France was key to all of this and the Auxil company gave him his first order. A small selection of other markets quickly followed - Italy, Germany, USA and Japan.

"From day one of the company, Brian was focussed on quality. As a new small player, if you didn't have quality then you were doomed to failure. Thankfully, back in the early 1990s there was good availability of high quality bulk whisky for his brands. Many of the distilleries which are almost impossible to source today were readily available if you had the right connections.

"The malt market back in 1992 was very different to today. There were only

Ben Inglis, Caroline James, Andrew & Brian Crook

a handful of single malt brands widely available so Brian felt there was space in the market for the exciting new brands he had in mind to create. Although back then the interest in smoky, peaty Islay whisky wasn't anywhere near the level of today, Brian's experience with Bowmore in the 1980s had shown him that there was a growing appetite for whisky of this style bottled in its own right, rather than just for adding character to blends. For some years he had the idea in his head that "Finlaggan" would make a great name for an Islay Single Malt Scotch Whisky so from day one establishing this new brand was his main focus and very much a "labour of love". However, he also felt it was

important to have more approachable styles too so the brands Glenalmond (A Highland pure malt) and Tantallan (a Speyside single malt) were established.

"In terms of independent bottlers, there was really only Gordon & MacPhail, Cadenheads and one or two others. However, these companies were cask bottlers and mainly used the names of the distilleries on their labels. Brian wanted VMW to be different and brand focused, hence the creation of his own brands, Finlaggan, Glenalmond and Tantallan, where the source distilleries were undisclosed. As the years passed and the company grew, additional brands were created.

"In saying that, it didn't take long before customers in certain markets began asking him if he could bottle single casks where the distillery name was disclosed. Although reluctant initially, it made sense commercially and in late 1992 "The Cooper's Choice" single cask series was born. The first bottlings were for Italy, USA and Switzerland. The name "Cooper's Choice" was actually suggested to Brian by Jim MacEwan, an old colleague and friend from his days at Bowmore. Jim had started as a cooper and felt their important role in Scotch whisky didn't get the recognition they deserved. The creation of a brand in their honour was long overdue. Brian agreed and the rest is history. Jim was given the first ever bottle of Cooper's Choice, a Caol Ila from the early 1980s."

Watt Whisky
www.wattwhisky.com

Mark Watt: "The Independent Bottling scene has changed a lot from when I first started in 2000 but they were always important, and always important in my work. I found a whisky list from the Quaich bar from 1998 when the bar was just beginning to grow its reputation as a world famous whisky bar. Of the 308 single malts or so on the bar nearly a quarter of them were bottled by independent bottlers. When you factor in that Macallan, Glenlivet, Glenfiddich and Glenfarclas, combined had nearly 40 different distillery bottlings it highlights how important the IBs were in the bar. More so when you consider out of the 113 distilleries represented on the shelves 30 of those distilleries were only available as single malts from IBs.

"Throughout my early career I always found the IBs offered the best value for money and allowed you to sell something to someone that they won't find in just any bar in the world (or from a distillery that many people had never heard of). It also allowed you access to closed distilleries; it is unlikely anyone would

Mark Watt & Kate Watt

241

Each colour is a flavour

have heard, let alone tasted, the likes of Banff, Brora and Port Ellen if it wasn't for the likes of Douglas Laing and Signatory.

"As I began my career, the main players were Signatory, Douglas Laing and Chieftains Choice (owned by Iain Macleod) - mainly due to what was available locally and in the bars. Cadenhead's were obviously well known but unless you hiked all the way down the Royal Mile you wouldn't see much of it in mainstream shops - which was obviously the same for the SMWS. They were a club and kept to themselves. When I started behind the SMWS whisky bar in Leith[263] there was an outcry when someone added a choice of three white wines and three red wines by the glass to the drinks menu; "This is not a wine bar!" several of the members scoffed - the very notion of a choice of wine in a whisky bar.

"A strange case for me is G&M and I mean that with the greatest of respect because they are such a big company with a long history of bottling – and such large offerings under the distillery labels. They never really felt like an Independent bottler when I first started, they were more semi-official bottlers, but obviously that was just my perspective then. Even though I loved a lot of their bottlings - the first bottle of whisky I ever bought was a 1982 St Magdalene from the Connoisseurs Choice - acquired in their shop in Elgin from a young Ronnie Routledge - I still have that bottle.

263. Known as The Vaults.

"Once at Duncan Taylor Co and seeing more people in various markets around the world it was interesting to see that different companies seemed to do well in different markets. The company were always pretty big in Japan, whereas Douglas Laing were successful in Germany and Signatory in France and Germany for example.

"I think IBs certainly had a big hand in the malt market growing, I don't mean they helped sell more of big brands like Lagavulin or Talisker but the sector was certainly more helpful in pushing the smaller brands. Some distilleries that have been championed by IBs for a while, whilst perhaps being overlooked by their owners, are now major brands in their own right now (think Tomatin or Benriach for example). I remember working at Royal Mile Whiskies and a Signatory bottling of Glenallachie was one of our best sellers; it was taken from a single cask; had individually numbered bottles; bottled at 46%; with natural colour and was non-chilfiltered. Amazing to think it retailed for about £23.00 a bottle. Not surprisingly, we sold absolute bucket loads of the stuff. Mainly because it was an amazing whisky the staff all loved it and no one had ever heard of the distillery.

"Things have changed a lot in the last twenty years and more so probably in the last five. There are so many IBs now it is difficult to get your head around who is behind a lot of them, but it just shows there is a demand for it out there. There has always been an interest outside of Scotland by companies wanting specific whiskies. The Italians, Germans and Japanese being some of the early players but now every corner of the world has their own local IB. Due to this growing interest, prices are on the rise and availability is in a downward spiral - as more and more people are chasing the same casks, prices have risen a lot and it is no longer the case that IBs will be considerably cheaper than distillery bottlings.

"As prices for the big names continue to rise more and more people are looking for the lesser known names, as these offer better value and remain of interest to the malt drinker. The internet has allowed a lot more people to have a little bit of knowledge and that has opened up the likes of Miltonduff, Glen Elgin and Glenlossie etc (to pick just a few distilleries) to be explored by malt whisky drinkers and championed by IBs.

"Starting Watt Whisky Co during the Covid Lockdown and the Brexit fallout was a challenge. But looking back now it was an ideal time as we felt if we could survive those hurdles, then hopefully it bodes well for the future. Kate and I have been very fortunate to work with a lot of people in the industry that we have built relationships with over the past twenty years. Many people have helped us get to where we are today, probably we are further ahead than we thought we would be at this stage. If you look at the markets we export to, Kate and I have worked with some of them for twenty years and relationships like that you just cannot buy. Oliver Chilton, Elixir Distillers, always claims that you can feel an IBs personality coming through in their whiskies and people should find an IB that they like the style of - more often than not they will like their style whether it is from a distillery they know of or not. This is certainly the case with companies like ours where there are only two people picking what is being bottled rather than picking by committee. I think people will see a style of spirit coming through when they look at Watt Whisky Co and probably a style that has followed me through the years."

Wemyss Malts

www.wemyssmalts.com

Founded in 2005, Wemyss Malts is a family-owned company with heritage rooted in Fife, Scotland. The impressive Wemyss Castle is the family's ancestral home. Connections to Scotch whisky can be traced back to the early 19th century when John Haig built Cameronbridge distillery on Wemyss land. Wemyss Malts are known for the quirky names they bestow on their single cask bottlings, such as An Antique Armchair, Mocha on the Deck or Tutti Frutti Zing. They also produce a range of blends and blended malts like Spice King, The Hive and Lord Elcho; and they have their own distillery, Kingsbarns.

Wm Cadenhead Ltd

www.cadenhead.scot

In its 180 plus years of existence, Cadenhead's has survived against all the odds. A shocking death in the 1930s; a notorious auction in the 1970s... The oldest independent whisky bottler in Scotland has quite a tale to tell.

To the modern whisky drinker, Cadenhead's – or William Cadenhead, if you prefer – is intertwined with Springbank Distillery. They share the same owner and conduct business using a similar philosophy. But Cadenhead's has been around for nearly two centuries, and for most of those years it wasn't part of J&A Mitchell in Campbeltown. The company is a fixture in today's whisky landscape but has travelled a long and bumpy road to get there. It all begins in 1842 in Aberdeen.

George Duncan established himself as a vintner and distillery agent at Netherkirkgate 39. One of the distilleries in his portfolio was Huntly, which closed in the 1860s. He was noted as "...a gentleman whose genuine kindness of heart and thorough integrity as a business man, were known and admired by everyone who enjoyed the pleasure of his acquaintance." In June 1858 he had been the guest of honour at a dinner organised by members of the Spirit Trade, where he was presented "...with a handsome Gold Watch and Chain worth nearly

forty guineas, and a beautiful Diamond Ring, of the value of fourteen guineas for Mrs Duncan."

One of Duncan's early employees was one William Cadenhead. When Duncan died in 1859 after a short illness, it was Cadenhead who acquired the business and quickly changed the trading name to his own. He even wedded his former employer's widow. Cadenhead's reputation had little to do with his distinction as a vintner. It was his renown as a poet that made him something of a local celebrity in Aberdeen. Whisky, however, wasn't on his mind when writing. The closest he ever came to mentioning it was in "Kittybrewster", one of his better-known poems:

'Her dram was good, but O, her ale!
'Twas it that did her credit,
Aboon a' brewsts it bore the bell,
And 'twas hersel' that made it'

At the first annual supper and ball of the Aberdeen wine and spirits trade in 1886, Cadenhead delivered a speech that offers an insight into the climate in which he and other colleagues operated. The Scottish temperance movement, which was most active in the years before the First World War, had already had an impact on society.

The Aberdeen Evening Express records Cadenhead as stating that 'their maligners blamed them for all the evils in the world, and he believed that if

Christie-Restell

CITY WINE SALE

at Beaver Hall

Following the recent cessation of trading

THE COMPLETE STOCK-IN-TRADE

OF

Wm. CADENHEAD

Wine Merchants of Aberdeen

which will be sold at Auction
WITHOUT RESERVE

by

CHRISTIE, MANSON & WOODS

J. O. CHANCE, C.B.E., J. A. FLOYD, A. G. GRIMWADE, GUY HANNEN, M.C.,
THE HON. PATRICK LINDSAY, JOHN HERBERT, A. J. H. DU BOULAY,
THE HON. DAVID BATHURST, W. A. COLERIDGE, J. M. BROADBENT,
W. A. SPOWERS, M. L. TREE, ROBSON LOWE, THE HON. CHARLES ALLSOPP,
NOEL ANNESLEY, HUGO MORLEY-FLETCHER, ALBERT MIDDLEMISS,
WILLIAM MOSTYN-OWEN, CHRISTOPHER WOOD, T. E. V. CRAIG,
ANTHONY DENHAM, PAUL WHITFIELD, T. MILNES GASKELL, GREGORY MARTIN

Incorporating W. & T. Restell

at Beaver Hall
Garlick Hill, Cannon Street, London, E.C.4

On Tuesday and Wednesday
October 3 and 4, 1972
at eleven o'clock precisely each day

ALL ENQUIRIES TO THE WINE DEPARTMENT
CHRISTIE'S, 8 KING STREET, LONDON, SW1Y 6QT
Telephone: 01-839 9060 Telex.: 916429 Telegrams: Christiart, London, S.W.1

PRICE: TWENTY PENCE

In sending commissions or making enquiries quote LYNX

they could change the text of Scripture, they would make it read that Adam was tempted with a glass of beer. Their opponents would not believe them, but they knew that their motto was: "Let your moderation be known unto men."'

Cadenhead lived to see his 86th year, which would have been quite a remarkable feat at the time, if not for his two sisters and three brothers, who all lived even longer. His oldest brother, Peter, died aged 97.

The death of William Cadenhead in 1904 meant that his nephew, Robert Duthie, who was already a partner by then, took over. Born in India, where his father was superintendent of the Scottish Orphanage in what is now Mumbai, Duthie came to Aberdeen as a young boy. He was quiet and unassuming but developed the products for which the firm became most famous: single malt Scotch whisky and Demerara rum.

Duthie advertised extensively. The Aberdeen newspapers had a good client in Cadenhead's, but Duthie wasn't confined to print. He advertised on the backs of buses, on theatre curtains and in concert programmes. The company's slogan? 'By test the best.' Duthie established whiskies such as the deluxe blend Putachieside and The Heilanman. This quiet gentleman turned out to be instrumental in pushing the company forward and establishing it as a brand, rather than just a merchant.

246

Then, in 1932, tragedy struck. In the depths of the Depression, the business was in poor shape. Legend has it that, while on his way to see his bank manager, Duthie was run over and killed by a tramcar. A bachelor, Duthie left Cadenhead's to his sisters, who had no knowledge of the spirits trade. And so, responsibility for the business was handed to Ann Oliver, a long-term employee, ushering in another new era.

Oliver was eccentric, running the business in her own way. She refused to change with the times or the market in whisky sales and was a perfect client for the Aberdeen salespeople of the time. She bought freely and liberally, from casks to bottles to boxes full of labels. When she was finally forced to retire and sell, it was discovered that Oliver was averse to keeping records. Without any documentation, the company was deemed unprofitable. The bonded and duty-paid warehouses may have been full to overflowing, but no-one knew the value of the stock held there.

The bank assumed that the company was in terrible shape, resulting in a now legendary auction of the entire stock of Cadenhead's. Not a single item of the over 1,500 lots had a reserve price. The sale took place at Christie's in October 1972 and, contrary to expectations, it netted a six-figure surplus above and beyond the firm's liabilities. The auction broke all records. Among the lots in the catalogue were five hogsheads of 1967 Macallan, 10 hogsheads of 1967 Glen Mhor, five hogsheads of 1965 Rosebank and two hogsheads of 1963 Talisker. Also included were many already bottled wines, rums and whiskies.

Meanwhile, someone in Campbeltown took notice of the situation in Aberdeen. That someone was Hedley Wright, owner of J&A Mitchell & Co, the firm that also owns Springbank. Wright is a modest man and notoriously private, never giving interviews and staying out of the limelight. One of the main attractions of buying the Aberdeen firm were the glass bottles, of which there was a shortage in the early 1970s. In his bid for the company, Wright stated that the glass bottles had to be included. Shortly after the Christie's auction, Cadenhead's officially became part of J&A Mitchell. The glass bottles, however, were nowhere to be found.

Under new ownership, whisky became an even bigger focus of Cadenhead's. In the following decades, the company opened dedicated Cadenhead's shops, not only in Edinburgh and London, but also on the European mainland. It also adopted the philosophy of its parent company, one that has made Springbank such a success story.

Everything at Cadenhead's is about giving back to the community and ensuring long-term stability. Keeping in mind the boom-and-bust cycle of the whisky industry, Cadenhead's would rather go slowly than quickly. To secure the future of his company, Wright has ensured that Cadenhead's (and Springbank and Glengyle distilleries) will pass into the ownership of a charitable trust when he dies. As the largest employer in Campbeltown, he doesn't want to jeopardise the future of his business. And so Cadenhead's – once again without a direct heir – will eventually go to the people of Campbeltown.

Whiskybase

Dirk Henst: "Whiskybase.com started in 2007 as a hobby to capture factual information about whisky bottles, keep track of personal tasting notes and scores all brought together into your 'personal collection'. It attracted a substantial group of like-minded whisky enthusiasts. After a few years it was time to offer the members a chance to purchase good independent bottlings. This first took place in 2011. We thought that a whisky specialist shop could not be considered a specialist without having our own range of bottlings. From the very start we focused on single cask, cask strength releases. This is still our main focus but has expanded over the years and actually became very selective. There are so many bottlers out there that it becomes hard to navigate the offering of new releases.

"Our own releases are still selected on the same principle we had in the beginning. CJ and myself taste samples from the casks we own and decide what to do with them: further maturation or bottling. The 'ready to be bottled' cask purchases that got us started are very hard to find nowadays. Several years ago we adjusted our approach to be more in control of the maturation. We like pure whisky, minimal cask influence where the spirit and time would be the main influence on the flavour of a whisky. Every bottler has their own approach to what they consider good whisky, we like to be known for a certain style. But it can change over time, we are all on a whisky journey and being a bottler doesn't mean we are not constantly learning as well.

"For us there have been two waves of inspiration; we have been lucky enough to be able to remember and try many of the famous bottlings from Italy by Samaroli, Sestante, Moon import and Silver Seal. But for our brand the biggest influence would be The Whisky Agency, Whisky Fässle and Whisky-Doris. It feels like these bottlings are now slowly turning into classics but the offering from indy bottlers in this period was much larger.

"My personal introduction to the IB scene was through a wild evening when I drank 1974 Millburn from Blackadder, 1964 Coleburn from the Bottlers and three different 1972 Caperdonich's from Duncan Taylor. From that moment I learned that price/quality from IBs was better than official bottlings and they released whisky that was not available as a distillery bottling. From a flavour perspective I was spoiled and that really got me excited about the works of an IB."

Wilson and Morgan

www.wilsonandmorgan.com

Fabio Rossi, founder of Italian independent bottler Wilson & Morgan, comes from a proud family of Venetian wine merchants. His father made the decision to expand to (blended) Scotch whisky in the 1960s, which eventually led to Rossi branching out as an independent bottler in 1992. He initially bought his casks at Cadenhead's to create the Barrel Selection label – part of Wilson & Morgan's product range to this day. In time Rossi started selecting his own casks, visiting distilleries and warehouses in Scotland and letting casks mature further in their original habitat.

Bibliography

Andrews, Allen 1977 "The Whisky Barons"

Barnard, Alfred 1887 "The Whisky Distilleries of the United Kingdom"

Brander, Michael 1975 "The Original Scotch"

Buxrud, Ulf 2006 " Rare Malts. Facts, Figures and Taste"

Buxton, Ian 2010 "Glenglassaugh A Distillery Reborn"

Buxton, Ian 2009 "The Enduring Legacy of Dewar's"

Buxton, Ian 2014 "But The Distilleries Went On: The Morrison Bowmore Story"

Buxton, Ian & Hughes Paul 2014 "The Science and Commerce of Whisky"

Charles, H Craig 1994 "The Scotch Whisky Industry Record"

Daiches, David 1969, "Scotch Whisky, Its Past and Present"

Eadie, James 2022 "The Distilleries of Great Britain & Ireland: 1922-1929"

Dron, Emmanuel 2018 "Collecting Scotch Whisky"

Grindal, Richard 1992 "The Spirit of Whisky"

Hills, Pip 2019 "The Founders Tale"

Kirsch, Harald 2004 "Independent Bottlers of Single Malt Scotch Whisky"

Manning, Sydney 1947 "A Handbook of the Wine & Spirit Trade"

Mantle, Jonathan 1991 "The Ballantine's Story"

Mackie, Albert 1973 "The Scotch Whisky Drinker's Companion"

MacDonald Aeneas, 1930 "Whisky"

McDougall, John 1999 "Wort, Worms & Washbacks – Memoirs from the Stillhouse"

McDowall, R. J. S, 1967 "The Whiskies of Scotland"

Morgan, Nick 2020 "A Long Stride, The Story of the World's No 1 Scotch Whisky"

Morrice, Philip 1983 "The Schweppes Guide to Scotch"

Moss, Michael S. 1981 "The Making of Scotch Whisky"

Murray, Jim 1998 "The Art of Whisky"

Paterson, Richard 2008 "Goodness Nose: The Passionate Revelations of a Scotch Whisky Master Blender"

Pugh, Peter 1987 "Is Guinness Good For You? The Bid for Distillers – The Inside Story"

Robb, J. M. 1950 "Scotch Whisky"

Ronde, Ingvar 2008-2023 "Malt Whisky Yearbook"

Simpson, Bill (& others) 1974 "Scotch Whisky"

Steadman, Ralph 1994 "Still Life with Bottle: Whisky According to Ralph Steadman"

Stirk, David 2002 "The Malt Whisky Guide"

Stirk, David 2004 "The Distilleries of Campbeltown"

Udo, Misako 2005 "The Scottish Whisky Distilleries"

Weir, R. 1995 "The History of the Distillers Company 1877-1939"

Wilson, Ross 1970 "Scotch. The Formative Years"

Wilson, Ross 1973 "Scotch Its History and Romance"

Magazines and Periodicals:

1994-2007 "Scotch Whisky Review"

1999-Present "Whisky Magazine"

1958-1986 "Wine and Spirit Trade Record"

Numerous articles on www.scotchwhisky.com

Acknowledgements

As has been noted, despite being a major industry, the Scotch whisky 'world' is like one big extended family. Without the help and assistance of the people within it I would never have begun my odyssey or been able to write this book.

Very special thanks go to 'Pinky', one half of Electric Coo and my oldest pal in the whisky biz; Mark Watt. I apologise for the continual pinging of messages with questions, queries, news articles and the odd bit of writing for checking. Also to Kate Watt, another dear friend, ex-colleague, mine of information and advisor; and for the more than several nights drinking in Campbeltown when there wasn't much else to do.

Thanks to; Thijs Klaverstijn for his editorial help and excellent contribution; Matt McKay, Angus MacRaild and Iain Russell for their editorial guidance and expert critique; to Serge for his Foreword and all that he has done for the industry and the independent bottling sector – and all that provided quotes.

Thanks to everyone I interviewed: Gordon Wright, Donald & Andrew Hart, Andrew Symington, Phil Thompson, Doug McIvor, John Glaser, David Boyd, Oliver Chilton , Ken Grier and Dr Alan Rutherford.

The research would not have been possible without the Glasgow Archives and to all that supported the CrowdFunder. A big dram is due to Tom and all at Dramtime NL, WIN Dranken, Katy Coltart and the team at Claxton's – thank you so much!!

Thanks to my cocker spaniel, Molly, who insisted that no matter how hard I was working, or even if I was in the middle of a really good part, I needed a walk, or to give her a belly-rub or a treat.

And finally, my thanks to the whisky industry in general. From that first Glenlivet, to the last tasting I hosted, festival I visited and cork I pulled, this industry has provided much more than I ever expected from it and considerably more than I feel I warranted. I was quite right on that sunny day in Islay when I concluded that this truly was the best industry in the world.

David Stirk

Thijs Klaverstijn

David Stirk began his life in whisky in 1996. From Whisky Magazine to Wm Cadenhead and The Creative Whisky Co Ltd he has pursued a career that kept him relevant and interested in, mainly, Scotch whisky. The author of "The Malt Whisky Guide", 2002 GW Publishing and "The Distilleries of Campbeltown" 2004 Neil Wilson Publishing, David has also contributed numerous articles to Whisky Magazine and The Malt Whisky Yearbook as well as several angry social media posts (mainly complaining about whisky investment companies). After selling The Creative Whisky Co Ltd in 2018 David set up as a *Whisky Consultant* and has worked with numerous companies including North Star Spirits, Campbeltown Whisky Co Ltd, Little Brown Dog and Claxton's Ltd. David spends much of his time drinking whisky, playing golf and reading WW2 books.

Thijs Klaverstijn is a whisky and spirits writer based in The Netherlands. He regularly contributes to titles such as Whisky Magazine, Gin Magazine (writing about his other boozy love Genever) and the Dutch magazine Whisky Passion. You might have also caught his musings on Distiller.com, the late great Scotchwhisky.com and his own blog Wordsofwhisky.com, which is celebrating its ten-year anniversary in 2023. When he isn't writing about or tasting whisky, you can usually find him consulting or writing for drinks related brands, retailers or startups. Or just badgering any unsuspecting soul who walks into his home to have a drink with him. Thijs enjoys watching movies and good television shows, travelling (mostly to Scotland and Ireland), usually with a dram not far afoot.